Street-Smart Advertising

Street-Smart Advertising

Advertising

How to Win the
Battle of the Buzz

MARGO BERMAN

ROWMAN & LITTLEFIELD PUBLISHERS, INC.
Lanham • Boulder • New York • Toronto • Plymouth, UK

ROWMAN & LITTLEFIELD PUBLISHERS, INC.

Published in the United States of America
by Rowman & Littlefield Publishers, Inc.
A wholly owned subsidary of The Rowman & Littlefield Publishing Group, Inc.
4501 Forbes Boulevard, Suite 200, Lanham, Maryland 20706
www.rowmanlittlefield.com

Estover Road, Plymouth PL6 7PY, United Kingdom

British Library Cataloguing in Publication Information Available

Library of Congress Cataloging-in-Publication Data

Berman, Margo, 1947–
    Street-smart advertising : how to win the battle of the buzz / Margo Berman.
        p. cm.
    Includes bibliographical references and index.
    ISBN-13: 978-0-7425-4136-8 (cloth : alk. paper)
    ISBN-10: 0-7425-4136-3 (cloth : alk. paper)
    ISBN-13: 978-0-7425-4137-5 (pbk. : alk. paper)
    ISBN-10: 0-7425-4137-1 (pbk. : alk. paper)
    1. Advertising. 2. Commercial art. 3. Graphic design (Typography).
4. Advertising media planning. 5. Creation (Literary, artistic, etc.) I. Title.
HF5823.B454 2007
659.1—dc22   2006016643

Printed in the United States of America

♾™ The paper used in this publication meets the minimum requirements of
American National Standard for Information Sciences—Permanence of Paper for
Printed Library Materials, ANSI/NISO Z39.48-1992.

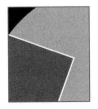

Contents

Preface

While reviewing the literature that existed, I realized that although quite a few volumes have been written on creative thinking, advertising, and design, few cover the conceptual process as it relates to creative strategy. While many of these books offer strong theoretical content and excellent visual examples, they don't necessarily take the reader from concept to execution, step by step, something I believed would be helpful.

In this work, I covered the elements and principles of design, methods to create sticky slogans, techniques to write powerful ad copy, global meanings of colors, case studies of inventive campaigns, creative process with insightful interviews, and examinations of self-promotions, plus tips from conceptual thinkers at some of the most imaginative agencies and design firms in the world. With this showcase of exceptional creative work, readers can be guided and inspired to look for novel approaches and unique solutions to marketing and advertising challenges.

Each chapter examines a particular aspect of creative development and showcases examples through quotes, visuals, commentary, and exercises. Readers can work at their own pace and refer first to the chapters they are most interested in. For easy reference, words in the glossary appear in italics, as do the titles of the campaigns being discussed. This way, readers can more easily refer back to a particular campaign.

Written with advertising professors and students in mind, the book will also be interesting to seasoned professionals who enjoy reading about campaigns that created a global buzz. This systematic explanation will also help marketing executives, business owners, and entrepreneurs gain a richer understanding of advertising and what it takes to create campaigns that generate press coverage. In addition, they will be able to better assess their immediate and long-term promotional plans.

After completing the book, readers will be able to:

- rethink traditional media usage
- write more compelling copy
- evaluate and or modify slogans they might be currently using
- instantly identify and classify slogans in advertising messages
- consider developing a self-promotion
- explore new advertising vehicles
- think in a more creative way

I hope the information in each chapter will prove useful to readers and will help them create innovative ideas to solve myriad marketing dilemmas. I am inviting readers who might be working at agencies, design firms, or portfolio schools and who have developed unusual self-promotions to let me know about them, at fiuberman@aol.com, for possible inclusion in future works.

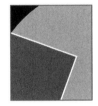

Acknowledgments

There are so many people without whose help this work would never have been completed, that I must take a moment to thank each and every one. Many may feel no thanks are necessary, but I totally disagree. If in the final push to complete this book, I inadvertently omitted someone, please forgive me.

First, I must thank my husband, Jack, who listened to my many iterations of "Sorry, I can't talk now," and second, Jennifer Minnich, creative director of M2Design, who constantly cheered me on. Each one encouraged me along as I moved down the long road from concept to final execution. Jennifer's help was invaluable in proofing, helping to design some of the graphics, and in pinch hitting wherever needed. Third, I must say a special thank you to my niece, Ronni Alexander, who always shared my vision.

Next, I must thank three people at Rowman & Littlefield Publishers. First, Brenda Hadenfeldt, acquisitions editor, communication and journalism, who believed in me from the start and patiently persevered until we found a literary vehicle. Second, Bess Vanrenen, her editorial assistant, who never grew tired of answering my endless questions. And third, Jehanne Schweitzer, senior production editor, whose editorial and visual expertise and attention to detail brought the manuscript to fruition.

I wish to thank all the creatives and executives at ad agencies who interrupted their busy schedules to assist me in obtaining visuals and participate in interviews; gathering pertinent campaign information; and reviewing chapter excerpts.

At BBDO Atlanta: Deborah von Kutzleben, senior vice president, account director, for providing the correct Cingular script credit.

At Crispin Porter + Bogusky: Steve Sapka, manager, agency communications, for diligently supervising all correspondence, image acquisition, crucial creative campaign information, permissions, and approval; Sarah Howard, content supervisor, who coordinated the review and approval of chapter excerpts, the compilation of campaign information, and ongoing correspondence; and to both of them for helping gain images and approval from Adrienne Hayes, at Burger King; Andrew Cutler, MINI communications manager for MINI USA; and Trish O'Callaghan, vice president of public relations for the Ad*itive.

At Deutsch: Jeffrey Wolf, partner/director of account planning, Deutsch NY, for his detail-driven phone interview, compilation of critical information, and content review, and Scott Lahde, vice president/associate director of corporate communications, Deutsch Inc., for his mastery of multifaceted correspondence, scheduling and detailed coordination of approving content, gathering and submission of images, and assembling of vital information, as well as gaining permission for visuals, interview quotes, and comments on the Deutsch Web site.

At Euro RSCG: Ron Berger, CEO and chief creative officer, RSCG Worldwide, New York and San Francisco, for his comprehensive phone interview and subsequent excerpt approval; Charlie Fabrizio, executive assistant to Ron Berger, for handling all the seemingly endless correspondence, scheduling, image compilation, and follow-up, in addition to gaining permission to quote from the Euro RSCG Web site.

At Fallon Worldwide: Brenna Brelie, global communications coordinator, for permission to use quotes from the Fallon Web site.

At The Kaplan Thaler Group: Linda Kaplan Thaler, CEO and chief creative officer, for her thought-provoking phone interview and subsequent content review; Tricia Kenney, managing director, corporate communications, who expertly supervised the complicated correspondence and permission to quote The Kaplan Thaler Group Web site; and Erin Creagh, account coordinator, corporate communications, who fluidly handled the intricate follow-up details of schedule coordination, excerpt approval, permissions, and image acquisitions and for assisting me in contacting Ellyn Fisher, director of corporate communications at the Ad Council, who helped obtain a visual from a Girls Scouts of the USA TV spot and granted content approval, and Al Johnson, second vice president, director of branding and advertising corporate communications, Aflac Incorporated, Worldwide Headquarters, who permitted me to use images of the Aflac duck and generously spent his time reviewing a chapter excerpt.

At Leo Burnett USA: Abby Lovett, corporate affairs senior associate, for tirelessly arranging interviews, images, permissions, and approvals, and Noel Haan and G. Andrew Meyer, executive vice presidents/group creative heads, for their engaging and creative-focused interview and content review.

At Ogilvy Worldwide: Toni Lee, public relations, for giving me generous permission to use several of David Ogilvy's quotes from his books and comments from the Ogilvy & Mather Web site.

At Saatchi & Saatchi: Bob Isherwood, worldwide creative director, for his insightful comments; Monica Hudson, executive assistant to Bob Isherwood, for her dedication to detail and for obtaining quotes, collecting and submitting images, gathering vital background campaign information, and gaining permission to use Saatchi & Saatchi Web site quotes; Jillian Stanton, account director, Saatchi & Saatchi New Zealand, for coordinating the acquisition of visuals; and John Vidal, worldwide visual communications director, Saatchi & Saatchi, for providing images for inclusion in this work.

At TBWA\Worldwide: Jeremy Miller, public relations director TBWA Worldwide and TBWA\Chiat\Day, for reviewing excerpts, obtaining an Adidas visual, gaining approval for all content, being so responsive to requests, and permitting me to quote from the TBWA\Worldwide Web site.

At Think Tank 3: Sharoz Makarechi, creative director, for her patience in answering my many requests for information and visuals and for her lucid interview; Harris Silver, president, for orchestrating the initial correspondence and guiding my efforts; and Matthew Dugas, art director, for patiently assisting in the conversion of the images into other file formats.

At Wieden+Kennedy: Liz Hartge, PR director, for allowing me to use quotes from the Wieden+Kennedy Web site.

At Young & Laramore: Tom Denari, president, for his thoughtful and extensive interview, image retrieval, content review of excerpts, and tireless assistance; and Megan Sams, business development coordinator, for handling all the details in correspondence and final image releases.

At the design firms that sent me images and granted me interviews, I would like to thank the following for all their help.

At Knock Knock: Jen Bilik, president, for granting me an interview and for providing visuals and permission approval, and Brianne Sheldon, at the PR firm handling Knock Knock, for conscientiously coordinating all correspondence and the acquisition of images.

At Modern Dog Design: Robynne Raye, creative director, for her interview, time and commentary; and Junichi Tsuneoka, art director, for his kind assistance in downloading the image files.

At Randal Grey Design & Illustration: Randal Grey, president, for granting me an interview and providing relevant visuals and permission approval.

For the assistance from different creative centers of learning, I would like to thank the following people for their generosity:

At Miami Ad School: Pippa Seichrist, president and cofounder, for her interview, creative visuals, and help in reaching a former student for an interview.

At the Creative Circus: Norm Grey, executive creative director, for his interview, other comments, and help in obtaining student work.

At Florida International University: Lillian Kopenhaver, dean, School of Journalism and Mass Communication, for permission to use visuals of students' creative work and for her ongoing support; and Cathy Ahles, advertising and public relations department chair, for her encouragement.

For help with the chapter on color, I would like to thank Ellen Meany, creative director, Isthmus Publishing Co. Inc., for her assistance in obtaining information on the use of color in print ads; Suzanne Raitt, vice president of marketing for the Canadian Newspaper Association, for permitting me to use statistical information about the power of color; and Victoria Herbert, director of strategic projects for COLORTEAM at the Pantone Color Institute, for providing relevant articles about the impact of color.

I would like to thank publishing industry professionals for their kindness in allowing me to quote from their articles. These include, but are not limited to, Brooke Capps, editorial assistant, *Advertising Age*; and Eric Rubenstein, assistant general counsel, VNU Inc. for *Adweek*. A special thank-you goes to Gary Ink, who handles rights and permissions for *Publishers Weekly*, for granting me permission to quote freely from various articles.

Two particular companies were of help in the acquisition of creative samples. I would like to thank the following people for their assistance.

At Cingular Wireless: Mark Siegel, executive director, media relations, for permission to use the script from a Cingular TV commercial.

At Vert Inc.: Linda Kelley, bookkeeper/office manager, who managed to send me an image of a taxi-top VID (Vert Intelligent Display Video) ad.

Two other individuals gave help for which I am thankful. These are Natalia Cova, franchise owner of Fast Track Kids2005, for her interview and insights; and Steve Timana, designer, for his thoughtful interview and wonderful images.

Rev Up Your Thinking with Creative Stimulation

> Good ideas do not just circulate information. They penetrate the public mind with desires and belief.
>
> —LEO BURNETT[1]

Taking the Pulse on the Street

Creating a buzz starts with hearing the heartbeat of the crowd, listening to the language of the street, and tuning into the message makers of the masses, namely the consumers themselves. Everyone targeting an audience is looking for the answers, so they can tap into the pulse of the public and really get street savvy. To succeed, they need to know what's hot. What's making a stir. What's all the rage. What's getting talked about. To get a handle on the market, they find out where their audience gets its information and then immerse themselves in the same media.

Creative advertising talents spend endless hours reading blogs; visiting creative Web sites; surfing the Internet, digesting articles in trade journals, magazines, books, and newspapers; and tapping into the lifestyle of their audience. They realize that in order to create advertising that gets noticed, they must understand what's capturing people's attention and why it is. In short, they constantly monitor the media, analyze the messages, and scrutinize new avenues that lead to street-smart advertising.

Breakthrough Thinking

Art directors, designers, and copywriters are also looking for inventive places to get their messages out. Seeing wonderfully ingenious new media developed by others sparks new thinking. Here are a few exceptionally creative campaigns.

The first was a unique and tremendously successful interactive online campaign, "Subservient Chicken," created for Burger King by Crispin Porter + Bogusky, a Miami-based agency renowned for campaign originality and media ingenuity. Someone dressed up in a chicken costume stayed in front of a webcam all day and would move in response to online commands (figures 1.1 and 1.2).

FIGURE 1.1 Photo of man dressed in a chicken costume from the "Subservient Chicken" campaign, created by Crispin Porter + Bogusky for Burger King. Photo courtesy of Burger King Corporation

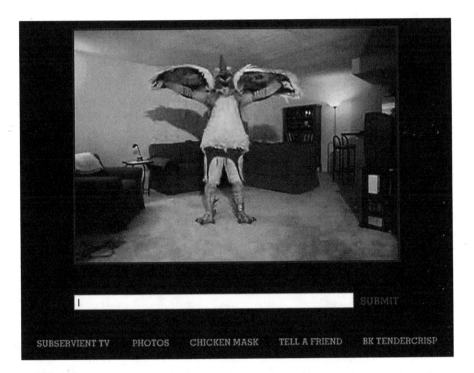

FIGURE 1.2 The "Subservient Chicken" Web Site, created by Crispin Porter + Bogusky for Burger King. Photo courtesy of Burger King Corporation

People could ask the chicken to flap its wings, spin in a circle, or dance around and could watch it follow their commands. If someone requested moves of a sexual nature, the chicken responded with a "naughty, naughty" motion of its wing. It was very entertaining and extremely funny to see—so much so that it became a smash hit on the Web, with more than 385 million hits and 12,142,314 unique visitors within one year of its launch on April 8, 2004. Visitors stayed online an average of seven minutes and thirty-five seconds.[2]

Although this offbeat campaign may be viewed as highly risky, it is exactly that kind of risk taking that succeeded in creating a buzz. "This odd bird is the product of CP+B's disciplined, ingenious blueprint of systematically producing work that is original, innovative, authentic, strategic, and most important, pretty damn effective. It's a creativity that, ironically, is liberated by the marketing game's strict limits on such things as media choices, budgets, and message content."[3]

Another breakthrough concept, created by the Omnicom Group unit of TBWA\Japan, involved "vertical soccer" played live on a billboard. Two players, suspended by 26.5-foot ropes, kick a ball tethered to the board. Five ten-minute games took place every afternoon and practically stopped pedestrian traffic by capturing everyone's attention. The creative director of TBWA\ Japan, John Merrifield, wanted to generate a "wow" for Adidas.[4] The cost was low, around $180,000, considering it created $150 million in press coverage across the world.[5]

Millstone coffee had a billboard with live people drinking coffee in a three-dimensional outdoor "kitchen." It didn't have the impact of the Adidas sign because it lacked these attention-grabbing elements: (1) the threat of danger, (2) the excitement of sports competition, and (3) the entertainment factor of live action. The Millstone board simply had celebrity athletes sipping coffee on highways in San Francisco, Atlanta, and Fort Lauderdale.[6] Although having live people on a billboard is eye catching and did gain some press, Millstone's didn't create the scope of media attention that the Adidas board did. What created the Adidas buzz wasn't just live soccer players; it was that they were dangling dangerously on ropes in midair. Watching their movements was almost hypnotizing. People just couldn't stop looking.

A campaign for Sega's Beta-7 combined multimedia with a significant emphasis on an online hoax presented through "live interactive theater." Created by Wieden+Kennedy, it integrated three Web sites. The first one, created by the agency, offered twenty-four-hour-a-day commentary by someone claiming to be a Beta-7 tester whose life had supposedly been changed dramatically because of the game. He complained on his Web log that Beta-7 created uncontrollable reactions, like spontaneously tackling people. The second two sites were created by actual fans who were responding to the first site.

It seemed believable because small ads looking for game testers appeared in places gamers frequented like the *Onion* and chat rooms, actual beta copies of the game were sent to a few testers, and direct-mail pieces appearing to be legitimate cease-and-desist orders demanding the games be returned were sent to the testers. In addition, viral videos, voicemail messages, broad e-mailings, and fliers were released, while TV commercials appeared on cable networks.

The whole idea was to create a fight between the Sega designers, who were only trying to introduce a new first-person football feature with Sega's ESPN football game, and a disgruntled game tester hired by Sega. The tester then ranted on his Web log that Sega is harmful and that the company is trying to cover it up while contesting the facts through a phony fan Web site named GamerChuck.com. To make the site and direct-mail materials look authentic, the art director created amateur-looking materials. Even funnier is the fact that several of the viral videos were developed by the filmmakers responsible for *The Blair Witch Project*.

It was so effective that the site generated more than two million collective hits. Plus, months after the Web site was taken down, gamers, believing this implausible Sega conspiracy, continued trying to log on in an effort to find out what had happened to Beta-7. But one of the most impressive aspects of the campaign is that it produced a 20-percent increase in projected sales.[7]

Ingenious campaigns like these that are as exceptionally brilliant in their concept as they are in their subsequent executions serve as creative juice for art directors and copywriters across the world. This is why everyone involved in developing the creative strategy, as well as working through the creative process, needs to be absorbing information from as many sources as possible on a daily basis.

> Example isn't another way to teach, it is the only way to teach.
>
> —ALBERT EINSTEIN[8]

Other New Ways to Advertise

In addition to new media vehicles, there have also been changes to existing media that offer more options for targeting a specific audience. For example, News Corporation's Fox network is utilizing the technology from Visible World, a New York firm, in an attempt to introduce adaptable TV commercials that can be customized digitally to be more relevant to an audience at a certain time. So, soup companies can include chilly outdoor temperatures in their ads to encourage sales. Or beer companies can have actors in commercials discussing different teams during an actual sporting event to bring more attention to their product. This means one ad could be altered many ways without the need to reshoot any part of the spot.[9]

In Asia, because of the social stigma of speaking in public on the phone, text messaging is even more prevalent than in the United States. So, Asians are very comfortable using their cell phones for e-mailing. Among the Chinese, cell phones are considered a status symbol, so much so that relatives at funerals burn paper replicas of cell phones to assure the dead will be able to communicate in the afterlife. It is so ingrained into the culture that most people today are unable to consider being dead without having their mobile phone. This cultural phenomenon is recognized by Genevieve Bell, a staff anthropologist at Intel Corporation who has studied Asian mobile phone use in seven countries for more than three years. More than just a technological device, the phone itself represents deep cultural values.[10]

Because Asian countries do not have the laws we have in the United States banning unsolicited advertising on cell phones, Asian advertisers are communicating with their consumers in many ways. Procter & Gamble has signed up 80,000 women in Japan to receive messages about Whisper, a brand of feminine hygiene products, such as "Your skin gets even more sensitive and dry, especially during this period. . . . Try not to use new skin-care products." Pfizer wanted Japanese teenagers to talk about their product, Acuvue contact lenses, so it strategically placed billboard ads near schools and attached free cell phone accessories with Acuvue's Web site address.[11]

In China, News Corporation's Star TV created a popular game show by enticing viewers to download bingo boards onto their mobile phones so they could play along while they watched. According to Geoffrey Handley, founder of New Zealand's Hyper Factory, an Asian cell phone marketing company, mobile phones can serve as another way to reach consumers who are harder and harder to reach because of their very busy lives. Now they can still be connected to the brand, while watching a TV show as well as when they are out around town.

In Asia, cell phones can be used as train tickets as well as game players. In America, companies are just starting to tap into the mobile phone market as a commercial message communicator.

Viewers of the TV talent competition *American Idol* are encouraged to call or text message their votes for the idol of their choice. This type of interactivity ties the viewers even closer to the contestants and the program.

Amazingly, ringtone downloads have grown into a $217 million market. Recognizing an opportunity, two radio stations, Viacom's Infinity Broadcasting and Clear Channel Communications, have expressed interest in offering songs, concert tickets, and promotions through cell phones. The power of cell phone communication should not be underestimated. This is evidenced by a new art form: original music specifically written as cell phone ringtones. Nokia, which introduced musical ringtones in 1991 with Tarrega's classical guitar piece "Gran Vals," has commissioned Ryuichi Sakamoto, a Japanese composer, to create original music and sounds for its latest line of phones. Consumers can even customize which part of a song they want as their ringtone, a decision once controlled by recording companies. Even Juilliard School professor Edward Bilous recognizes the shift in power: "Ringtones are pointing towards a kind of new interactive media in which the user and the creator have a more democratic relationship."[12]

Constantly Examine Inspiring Work

Constantly look at campaigns that introduce new media or that use existing media in novel ways. According to Chuck Porter, chairman of Crispin Porter +

Bogusky, creative talents must consider many different media, not just one: "The dumbest thing you can do is think in terms of one medium. The biggest problem this industry has is laziness. It is a hard thing to do to think differently."[13]

One example of CP+B's unusual approaches is the MINI Cooper "Counterfeit" campaign, which directed people to a site that sold DVDs that cautioned against buying fake MINIs. The whole story was a fabrication, but people enjoyed punishing counterfeit MINI owners who were tricked into buying phony, discounted copies of real MINIs by using their mouse to hit them.[14]

An excellent example of using traditional media simply incorporated an unexpected visual. "Street Building," created by Ogilvy & Mather, used a billboard that showed a picture of a building with one Lego-like piece missing on the outside.[15] The Lego logo appeared just above the left corner of the Lego-shaped opening.[16]

The Power of Product Placement

Sometimes it's a promotional idea that creates a tremendous amount of press. When Pontiac teamed up with Oprah Winfrey and gave away a free Pontiac G6 to everyone in the audience, news networks across the country took notice. Part of the appeal was that the audience was hand-picked from letters from people begging for a new car for someone they knew who desperately needed one. The audience was flown in believing that one of them would win a new car. So, when everyone won, the whole audience was screaming all at once. They were all asked to go outside of the studio and pick a car. The parking lot was filled with Pontiacs wrapped in huge red bows. Of course, the winners, all 276 of them, received their cars sometime after the show. They were told to go to their local Pontiac dealers and choose which color and options they wanted. So, not only did they win a car, but they even had the opportunity to select the one they wanted.

The $7 million cost, which was more than double the rate of a thirty-second Super Bowl commercial that year (2005), created so much publicity that GM continued giving away vehicles. It followed that up by giving away one Montana SV6 minivan on ABC's *Live with Regis and Kelly* morning show every day in February. That promotion garnered even more sales leads.[17]

Pontiac, of course, is only one of many companies that use giveaways to increase sales. The key, according to Matthew Creamer and Jean Halliday, is to follow these five guidelines for a successful giveaway: (1) Check that there is an overlap between the show's audience and the target audience; (2) Realize the emotional connection with the host is stronger than that with the product; (3) Be prepared for a gradual increase in sales, not the sudden spike that happens to products featured on *The Oprah Winfrey Show*; (4) Continue the emotional connection long after the show is over to create viral marketing; and (5) Support each giveaway with PR and advertising campaigns.[18]

Product placement, on the other hand, does not have to include giveaways. The medium can be so powerful by itself that it can propel a hardly known product into stardom. One clear example is the inclusion of Reese's Pieces candies, instead of M&M's, in the film *Star Wars,* which grossed $460,998,007 and catapulted the astronomical sales of the candies. Another example again involves Oprah Winfrey. Every writer knows the power of Oprah Winfrey's book selections, known as the "Oprah effect," which turns almost any book into an overnight best seller.[19] Her choices have even helped to launch a book into a major motion picture, like author Rebecca Wells's *Divine Secrets of the Ya-Ya Sisterhood*.

Some popular television programs blatantly show products in use during the show. For example, on *American Idol*, contestants and judges both drink Coca-Cola in cups on which the bright red logo is clearly visible. It has not at all negatively affected the number of devoted viewers, which is in the tens of millions. The audience recognizes Coca-Cola as the program's sponsor and accepts the product placement as easily as they do the TV commercials.

Of course, product placement isn't new. It's been around since the 1930s. Here are a few examples of products placed in early films. In 1932, White Owl cigars were shown in *That Uncertain Feeling*. In 1944, Bell telephones were included in *Arsenic and Old Lace*. In 1950, Coca-Cola was shown in *Father of the Bride*.

However, today product placement functions in a much more sophisticated manner, pairing up networks, talent agencies, producers, and prop coordinators. In fact, with the advent of digital technology, products in films are easily changed when shown in different parts of the world. For example, in the United States, Pepsico's Taco Bell was the restaurant featured in the 1993 futurist police-state film *Demolition Man*. But overseas, Pepsico's other chain, Pizza Hut, received the plug in the same film. Just being able to change the soda can in an actor's hands from one market to another increases the product placement's ability to generate new revenue. The industry is developing new opportunities and is evolving very quickly.[20]

But as influential as product placement in movies is, nothing surpasses the impact of a presidential approval or rejection. For example, when former president George Bush (Senior) said he didn't like broccoli, the entire industry of growers was up in arms. Likewise, when Bill Clinton frequented fast-food restaurants, it encouraged millions of people to indulge as well. Former president Ronald Reagan's love of jelly beans just enhanced the candy's already popular status. These unpaid endorsements are truly priceless, because they are genuine preferences of those presidents.

Just as quickly as a presidential seal of approval can give a brand instant visibility, strong placement of a recognized brand can create "branded entertainment." That was what occurred in the case of a TV show character's fascination with a brand, such as *Sex and the City* character Carrie Bradshaw's passion for Manolo Blahnik shoes. Likewise, placement of a small company's product in a TV show can also catapult it into the spotlight. According to Schuyler Brown, associate director of strategic trend spotting at Euro RSCG Worldwide, producers are striving to imbue their shows with authenticity and real-life credibility. This is why a novel brand can add a unique flavor to a scene. Programs offer a wide range of opportunities for small, lesser-known firms.[21]

As an indicator of the magnitude of product-placement spending, a 2005 research study by Stamford, Connecticut-based PQ Media indicated that there was a 23-percent spike in one year, reaching a total of $4.25 billion. Audience fragmentation is partly responsible. According to Patrick Quinn, PQ Media's president, "Technological advances, most notably PVRs (personal video recorders) and continued audience fragmentation, due to the growing popularity of new media like the Internet and video games, have led major marketers who are already skeptical of their return on investment in traditional advertising to become even more dispirited with the old means of reaching target audiences."[22]

> We believe passionately in the power of ideas to create sustainable growth for our clients. We're also driven by the simple belief that NOTHING IS IMPOSSIBLE. We can go deeper into what we believe right here.
>
> —SAATCHI & SAATCHI[23]

Unusual Places to Advertise

Product placement has gone in a new direction. Companies now are paying people to wear temporary tattoo logos on their foreheads. Snorestop won an eBay bid to imprint its logo on Andrew Fischer's forehead for one month. The cost was $37,373. It followed up that campaign by advertising to find the next human billboard for the company. This time, Snorestop wanted the *headvertisers* to show off their own unique talent. They could dance, model, sing, recite poetry, do stand-up comedy, or even snore, just so long as it helped promote the company.[24]

As if head advertising were not eye-catching enough, there is another way for companies to "walk" their message around in trade shows or other heavily trafficked spots. The Walking News, created by Miami-based Multivision, a commercial production facility, offers a "walking TV." A person can stroll through an exhibit hall or shopping center with the advertiser's message appearing on a TV screen that is worn over the body. These new message boards can also show news and weather and can link to the Internet and offer MapQuest information as well.[25]

Bringing the message to the consumer is the idea behind using the sidewalk as a canvas. TBWA\Paris used the sidewalk much like a supermarket *floor talker* to advertise K2r Stain Remover. It painted a large white outline of a shirt on the pavement. A dark stain appeared to be on the "shirt," when actually it was on the pavement. Two words in white appeared on the bottom right side under the shirt encouraging passersby to "Try K2r."[26] This visual was impossible to ignore. What an effective way to showcase a product's benefit in full public view!

Other advertisers have used local sidewalks by painting footsteps that guide pedestrians into a particular store or salon. Some agencies, like Think Tank 3 in New York, have used sidewalks to highlight the dangers of traffic by stenciling an outlined body, with statistics, at various sites where pedestrians have been hit.

Advertisers like Nike, Apple, and Swatch, among others, have used entire buildings to project their messages. Apple's "Think Different" message was clearly visible in the form of wallscapes in Los Angeles. This was later followed by the Apple iPod's *Silhouettes* by TBWA\Chiat\Day. Nike's oversized images of athletes seemed actually to be participating in sports on the sides of buildings. And in 1983, when Nicolas Hayek took over as head of the Swatch Group, an enormous Swatch watch was very prominently draped down the sides of buildings. (Hayek was recognized for his innovative marketing tactics, which were the driving force behind the Swatch phenomenon.) But Taxi Advertising & Design's *Bernard Wall* for Nike has taken the concept of wallscapes even further. Here two buildings are used. The first has a visual of an athlete who seems to have crashed through the building onto the next building. The visuals' paired impact is unforgettable.

Being able to get noticed has become more and more difficult. It's only a few years ago that researchers claimed the average person saw 1,500 messages a day. Now, the estimate is more than 7,000, and this number is expected to climb past 10,000. Even the tiniest budgets must compete with the biggest spenders, as well as with all the "oh, wow!" messages.

Every now and then, an original idea is so simple that it captures the imagination. Stores in New York carrying the fragrance Bond No. 9 created a new way to give away free samples—no, not a new bottle or a new tube, but an entirely novel way to use a preexisting package design. They handed out vials of perfume dressed in bright, foil candy-like wrappers in beautiful shimmering colors. When twenty-three new fragrances for both men and women were introduced, they flew off the shelves. People were rushing in to raid the samples because they were so appetizing, yet totally calorie-free.[27]

Another innovative way to deliver a message is when the object itself makes the point for the advertiser. Creative talents at Leo Burnett USA chose to write a weight-reduction headline on a red six-pound weight. It challenged the reader to "drop the weight." The client was Kellogg's Special K, a breakfast cereal with campaign messages that have focused on helping people achieve their weight-loss goals. Although there are many diet products on the market, none have used such a well-targeted message site.

Messages on the Move

Sometimes it's not the venue (billboards, sidewalks, foreheads), but the vehicle that is delivering the message. Although outdoor advertising has been a standard vehicle to target an on-the-go society, mobile ads have become increasingly more popular. Many companies have used unusual vehicles on the road to catch consumers during their everyday travels. There's something entertaining about seeing theme-designed vehicles in the middle of a big city or even an image of one in the newspaper.

Although advertising-themed vehicles date back before the car was invented, they never seem to lose their appeal. As early as the 1890s, a horse-drawn Moxie Bottle Wagon pitched the soda at amusement parks and dance halls. Pep-O-Mint Life Savers hit the road in 1918, followed years later in 1947 by the Zippo Car, which was created from a 1947 Chrysler Saratoga and featured a pair of lighters flipped open with what appeared to be flames. It's hard to believe that Oscar Mayer, which was introduced in 1936, was revitalized five decades later, when it brought out its Hotdoggers—huge vehicles shaped like giant hot dogs on buns—in 1986 to celebrate its fiftieth anniversary. Then in 1993, the Wienermobile was redesigned and has been traveling the country ever since. It has been joined on the road by a giant Goldfish, three huge Hershey's Kisses on the Kissmobile, Mr. Peanut, and other icons in advertising. It might surprise people to know that in the middle of the three Kisses in the 13,250-pound Kissmobile is a karaoke for kids. The third Kiss is a gigantic refrigerator that houses more than 230,000 Kisses, which are given out to children. The first one is the command station that controls the vehicle.[28]

The publishing industry has jumped on using oversized vehicles to promote some books. For example, for a BBQ grilling book, the author toured the country in a large recreational vehicle with the book title appearing across it in gigantic letters. The author would go to the predetermined stop and conduct a BBQ cooking class, showcasing the recipes in the book.

The Harry Potter book and film series craze continued to generate enthusiasm when a double-decker bus traveled around Singapore dressed in the story's signature color, purple. The Knight Bus was designed to promote the opening of the Warner Bros.' book-based film, *Harry Potter and the Prisoner of Azkaban*. The bus was supposed to look like the magical double-decker bus that raced throughout London in the film.[29]

In an effort to reach the burgeoning Hispanic population, Johnson & Johnson created the VidaNuestra (Our Life) trailer, which took a thirty-four-week tour around the country in March 2005. Life-size cutouts of members of a fictional family named Bueno were inside the trailer, which showcased fifteen Johnson & Johnson products. The fifty-three-foot trailer's trip covered one hundred Wal-Marts and twenty Hispanic festivals, or fiestas. The van advertised the bilingual Web site VidaNuestra.com, as well as brands with other sites in Spanish. The huge vehicle stayed in Wal-Mart parking lots for around eight hours, allowing visitors to walk through and see all the products up close. Not only did this campaign target the Hispanic market, but it also tackled the challenges of multibrand promotions.[30]

Not only are there oversized, unusually shaped vehicles on the road, but decorated regular model cars are also used for promotions. For years the Truly Nolan company has used the VW Beetle, adorned with mouse ears and a tail, to move its name around town. Even Edy's has introduced a car decorated with pictures of Dibs, their bite-sized chocolate-coated ice cream, complete with a refrigerated trunk to keep the free samples ice cold. HBO Video wrapped buses with an image of a hearse to advertise the DVD version of its popular TV series *Six Feet Under*. The wrap was so distinctive and accurate, the buses in New York, Los Angeles, Chicago and San Francisco each looked like a giant hearse.

The use of vehicles to promote products was taken to a new level when the MINI Cooper was driven around on top of a Ford SUV in a groundbreaking 2002 campaign. Seeing a small car chauffeured around raised eyebrows and instant awareness. Since then, the MINI Cooper—yes, the entire car—has even appeared on billboards in Canada and New Zealand.

Placing products in locations other than a store shelf may seem ho-hum. Everyone has seen the ice cream truck or the mobile dog-grooming units, or even hot dog and other food vendors outside office buildings or in street festivals. However, it takes some imagination to place a product in a venue that is so ideal that it's hard to believe it was never considered before. For years, people have gone to South Florida for a break from the cold winter. But it wasn't until 2003 that visitors could get off the plane and purchase Banana Boat skin and sun care products from a vending machine inside the terminal. What a brilliant idea. So many people get sunburned on vacation because they forgot to bring or buy lotion. Now, they can pick it up before they leave the airport.[31]

Other Promotional Ideas in the Publishing Industry

With the battle to gain the consumer's attention, advertisers are thinking of smart ways to get their message across. If there is a way to stay in the consumer's mind before, during, and after a purchase, this is what advertisers are seeking to do. Publishing houses have become adept at turning author tours into attention getters by having them arrive in unusual vehicles or by creating excitement online with scavenger hunts and sweepstakes.

To promote his second novel, Brooklyn author John Wray decided a standard book tour wouldn't be as effective as a two-week trip down the Mississippi River on a beat-up homemade raft, to replicate the book's setting. He traveled from Helena, Arkansas, to New Orleans and received some press coverage he might not have had otherwise. Presence in the media equals awareness, which can drive sales.

The online clues to solve author Dan Brown's *The Da Vinci Code* scavenger hunt on the book jacket's cover art resulted in 40,000 people solving the problem and one winning a free trip for two to Paris. The entire story received national attention, and the winner was announced on *Good Morning America* in New York. Even long after the game ended, people could log on to Random House's Web site and see the original Web Quest. In addition, the author continued to have another site up for people to crack other codes. Both sites, with hypnotic music, ancient-looking type, and rich red colors, allow visitors to opt to receive Dan Brown's newsletter. This has allowed loyal *Da Vinci Code* enthusiasts to maintain a relationship with the author, while welcoming newcomers to the "inner circle." This connection only strengthened fans' desire to see the film version, which was released in 2006.

Even as early as 1999, publishers and authors of mysteries quickly recognized the power of the Web. One author, Lisa Scottoline, posted her first chapter on her Web site and asked for people to "edit this." Not only did she get hundreds of responses, but she also received attention from the press. Readers felt closer to her and were more eager to buy her book. According to industry insider

Kat Berman, then director of online business for Penguin Putnam, "Mystery readers are generally very 'wired and Internet savvy.'"[32] In addition, they enjoy talking to each about their favorite authors. Because of this, the Internet became one of the choice media to promote new books and connect with readers.

To explain how to reach mystery readers online, seven clues were offered in a 1999 James A. Martin article. These clues, shown in box 1.1, are still relevant today and are applicable to a wide range of industries.

At this point in time, using the Web is an integral part of many promotional campaigns. But it's using the Web in a new way that gains notice. For example, in 2005, when Crispin Porter + Bogusky introduced a PG-rated online "Striptease" for Gap, a trendy clothing retailer, the Web site was designed with no advertising support. Instead, the interactive campaign relied on word-of-mouth or viral marketing to drive consumers to www.watchmechange.com for a visit. Once there, visitors could type in their measurements and physical description and wait until the computer generated their likeness. Then, the computer model would come out and undress down to its underwear, go into a dressing room, and return modeling different outfits for the consumer to see. It was like having a personal runway show, and each consumer was the model.

The interesting thing is that consumers couldn't make a purchase on the site, and the logo was only shown briefly. Instead, site guests were able to develop a cartoon-like character and e-mail it to their friends. The site's only call to action was the furtive online invitation to meet in the back of Gap, used to entice guests to visit a Gap store.[33]

Likewise, the use of book tours is not new. But connecting a book tour to a special promotion or sweepstakes can enhance its impact. For example, Workman Publishing promoted its top-selling educational question-and-answer-based card game, *Brain Quest*, by sending twelve teachers who were frequent product users on a tour across the country during the summer of 2005. This book tour not only promoted the product, but it also added visibility to *Brain Quest*'s Win Your College Tuition sweepstakes, with its generous $150,000 grand prize college scholarship and five $10,000 runner-up scholarships.[34]

Another company, Cisco, wanted to stimulate more support from industry professionals without a big marketing budget. To accomplish this, it used viral marketing to create a business-to-business buzz for its new vodka, Triple Eight. It targeted four hundred bartenders and enticed them into selling more of its product by promising 150 all-expenses-paid trips to Nantucket to visit its vineyard and brewery. To support participating bartenders' efforts to win, Cisco kept in touch with them throughout the promotion, giving them updates on their progress in the contest and offering them new vodka recipes.

BOX 1.1 SPINNING A NEW WEB

Clue #1: Little-Known Territory. The Web is a wild and woolly place. There are very few rules.

Clue #2: Imagination Is Key. The possibilities on the Net are limited only by your imagination. This is evident in all the online book-related scavenger hunts and interactive games.

Clue #3: Simple Is Okay. Getting creative is great, but don't ignore the basics. Online author chats and book excerpts are still effective.

Clue #4: Flexible Budgeting. You can spend a lot of money—or next to nothing—promoting on the Web. Posting an ad or book chapter on a site frequented by a targeted group can be ten times more effective than running an ad in the subway.

Clue #5: Calculating the Payoff. White the costs of online marketing can be minimal, the rewards aren't easy to calculate. Not all book consumers buy them online. They might go to a local bookstore to make a purchase.

Clue #6: Reaching New Readers. The Web's biggest advantage could well be helping readers discover mysteries they might not have found otherwise. By using a few keywords and specific topic categories, publishers can introduce the reader to new books and authors.

Clue #7: Expanding Popularity. Online bookselling has the potential to expand the popularity of mysteries. Many mysteries are based on repeat characters and are created in series. Bookstores don't stock backlists, but the Internet e-stores do.

Clue #8: Staying on Track. It's easy to get lost on the Web. Surfers can just as easily connect to online content as they can get lost by browsing and wandering off.

Clue #9: Copyright—or Wrong? Copyright issues can get thorny in cyberspace. Because each author has a different rights deal, publishers may use the Internet on a book-by-book basis, not as part of an integrated plan.

Clue #10: It's Just Beginning. To many players, the future of mysteries in cyberspace seems limitless. Authors not only use the Web for promotion and contact with readers, some even use it as a place to publish their work. Some genres may eventually be very popular in an electronic format.

Source: James A. Martin, "Spinning a New Web," Copyright 1999 *Publishers Weekly*. Published by Reed Business Information.

This ongoing contact also helped increase the company's one-to-one relationship with its selected target. Cisco had the opportunity to interact with the winners throughout the trip, and the winners enjoyed the chance to participate in the production process. Some even added labels to the bottles. The highlight of the trip was the revered Bartenders Ball and the stories the bartenders took home with them. The result? In just four years Cisco's revenue increased to $1.2 million, double what it originally was.[35]

Advertising and promotional campaign strategists need to think beyond broadcast and print, outdoor and online. They need to look at all media. They need to consider how the target market thinks. How this group gathers information. How it likes to be approached. How it connects with others. How it responds to interactive promotions. How it can be intersected during daily activities. Most importantly, they need to be able to answer this question: How can this group be energized into creating a buzz about this product?

The creators of every campaign that created attention first understood how to approach their audience in an interruptive or novel way. Today, because of satellite feed and wireless Internet links, advertisers can customize messages on top of taxicabs according to zip codes, geographic areas, time of day, and even streets, as in figure 1.3.[36] So, if McDonald's wanted to advertise a breakfast special on streets

FIGURE 1.3 "Harpoon Beer" VID (Vert Intelligent Display) ad on top of taxicab, created by Vert Inc. Photo courtesy of Vert Inc.

surrounding its restaurants, it could, because the digital cab-top billboards are programmed to change throughout the day. In financial districts, the screens could display current stock prices. Major cities like New York and Boston already have VIDs, or Vert Intelligent Display videos, named after the company that created them, Vert Inc. Cofounder and chief executive officer Brad Harkavy found a way to take standard cab-top signs and turn them into high-tech message boards.[37]

Sometimes the most innovative campaigns are paired with equally creative media placement. Stay alert in order to notice new approaches or even to think up new campaign and product placement. Study billboards, bus wraps, taxicabs, and even store floors and sidewalks. Messages are everywhere, yet there's always a new place that's always been there but has previously been overlooked. In London, you may even see messages on the top of double-decker buses. These are there for people who work in high offices. When they look down, a promotional message awaits.

Some companies have used the sand on beaches to imprint their logos as a reinforcing reminder to sunbathers. Beer companies like Heineken have even used the bottoms of urinals to place their ads. Other companies like Country Music Television placed automated talking messages called "urinal communicators" in urinal covers to promote CMT's *Greatest Outlaws: The Dirty Dozen*. Those who find the medium distasteful will probably also object to the message, which reminds users not to miss *Outlaws* on CMT, even though they might miss everything else. Although these motion-activated ads last for more than 10,000 flushes, some critics have added them to the "bad ad" list. Ads that fall into this list are those that (1) are intrusive and costly (i.e., fax blasts), (2) do not allow the audience to shut them off (outdoor ads), (3) are uninvited house guests (direct mail), and (4) talk to a captive audience (urinal ads).[38] Whereas some new media are entertaining and exciting, others may be considered socially incorrect. Although it is difficult to stimulate media attention, this question still needs to be asked: Is it the right kind of attention? Or, as some believe, is any form of attention some kind of valuable recognition?

Some Important Sources

Everyone needs inspiration, including the most brilliant creative minds. They battle the same difficult challenges every day: how to develop exciting, breakthrough solutions to exceptionally complex problems. In addition to studying breakthrough ad campaigns, such as the ones we've seen in this chapter, even the most seasoned creative talents use numerous references to jump-start their imaginations. Here are a few sources they explore to help stimulate new ideas.

Often, they refer to unusual examples of inventive brochures, ads, direct-mail pieces, banner ads, and advertising articles they have saved over the years. Many have various editions of graphic design books, award annuals, and magazine subscriptions. Some find instant inspiration in popular advertising and graphic design publications, for example, *HOW, Print, Communication Arts, Dynamic Graphics, Adweek,* and *Advertising Age.*

They also go online to view ads on www.adage.com, www.adweek.com, www.adcritic.com (which has downloadable videos of spots from the Ad Age Group's *Creativity* magazine), and AdForum.com (including AdFolio's library of award-winning ads and commercials from around the globe). They may frequent www.adrants.com to look for innovative campaigns and to explore the site's extensive list of ad resources. Or they may check out other sites such as www.adblather.com for more creative work and lists of talented "idea people," related blogs, and other important resources. They may even bookmark the lists for future reference. These sites usually change frequently and even close down. It's important to continue searching for new sites that offer examples and insight into creative thinking. One such site is www.ihaveanidea.org. It has excellent visual work, as well as one-on-one interviews with the heads of many of the world's largest agencies.

In addition, they stay on top of the freshest creative ideas by reading current issues of publications like the daily Marketing section of the *Wall Street Journal* and the Business, Style, and Sunday *Magazine* sections of the *New York Times.* They visit recent work from ad agency Web sites, including Saatchi & Saatchi; Crispin Porter + Bogusky; Wieden+Kennedy; Ogilvy & Mather; TBWA; JWT; Leo Burnett; Euro RSCG Worldwide; Fallon; Goodby, Silverstein & Partners; Grey Global Group; and Young & Laramore, among many others. They also log on to the Web sites of top design firms or imagination centers like The Brooklyn Brothers, The Johnson Group, and Think Tank 3 to see what they're creating. The following list provides the current Web sites for these creative firms.

www.thebrooklynbrothers.com	www.leoburnett.com
www.cpbgroup.com	www.ogilvy.com
www.eurorscg.com	www.saatchi.com
www.fallon.com	www.tbwa.com
www.goodbysilverstein.com	www.thinktank3.com
www.grey.com	www.wk.com
www.johngroup.com	www.youngandlaramore.com
www.jwt.com	

Serious creative professionals read graphic design articles both in hard copy and online through www.allgraphicdesign.com, www.printmag.com, and www.howdesign.com. They also search for new information at dir.yahoo.com/Arts/Design_Arts/Graphic_Design/Magazines, www.world-newspapers.com/graphics.html, and desktoppublishing.com/design.html, to name a few. This last site offers links for graphic designers with tips about Web design and layout, plus information about organizations like Graphic Artists Guild, American Institute of Graphic Arts (AIGA), and Society for News Design (SND). The blogs like these listed in box 1.2 from the informative AdBlather site are very popular.

BOX 1.2 **INTERESTING ADVERTISING BLOGS**

Ad Pulp	Ernie Schenck
Adfreak	Gapingvoid
Adland	Grow A Brain
Adrants	Influx
Advertising/Design Goodness	Mindless
Adweak	Ordinary Advertising
Agenda Inc.	PSFK
Brand Autopsy	Seth Godin
Brand New	TBLOGWA
Brand Noise	The Hidden Persuader
CMO Magazine	The Origin of Brands
Coudal Partners	Urban Intelligence
Creative Classics (Italy)	Welcome to Optimism
Cup of Java	Y Pulse

Source: http://garicruze.typepad.com/ad_blather

A Few Techniques to Notice

By looking at award-winning examples, creative minds are inspired, motivated, and challenged to demand more imaginative, less expected solutions. Both graphic designers (those who create product packaging and indoor-outdoor signage, plus other graphic solutions) and art directors (those who design multimedia advertising campaigns) are always looking for new stimulants. When reviewing creative work, graphic designers and art directors examine the use of these and other layout components.

1. *Typography*—the selection, manipulation, treatment, and placement of type to create text portions and graphic components
2. *Color*—the use of specific colors and color combinations for specific products and emotional responses
3. *Visual techniques*—like *layering, ghosting back* type or images, lines, repeat graphic elements, *bullets* (icons used in front of word lists), illustration (realistic, abstract, cartoon, line art, etc.), and photography
4. *Shape*—the inclusion of a particular geometric *shape* used to organize or divide the page
5. *Value*—the use of dark and light to show contrast between different layout components or draw the reader's attention (closer objects have more detail, while dark or bright areas are seen first)
6. *Texture*—the use of visible patterns by grouping shapes together (like repeated squares), or contrasting light with dark areas and showing texture (like depicting sand, fabric, rocks, wood, etc.)
7. *Volume*—the portrayal of three-dimensionality with the use of *drop shadows* behind objects and borders around images
8. *Legibility of type*—the clarity of the type (ability of the reader to see the letters):
   - Is the font easy or difficult to read? (for example, *novelty type,* with its irregular shaped letters or unique design, is harder to read than many other fonts)
   - How does the background enhance, rather than compete, with the text?
   - Is the type the appropriate size and weight (not too small or thin) to be set in *reverse* (light type over a darker background; for example, white type on a black background)?
   - How much room was left around visuals to avoid *crowding* the type (making the type look as if it needs more space)?
9. *Layout*—the arrangement and relationship of all the components to each other (how the type, color, visuals, and icons work together)
10. *Overall impact*—the impression the overall design leaves with the audience
11. *Unusual components*—the inclusion of novelty fonts (like *Critter*), unexpected visuals (like one image *morphing* into another), or tiny type tucked away (which forces the reader to look closer)

Copywriters also analyze promotional literature to stimulate their creative thinking. They may be excited by these aspects of the copy (written words or text in the material):

1. *Marriage of a visual and headline*—the integration of both into one inseparable concept

2. *Message of the headline*—its relevance and impact. Does it
- have *stopping power* (ability to demand viewer's immediate attention)?
- surprise, amuse, entertain, or shock the audience?
- challenge the reader's imagination (for example, *teaser campaign*)?
- make the audience react?
- engage the reader's imagination?
- stimulate viewer participation?

3. *Writing techniques*—these will be discussed in later chapters and include:
- *alliteration* (the repetition of the first letter or sound)
- *parallel construction*—the repetition of a word or phrase (for example, "The Energizer Bunny keeps going and going and going")
- *weave*—the integration of one idea from the main concept throughout the copy
- *buttons*—the use of a clever line to close the copy
- *ABA*—the reference back to the headline's main idea in the closing line
- *connectors*—conjunctions and other words that tie sentences and paragraphs together
- *contractions*—combining two words into one shorter one (for example, "I'm," not "I am"; "you're," not "you are"; "we're," not "we are"; "they're," not "they are"; "who's," not "who is")
- *vernacular*—casual, everyday speech (for example, "coulda," "wanna," "gonna," "gotta")
- *flow*—takes readers by the hand and walks them through the copy without interruption

4. *Readability*—copy written in a clear, easy-to-read style

Creative thinkers are always on the lookout for great work. *All-type ads* rely solely on the power of the words and the typographic treatment. If these are sharp, insightful messages and differentiate this product or service from its competitors, they can be excellent references. For example, an ad created by the former Huey/Paprocki agency and once posted on its site was for the WeatherBug, an online weather service. The all-type headline was set in four lines, stacked one over the other in all capital letters. Using a stencil-like effect, it cleverly stated that more than 6 billion people would visit the site on a good day, and even more would visit on a bad one. Another one of Huey/Paprocki's all-type ads was a campaign for MedCareer. One horizontal strip ad's headline offered this type of clever promise: there were more job opportunities at MedCareer than there were streptococcus bacteria in a room filled with kindergarten-aged kids. These types of headline messages respect the audience and expect that readers will immediately grasp the message.

A Glimpse of Tomorrow

Discovering or creating new vehicles to reach the audience is always challenging. What other media vehicles will emerge in the future? We may be looking at some types of alternative advertising right now and not see the opportunity, like programmable taxi top ads. Consider the growth of eBay over just a handful of years. Here is an entire advertising venue that was created by individual sellers, not necessarily large corporations. People just placed the item on sale on eBay. They didn't need a storefront or a business license or incorporation fees. They just needed products to sell, a digital camera to photograph them, a short description of the items, a listing fee, and other eBay requirements, and they were in business. The entire site is one giant advertisement, yet people see it as an enormous e-store. Many people use it to discard personal possessions, much like an unending series of concurrent yard sales going on globally.

What will be the next unforeseen media blockbuster? Perhaps someone reading this right now will be the creator of a brand-new advertising medium.

■ EXERCISE

Assemble an ongoing swipe or clip file of excellent creative examples. Look for exciting visuals, interesting use of color, imaginative applications of type, and unexpected use of media. Create or obtain a container for your samples. It can be a notebook, a large box, an accordion file, a file cabinet, or a digital file. Divide your samples into easy-to-find categories: ads, brochures, flyers, billboards, banner ads, coupons, logos, letterhead, business cards, slogans, annual reports, cool copy, great campaigns, super headlines, unusual visuals, typographic creative treatment, Web sites, online interactive campaigns, advertising-themed vehicles, photos of alternative media, etc. Also collect a few poor examples: illegible type, poor color combinations, weak graphics, vibrating type (see page 152), unbalanced layouts, etc. ■

■ PROJECT

Select a product or service to advertise. Choose one you use personally—it can be an iPod, a computer, or an online or a direct-mail company (such as www.amazon.com or 1-800-flowers). Think seriously about your target and how to reach these people. Do some research about your audience. If it's a product you use, why did you buy it? Was it word-of-mouth, or a TV spot that you saw? Next, consider using several media. Which one would first capture your attention? Can you think of a medium that has not been used that would be effective?

Now, you're ready to begin to create an ad using one of your great examples as a reference point. Look carefully at your samples. Can any of the elements inspire you, like the use of *typography* or photography or *vernacular* language in your sample? Did one of the headlines you collected generate a strong response within you? If so, how can you generate a similar reaction to your ad?

After you create your ad, ask yourself, Can I fine-tune it? Can I make it more relevant to my audience? Can I make it more believable? Can I use a better medium? Or visual? Or headline? Just the act of compiling examples forces you to analyze promotional materials for their overall impact. This will help you become more judicious in your choice of colors, fonts, and graphic elements. ■

Suggested Reading

Amy Merrick, "Gap Deploys 'Viral' Online Promotion to Pump Up Sales," *Wall Street Journal*, August 10, 2005: B1, 3B.
Tim Nudd, "HBO Videos' Scare Tactics: Some Run Screaming from Boone/Oakley's Hearse Wrap," *Adweek,* August 1, 2005: 30.

Notes

1. Leo Burnett, www.leoburnett.com/belief/index.asp (accessed June 27, 2005).
2. Steve Sapka, personal communication, December 11, 2005.
3. Ryan Underwood, "Ruling the Roost: Wacky Campaigns Have Made Crispin Porter and Bogusky the Hottest Agency in the Ad Business," *Fast Company,* April 2005: 70–75.
4. Geoffrey A. Fowler and Sebastian Moffett, "Adidas's Billboard Ads Give a Kick to Japanese Pedestrians," *Wall Street Journal*, August 29, 2003: B1, 4.
5. Joan Voight, "Living It Up," *Adweek,* September 26, 2005: 26–27.
6. Jeffery D. Zbar, "New Board Game," *South Florida Sun-Sentinel*, November 12, 2002: B1, 2.
7. Barbara Lippert, "Wieden's Great Hoax," *Adweek,* May 24, 2004, www.adweek.com/aw/magazine/article_display.jsp?vnu_content_id=1000517454.html (accessed June 26, 2005).
8. Creative Quotes and Famous Sayings, 1993–2006, http://home.att.net/~quotations/creative.html (accessed July 7, 2005).

9. Brian Steinberg, "Next Up on Fox: Ads That Can Change Pitch," *Wall Street Journal*, April 21, 2005: B1, 4.

10. Geoffrey A. Fowler, "Asia's Mobile Ads: U.S. Firms Study What Flies on Hot Medium and Why—and How to Try It at Home," *Wall Street Journal*, April 25, 2005: B1, 6.

11. Fowler, "Asia's Mobile Ads," B6.

12. Melena Z. Ryzik, "Fugue in G Major," *New York Times,* July 10, 2005: AR24.

13. Lisa Sanders, "Great Minds Think Alike," *Advertising Age,* June 27, 2005: 55.

14. Laurel Wentz, "At Cannes, the Lions Say 'Grrr,'" *Advertising Age,* June 27, 2005: 55.

15. Wentz, "At Cannes," 55.

16. "Cannes Winners: Press and Outdoor," *Advertising Age,* June 27, 2005: 58.

17. Matthew Creamer and Jean Halliday, "Dead Giveaways," *Advertising Age,* March 14, 2005: 1, 39.

18. Creamer and Halliday, "Dead Giveaways," 39.

19. Natalie Danford, "Reader, Heal Thyself," *Publishers Weekly,* June 27, 2005: 30.

20. Charles Goldsmith, "Dubbing in Product Plugs," *Wall Street Journal*, November 6, 2004: B1, 5.

21. Ellen Neuborne, "Ready for Your Product's Close-Up?" *Inc. Magazine,* October 2004: 48–49.

22. Marc Graser, "Product Placement Spending Poised to Hit $4.25 Billion in '05," *Advertising Age,* April 4, 2005: 16.

23. Saatchi & Saatchi, 2004, www.saatchi.com/worldwide (accessed November 29, 2005).

24. Adrants, 2006, www.adrants.com (accessed July 30, 2005).

25. Laurance Feingold and Randall Hilliard, "Walking News. Walking TV Station?" *Miami New Times,* April 1–7, 2004: 4.

26. Jeremy Miller, personal communication, January 13, 2006.

27. Ellen Tien, "A Little Candy behind the Ear," *New York Times,* July 31, 2005: ST3.

28. Jim Motavalli, "Hot Dog! They're Not Just Cars, They're Commercials," *New York Times,* December 8, 2002: SP15.

29. Laura Wentz, "Magic Bus Touts 'Potter' in Singapore," *Advertising Age,* June 14, 2004: 16.

30. Laura Wentz, "J&J Takes Hispanic Outreach Effort on the Road," *Advertising Age,* March 21, 2005: 3.

31. Elaine Walker, "With Vending Machines, Banana Boat Gets 'Em Right Off the Plane," *Miami Herald*, September 1, 2003: BM15.

32. James A. Martin, "Spinning a New Web," *Publishers Weekly*, April 26, 1999: 36.

33. Amy Merrick, "Gap Deploys 'Viral' Online Promotion to Pump Up Sales," *Wall Street Journal*, August 10, 2005: B1, 3.

34. Joy Bean, "On a Quest for Smarter Kids," *Publishers Weekly,* May 16, 2005: 13.

35. Lora Kolodny, "Intoxicating Results," *Inc. Magazine,* June 2005: 38.

36. Associated Press, "Boston Taxis Feature Variable Ads," *New York Times,* July 15, 2001: www.vert.net/press_pages/newyorktimes_2.html (accessed July 16, 2005).

37. Tricia Long, "Vert Turns Taxi-Top Signs Into Web-Style Banner Ads," *Wall Street Journal*, June 8, 2001, www.vert.net/press_pages/wallstreet_journal_1.html (accessed July 16, 2005).

38. Dave Carpe, "When an Ad Goes Bad (Think 'Talking Urinals')," October 12, 2004: www.passingnotes.com/index.php/when-an-ad-goes-bad-like-talking-urinals (accessed August 14, 2005).

Play with Typography's Multiple Personalities

Fonts have their own unique tone of voice. Some are whimsical, like Mister Frisky, Jokerman, Double Remedy, and Curlz. Others are authoritative, like the *New York Times* logo, or personal, like many handwritten fonts, including Bobbo, Dana, Kudasai, and Fink Heavy. Still others are imaginative, like Critter and Stencil. And some offer a sense of old Europe, like Old English Text, Harrington, and Lucida Blackletter. Others are simple yet distinctive like Techno, Copperplate, and Base.

Whatever your tone of voice—the way you speak to the audience—the typography should match. For instance, you wouldn't choose a *novelty font* with a whimsical look for a medical or surgical center. Nor would you choose an authoritative or old-fashioned European-looking font for a children's party. Take a quick look at figure 2.1, and you will get a sense of some different font personalities.

Although there are thousands of fonts, there are several main categories of type used today. These include those listed below. Roman type, which introduced the twenty-six-letter alphabet that is still used today, was created by the early Romans in the first century BC via Greece, directly from the ancient Phoenicians' twenty-four-letter alphabet around 850 BC. The lower-case letters were not completed until the Middle Ages, when the addition of the letters *j, v,* and *w* was made. Roman type was later refined by Francesco Griffo in 1495, during the Late Middle Ages. Its contrasting thick and thin stroke weights are still in use and are exemplified in the typestyle Bembo. The most recognizable font classifications used today are listed here:

Mister Frisky
Jokerman
RemedyDouble
Curlz
Bobbo
Dana
Kudasai
Fink Heavy
CRITTER
STENCIL
Old English Text
Harrington
Lucida Blackletter
Techno
COPPERPLATE 30 BC
BASE

FIGURE 2.1 Examples of Font Personalities

1. *Text letter or Blackletter*—Introduced in the 1200s and regaining popularity today, this Gothic form of lettering, called Textura, emerged with distinctive angular strokes, angled serifs, and tight kerning so that artists could use as little space as possible on costly parchment (includes Lucida Blackletter and Old English Text).
2. *Old Style*—Around 1530, Claude Garamonde sought to perfect Roman fonts through type that had less contrast between the thick and thin strokes with slanted or bracketed serifs (includes Garamond and Palatino).
3. *Transitional*—This type evolved during the 1700s as a transition between Old Style and Modern, resulting in a blend of both (includes Baskerville and Century Schoolbook).
4. *Modern*—Created in 1769 by Giambattista Bodoni, this lettering has acute differences between the thick and thin strokes (includes Bodoni and Tiffany).
5. *Egyptian*— In 1815 Vincent Figgins used the name "Antique" to introduce this font, which displays slab serifs (tails) with thick square or rectangular tails (includes Clarendon, Egyptian, and Rockwell).

1. 𝕿ext letter or 𝕭lackletter (Lucida Blackletter)

2. Old Style (Palatino)

3. Transitional (Baskerville)

4. **Modern (Bodoni)**

5. Egyptian (Rockwell)

6. Serif type (Times New Roman)

7. Sans serif (Arial)

8. *Script* (Edwardian Script)

9. Novelty (Sheryl)

FIGURE 2.2   Examples of Basic Font Classifications

6. *Serif*—There were always tails are on the ends of the letters of all fonts (like Courier, Times, and New Roman), including those listed above, until Sans Serif fonts were created.

7. *Sans Serif*—Making its first appearance in an 1816 type book released by William Caslon IV, this font has no tails at all on any of the letters (includes Arial, Caslon, and Futura). *Sans* means "without" in French.

8. *Script*—Introduced in 1557 by Robert Granjon, this type, also called cursive, imitates handwriting so that the letters are connected (includes Edwardian Script and Mistral).

9. *Novelty*—This name covers a wide range of typefaces that are ornate or decorative in their design. They are often whimsical or funky (for example, Critter, Jokerman, Mister Frisky, Curlz, and Sheryl).

Figure 2.2 shows examples of the basic groups of type. By closely comparing them, you can discern the differences among them.

It's important to start looking at typography everywhere you can. Go online. There are numerous type foundries (companies that create new fonts) that you can visit. This will instantly make you realize how many different fonts there are. In fact, with so many new fonts being developed so frequently, it may be almost impossible to have an accurate count. But, just to get a glimpse of the variety of styles and personalities, be sure to visit these sites:

A List of Online Type Foundries

www.abstractfonts.com

www.adobe.com

www.chank.com

www.coolarchive.com

www.emigre.com

www.fontboy.com

www.fontcraft.com

www.fontfoundry.com

www.fonts.com

www.fonthaus.com

www.fontshop.com

www.fontsworld.com

www.free-fonts.com

www.garagefont.com

www.houseindustries.com

www.itcfonts.com

www.larabie.com

www.linotype.com

www.myfonts.com

www.philsfonts.com

ww.psyops.com

www.p22.com

www.renaesroom.com

www.sharkshock.com

www.smackbomb.com

www.smartsoftware.com

www.t26.com

www.2rebels.com

www.typfonts.com

www.veer.com

Font Sites Specializing in Free Fonts

www.acidfonts.com

www.fontfreak.com

www.fontheaven.com

www.free-fonts.com

www.1001freefonts.com

Font Sites Specializing in Handwritten Fonts

www.a1fonts.com

www.ezgoal.com

www.fontgarden.com

www.geocities.com/compyater

www.1001freefonts.com

perso.orange.fr/dephitro/fonts.html

www.schoolhousefonts.com

www.letter.com

Be sure to wander around online and see the different font foundries up close. Just to entice you, here is a small sampling of what you'll find on a few of the larger type foundry sites:[2]

1. *www.adobe.com*—Long recognized for its library of fonts by leading type designers and foundries, Adobe offers so many products that it's difficult to find the area on fonts. Just type in "fonts" at the Search prompt. You will be taken to a page where you can choose from different classifications of fonts. Each category allows you to type in your own text and see it set in all the fonts on that page at the same time. You can click on another category, and your line of type will reappear in all the fonts on that page as well, without having to retype anything. If you want to obtain Adobe's useful type specimen catalog, you can order it online through the Adobe e-store. For a handy typography reference and glossary, download Adobe's PDF font guide.

www.fonts.com—Starting with the Agfa font collection (now known as Monotype Imaging), this site added many other font libraries, including the Monotype ITC typefaces, plus fonts from several other foundries and type designers. To see the entire range of fonts it carries, just ask for its free catalog. Under "About Fonts," you'll find articles about type designers, a brief terminology glossary, and explanations of the latest developments in font technology, including OpenType, a versatile new kind of font with multiplatform uses.

2. *www.fonthaus.com*—This easy-to-navigate site offers its own fonts as well as those from other font foundries. It also offers packages of best-selling fonts, retro clip art, illustration CDs, royalty-free photography, and more. Its online magazine, *x-height*, discusses type design, fonts, and technology updates plus features interviews by top designers.

3. *www.fontshop.com*—Fontshop dates back to 1989 as an independent font source. Today, it offers a wide range of fonts, including some exclusive to the site; a glossary; some site links; and its online publication, *Magazine Font*.

4. *www.itcfonts.com*—This e-store font shop, which in the 1970s was an icon of typographic design, allows you to purchase many fonts like the ITC classics Korinna, Kabel, and Clearface and to see the top five ITC fonts, including Officina and Avant Garde Gothic. It also gives you the opportunity to submit your own type design and have ITC help market it. ITC introduces around thirty new typefaces each year.

5. *www.linotype.com*—Here you can find 6,000 fonts, from all-time standards like Frutiger and Neue Helvetica to imaginative designs like Linotype Fresh Ewka and Linotype Drop Ink. Some of the most widely recognized type designers, both past and present, like Giambattista Bodoni and John Baskerville, are included. What makes the site extremely user friendly is the easy-to-understand font categories like "Handwriting," "Western," and "Cool" fonts. The "Font Lounge" allows visitors to see the top-selling fonts, link to hundreds of designers' home pages, view the entire type gallery, and view Linotype's complete portfolio of selected designers.

6. *www.myfonts.com*—This site has an extensive library of thousands of fonts. Particularly helpful is the "Font Category" page, which visually identifies specific groups of fonts. Another useful feature is the multiple font comparison function, which lets you compare several fonts at a time. You can also set any font, in any size, right on the screen and see how it looks in various sizes. The "What the Font" area allows visitors to submit a font by uploading GIF, JPEG, TIFF, or BMP scanned images for quick identification or submit it to the "What the Font Forum," where people all over the world help determine the font's identity.

7. *www.philsfonts.com*—With more than 35,000 fonts from seventy-five foundries, Phil's Fonts has many choices but less information than some of the other sites. But it does have some helpful services: it will help you identify a typeface that you submit by fax or by e-mail; convert fonts between PostScript, TrueType, and OpenType; organize your type library; custom design type; and more.

8. *www.veer.com*—Along with some very innovative fonts, this site also offers some entertaining aspects. You can take a short online typography workshop with fun interactive exercises, created by the University of Delaware's Visual Design Department. You can enter the John Lennon Songwriting Contest for a $20,000 prize or schedule a visit with the John Lennon Educational Tour Bus, which will visit your school for a hands-on recording session using the most technologically advanced recording equipment. You can even submit your own "inkjet haiku." Or you can see some visual and typographic solution ideas created from fictional briefs.

Today, some of the most popular fonts have been created in some of the smaller font foundries. These include Emigré's typeface Mrs. Eaves (based on the Baskerville font and created by designer Zuzana Licko in 1996), P22's Cézanne (reminiscent of the artist's handwriting and designed by Michael Want in 1996), Plazm Fonts' font Inky-Black (a fat, funky face designed in 1994, by Pete McCracken, the firm's director) and Retrospecta (with irregular serifs on ascenders and descenders, created in 1994 by Christian Kusters), Hoefler & Frere-Jones's formal Requiem (created by Jonathan Hoefler and Tobias Frere-Jones and inspired by wood engravings), House Industries' font Neutraface (a straightforward sans serif font that mimics commercial blueprints for buildings and homes, developed in 2001), and Powerhouse (a chunky, retro typeface at a slight slant, used for vehicle lettering and logos, as in the Powerpuff Girls, was also created by House Industries in 1995).[3]

Chank (Charles Anderson) is another type designer whose work today is instantly recognizable because one of his whimsical fonts, Mister Frisky, appeared on Taco Bell food wrappers and Welch's Grape Soda cans (see figure 2.1). There are many playful fonts on his well-known site, www.chank.com. His sense of humor is not only evident in his fonts—it's also apparent in his Web packaging. At one time, he grouped fifty fonts and called them Chank's Dental Pack in honor of his extensive dental work. When clients want an exclusive Chank font created just for them, they'll pay thousands of dollars. Ocean Spray hired Chank to depict its products' "zing" and paid $6,000 so no other company could use it.[4]

One site, www.fontcraft.com, offers special fonts designed to work well on the Web, as well as historic calligraphic fonts based on ancient, medieval, and modern lettering. Here you can find Celtic, Viking, Gothic, and even psyche-delic and futuristic fonts. There is also a collection of antique art and ARType packages that include art and fonts inspired by particular artists.

Another type site, www.2rebels.com, has creative fonts and hypnotic music in the background to escort visitors musically while they browse. Arranged alphabetically, the library is easy to navigate and rewarding when you stumble upon fonts like Hanbuhrs, Junk, Perceval, and Toxin. At www.zinzell.com you can browse though designer Don Zizell's creative works, including typographic designs. Here the fonts are integrated into exciting layouts, instantly trans-forming them from letter shapes into active design elements.

An artistic type book with unique fonts is *Extreme Fonts: Digital Faces of the Future* by Spencer Drate and Jutka Salavetz. Instead of just consisting of pages of new typography, the book presents each font set accompanied by bold layouts implementing the type. This helps designers see the font in use so that they do not have to try to visualize how it will work. It also lists the font name, designer, and font foundry, plus it cites clients, fonts used, illustrators/photographers, and graphic designers.

Unfortunately, now that so many people are able to create fonts with font edi-tor programs like Fontographer, FontLab, Font Creator, TypeTool, BitFonter, and AsiaFont Studio, piracy is prevalent. These programs are available for pur-chase online on many sites including www.fontlab.com, www.websitetips.com, www.high-logic.com, and www.fontcraft.com.

Of course, looking at different fonts is just the beginning. Now start to look at fonts more analytically. Do the letters have a tail like this font (Times New Roman)? If so, those kinds of fonts are serif fonts. If the letters do not have a tail, like the font Arial, those fonts are sans serif. Now think about the stroke weights. These are the thick and thin lines that create each letter. Are they similar, with equally thick or thin lines? Or are they different, with some lines thinner or thicker than others? Look carefully at each font and what makes it distinctive.

Examine the characteristics of the *ascenders*, those lines above the body of the letter, like the tall, vertical line in the letter *b*. Consider the particular traits of the *descenders*, the lines that hang below the body of the letter like in the letter *p*.

All these qualities help constitute the specific voice that the font uses. Some are bold and boisterous. Others are soft and whispering. Some are formal. Others are casual. Look at every part of the letters in a particular font. Then, decide which ones you want to use. Just as you created a clip file of excellent and poor advertising work, now collect examples of special or unique fonts and interesting typographic treatment. Go beyond just rotating type, or compressing or expanding the type by adjusting the *kerning* (the amount of space between the letters), or modifying the openness or tightness in lines of type by changing *leading* (the amount of space between the lines). Your attention to type will make any layout look more polished. Slight changes in the alignment of type, or its proximity to other objects, type boxes, and margins, as well as the rotation and wrapping of type, can enhance or detract from a layout.

One important consideration is the *legibility* of the type. This type characteristic is defined by this question: how effortlessly can the reader distinguish each character? If readers struggle to decipher the letters, as in some novelty fonts, the type is considered less legible. If readers easily recognize the letters, as in many serif fonts, the type is labeled very legible.

Also, think about the *readability* of the type. This has two specific meanings: first, how the type is set in the layout, and, second, how easily the reader can digest the information. In the former, the question is this: how long can readers read without becoming fatigued? How is the type set? In narrow columns? Small copy blocks? In screened (shaded) areas? In a straight line or at an angle? In a box or set as a shape (like a circle)? All of this affects the type's readability. Although sans serif type is generally easier to read set in reverse, research has shown that there is no perceptible difference in general readability between serif and sans serif type when it's not set in reverse.[5]

Serif font
Sans serif font

However, what affects readability is the ascenders. The reason for this is that we recognize letters more from the right side of the letters than the left side (except for *b* and *p*). We also identify letters more from the top parts of the letters (the ascenders) than from the bottom parts of the letters (the descenders). Place a sheet of paper on the line. First cover the bottom half of the letters. Then, cover the bottom half. Do this with several sentences. Do you see the difference? Did you notice how you could identify more of the letters from their top parts than from their bottom parts?

One more aspect of type readability is the height of the body of the letter. This is called x-height. The taller the x-height, the more area there is to show the letter's details. Type designer Adrian Frutiger ignited a new approach to type design when he created the font Univers with a larger x-height. This helped the reader discern the letters more easily. This is still true today. Therefore, when choosing type, compare x-heights of various fonts before making your final decision. Even when you are down to two fonts, the x-height may influence your choice.

Color combination also affects the type's legibility, because certain combinations are read more easily than others. What two colors do you think top the legibility chart? Black type on white, right? Would it surprise you to know that the most legible combination is black type on yellow? Then, second is black on white. Third is yellow type against black. Fourth is white type on black. According to the Pantone Color Institute, yellow and black are "opposites in chromatic value," with an "85% lightness contrast between the two colors."[6]

Here's the basic legibility list for outdoor ads using bright colors[7]:

1. Black on yellow
2. Black on white
3. Yellow on black
4. White on black
5. Blue on white
6. White on blue
7. Blue on yellow
8. Yellow on blue
9. Green on white
10. White on green
11. Red on white
12. White on red
13. Red on yellow
14. Yellow on red
15. Pink on white
16. White on pink
17. Pink on yellow
18. Yellow on pink

According to T. H. Nilsson of the Department of Psychology at the University of Price Edward Island, Canada, in measuring the legibility of color graphics and type, six combinations were found to be more legible than black on white.[8] These are, in descending order:

Type versus Background

1. Black on pink
2. Black on yellow
3. Black on orange
4. Dark green on yellow
5. Black on red
6. Dark green on white
7. Black on white

Other studies by Miles Tinker, his students, and associates back in the 1960s examined legibility of type. Their research and recent studies of screen legibility show that black on white is still considered by many the most legible combination.[9] Numeric values are given to combinations to indicate legibility in two books still referred to today: *The Legibility of Print* (1963) and *Bases of Effective Reading* (1965). Although more research on the subject is needed, the results reported indicate that the next most legible combinations were green on white, blue on white, black on yellow, red on yellow, red on white, green on red, orange on black, orange on white, red on green, and black on purple. Some might argue against the legibility of a few of these combinations, namely green on red (or vice versa) and black on purple. But Christmas cards and signage abound with green and red every year.

However, one conclusion agreed on by all researchers is that dark type on a light background is most legible. Many agree black type on a white or yellow background is most legible in many media, including print both outdoor and online.

The Importance of Type

By realizing the importance of all of type's aspects that affect legibility like type size, ascenders, x-height, stroke weight, kerning, alignment, column width, and type characteristic, designers are able to determine which fonts to use and in what manner. Graphic designers and art directors who handle type very creatively understand that it is a communication device, just like a language. It has its own syntax, which is created by the use and placement of the letters, words, rules, copy blocks, and space around the page, or *margins*. All these elements are then organized by (1) priority to indicate a *visual hierarchy*, (2) *ABA,* a literary form that gives a sense of order and completion to writing as well as visuals, and (3) an underlying division of the page based on an invisible *grid*.[10]

When examining the specific characteristics of a font, consider how the letters will work together to form words and sentences. Comparing several fonts online side by side is a particularly helpful guide. Also consider the arrangement of the words into columns or copy blocks. How much information do you have? How much space to you need to say everything? Next think about the inclusion of rules or lines to (1) emphasize type, (2) separate copy blocks, (3) create a graphic element, and (4) add balance. Lastly, picture an invisible border, or margin, all around the page. This frames the layout and allows breathing space for the eye to absorb the information. Sometimes there is so much information that layouts look jammed with content.

> There are only two kinds of advertising—great and invisible.
>
> —MICHAEL NEWMAN[11]

What Is Visual Hierarchy?

When designers and art directors talk about *visual hierarchy*, they mean that the layout uses the location, weight, size, and proportion of the type and visuals to show the reader exactly what is important. There is an ongoing dialogue between all the parts. Just like in a play, there are leading and subordinate roles. Think of your layout as a performance, with you as the director. Who needs to be outspoken? Who needs to be subtle? With visual hierarchy, you bring to center stage what you want the viewer to see first, second, and so on. If all the type is set large and bold, every word is commanding the audience's attention. Likewise, if the visual is overwhelmingly powerful, it becomes dominant. With contrast in the layout, only certain parts are prominent.

Ways to Use ABA

One helpful organizational tool is *ABA*. It creates a conversation between specific aspects of the layout, as well as recognized order and palpable rhythm. It can be used four ways:

1. Visual ABA organizes graphics that repeat or create contrast.
2. Typographic ABA groups similar and dissimilar copy blocks to create a visible dialogue.
3. Combined ABA exchanges type or visual components to continue a pattern.
4. Copy ABA reiterates the headline by referring back to it in the last line of copy, thereby reiterating the basic message. Figure 2.3 shows a number of examples of ways to use ABA. (This writing technique will be discussed further in chapter 5.)

The whole point of ABA is to guide readers' focus and make the layout and copy more easily digestible. It enhances message comprehension by carefully juxtaposing repetitive and contrasting elements. The result is a harmonious union that communicates well.

Using a Grid

Many designers work from an invisible *grid*, which divides up the page into little squares like a checkerboard. Think of a grid as the lines of a cutting board. Now mentally drop that measurement system behind the page. Picture a line that cuts the page in half, first vertically, then horizontally. Then cut again and again. You can divide the page up into small boxes, like a calendar, or just two or three columns. It depends on the layout you plan to create.

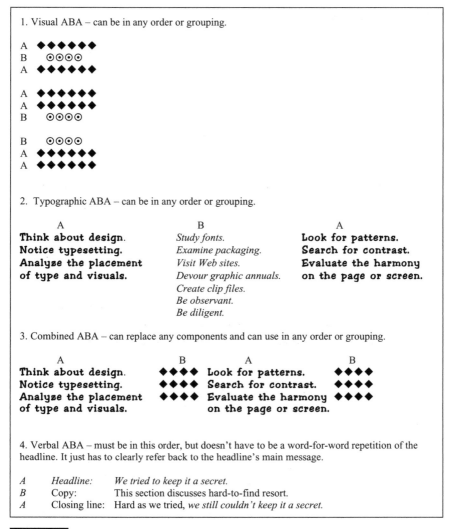

FIGURE 2.3 Examples of Ways to Use ABA

The beauty of using a grid is that it helps align columns of type and repetitive visual icons. With a grid, designers can quickly see if one line of type is lower than another. Or see if one visual is slightly higher than another one. Of course, some designers prefer to use the rulers in the design programs. They "drop a rule" or pull a "line" down from the horizontal and vertical guidelines as needed, rather than drawing an entire grid behind the page. These rules do not print. They are for the designer's reference only.

What Is Easier to Read

The actual characters in the font set are important in designing. But equally important are the weight and size of the letters. New designers sometimes use type that is too large for both the headline and the body copy. They may also fail to distinguish between the headline and subhead (secondary line that supports the headline). This lack of contrast confuses readers, leaving no road map for them to follow. With so much similarity, it is impossible to discern what is significant and what is secondary.

One interesting fact is that researchers have found that people can read ten- to eleven-point text faster than twelve-point type and larger. Considerably smaller sizes are more difficult to see, and type sizes above twelve points slowed the reader down and changed the way the eye moved across the page in saccadic eye movements.[12] One critical consideration is the age of your audience. People over forty generally lose their ability to read up close. Therefore, for a forty-plus market, the type should be set at thirteen-point for greater facility in communicating your message.

Research conducted in 1932 by American researchers Miles Tinker and D. G. Paterson, which is still accepted today, has shown that the eye grabs groups of words in "saccadic leaps" and briefly rests in regular "fixations."[13] The saccadic leap takes approximately one-tenth of a second, and the fixations to absorb the information between one-third to one-half of a second.[14] Larger type interrupts this process, preventing the reader from reading word groups.

You would read   this group of words   with little rests   like this.
The word groups approximate how the eye reads groups of type in saccadic leaps. The large space represents the little rests, or fixations, the eye regularly takes.

Another decision facing the new creative talent is where and when to use all caps or upper- and lowercase letters. Generally speaking, all caps should be reserved for headlines and places where there is very little text, like business cards. The use of all caps also affects saccadic leaps, because there is no height difference as there is in upper- and lowercase. However, some art directors like the look of all caps and like to use full-size caps followed by small caps. Again, if used judiciously, all caps or regular and small caps can work. But just notice HOW MUCH MORE SLOWLY YOU READ THIS LINE than you do this line of information.

One interesting point, however, is that although all caps are considered harder to read, they are preferred by radio announcers and voice-over talents. Radio scripts are the few places where the copy is set in all caps and double spaced.

More about Readability and Legibility

Kerning (the space between the characters) also affects *legibility*, as do weight, justification, and letter design uniformity (the thick and thin parts of the letters). Tight kerning, skinny fonts, wide spacing caused by justified type, and inconsistent letter design make the type harder to read (figure 2.4).

Reverse type, although eye catching, is also harder to read. To ensure legibility, a chunky sans serif font is a safer choice. Skinny type can seem to fall apart when set in reverse. Script and novelty fonts, as well as those set in italics, add to the challenge, making them even harder to read in reverse.

When you are considering a wide or narrow copy block, take a look at newspapers. What do you see? Narrow columns. Why? Because the eye moves faster vertically than it does horizontally. Although you may see ads with a small amount of copy set in a wide block, you'll probably notice that although the copy looks good graphically, you can't read it quickly. If the message is important, avoid using two or three lines that go across the width of the page—better to use six lines in a narrower block of type.

> Some designers prefer to use wide copy blocks like this because they like the way it sprawls across the page. But people read wide copy blocks slower than more narrow ones like this:

> The same copy would be read faster
> when set in a slightly more
> narrow block like this.
> The eye can move along
> in its regular *saccadic leaps*,
> looking ahead and anticipating
> the end of the line.

Easier to read	Harder to read
Regular kerning is better.	Tight kerning is more difficult.
Darker, bolder type.	Skinny fonts
Uniform letter strokes	Uneven strokes (thick & thin)
Flush left Type with even spacing between the words	**Justified with open spaces** T y p e t h a t ' s w i d e o p e n
Regular type	Novelty Fonts (Almagro)
Regular type	*Italics*
Regular type	*Script* (Edwardian Script)
Regular type	Cursive (Sheryl)
Regular type	Text letter (Lucida Blackletter)

Easier to read in reverse type:
Heavy, sans serif font (B Folio Bold).

Harder to read in reverse type:
Thin, serif font (Times New Roman).

Script font (Brush Script MT).

NOVELTY FONT THAT COMES IN ALL CAPS (HERCULANUM).

FIGURE 2.4   Reference Chart of Type Legibility

Although we discussed the problem created by wide copy blocks as well as open spaces between the characters caused by justified type, we haven't looked at the difference between flush left and centered type. Generally speaking, if there is a very small amount of copy, as in wedding invitations, centered type is acceptable. But where there is one full paragraph or several blocks of copy, flush left is easier to read than centered type. When you set type flush right, use it judiciously in layouts that wrap around an image, or for front covers of annual reports or magazines, or for letterhead. Reading flush right type is distracting when the text continues for any great length.

More about Type

Always remember that the reader's comfort must be considered seriously before you set type. Of course, there are times when the design seems to dictate the type. However, before allowing the type to succumb to the layout, ask yourself, how important is the message in this circumstance? Sometimes, obscuring or considerably reducing the type forces readers to pay attention and makes them take a closer look, thereby highlighting the message. There have been many ads that use very tiny headlines, the purpose of which is to draw the reader in.

Also consider if you want to use drop initial caps, to set any type in a box, to use a *screen* (light color) behind the text, to rotate the type, to wrap the type (*text wrap*) around an image or type box, or to have the type follow a shape or path (see figure 2.5 for examples of these techniques).

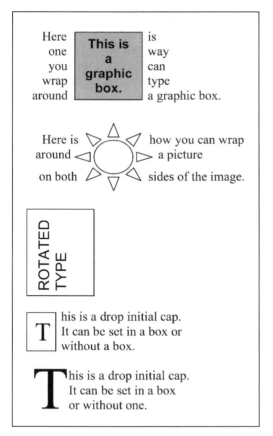

FIGURE 2.5 Examples of Text Wrap, Rotated Type, and Drop Initial Caps

> As Linda Kaplan Thaler told *Elle Magazine* in May, 2004:
> Ideas are like fish—they don't get better with time.
>
> —LINDA KAPLAN THALER, CEO and
> chief creative officer, The Kaplan Thaler Group[15]

A Quick Type Guide

Using type effectively is not based on graphic tricks like WordArt. Instead, it means setting type so it clearly prioritizes the information, quickly communicates the message, guides the reader through the copy, and works in harmony with the other components in the layout.

With so many typefaces, typestyles (bold, italics, three-dimensional, *drop shadow*, *outlined*), and type effects (rotation, open and tight *kerning*, and *leading*), new creative talents often feel compelled to use too many fonts, too many styles, and too many effects. Just because there are so many choices doesn't mean you have to use them all. Using too many fonts and effects in the same layout looks as if you opened up your closet and put on everything you owned. That may be an exaggeration, but you get the point. The layout looks like a disorganized mess. When it comes to typography, less is definitely more.

That means that if you're creating a brochure or newsletter, you should choose no more than two or three fonts. Use one font and type size for the headline, a smaller size for the subhead, a second font for the body copy, and possibly a third font for a *slogan* or tagline (the main message of the campaign), a *caption* (line of type, set under or next to image, that explains it), or any other ancillary comment that is not part of the copy.

This basic question often arises: what is the standard type size used for body copy and headlines to ensure legibility and good contrast? Here is a safe guideline: depending on the font, ten- to eleven-point type for body copy and fourteen- or sixteen-point type for subheads in newsletters and articles. Display type for headlines varies widely. This little guide will help.

Headline—sixteen point and above
Subheads—between fourteen and sixteen point (all the same font and
    color)
Body copy—ten or eleven point (depending on font, could go to twelve
    point)

For the brochure cover or newsletter masthead (name of the publication), choose a font with personality and strength. Trendy or novelty fonts are reserved for headlines rather than body copy. However, you can use any style of typeface as long as it reflects the image of the company or product. The size will depend on the overall layout. You may need to use oversized type, for instance, when you are creating a sprawling *double-truck* ad (a layout that goes across two pages) or a single-page ad that requires thirty-six-point type or larger.

For ads, the headline can be placed anywhere and can be any size. Watch that the subhead does not overshadow the headline. For the body copy, ten to eleven point is usually a safe choice. If you have a lot of body copy and want to use bold subheads to break up the sections, make sure they are all the same size and not nearly as large as the subhead that sits near the headline.

More about How We Read

You already understand that we absorb ideas through one- to three-second fixations between saccadic leaps and that we read narrow columns more easily than we do wide lines of type. The next thing to grasp is that the eye sees first whatever is most prominent. Therefore, if everything has equal weight, readers don't know where to begin or how to proceed.

People read from left to right and top to bottom. When looking at an ad, for example, the eye starts at the upper left corner then scans down to the bottom right corner and sweeps up to the middle. This is a quick one-two-three movement. If the visual emphasis is in the center, the eye will gravitate to it, and the reading pattern is altered. One interesting survey conducted by MediaAnalyzer Software and Research in Massachusetts compared what two hundred men versus two hundred women looked at first in ads. The online survey compared what was seen first in sexually charged ads versus nonsexual ads. Who looked at what first varied depending on the product and the visual content. Women responded better than men to nonsexual ads for Polo and Sketchers but had the same viewing pattern for a nonsexual alcohol ad. Sexual content changed the viewing pattern more for men than it did for women. However, both men and women had a more difficult time recalling the advertiser in ads with strong sexual content.[16]

But before reading an ad at all, people spend just *one* second deciding whether to look at the ad. Yes, just one second. If they actually decide to read it, they spend around *three* seconds to digest the message. That's all, three seconds. So the maximum total time you have with most readers is four seconds.

If your ad doesn't have stopping power, you don't even have those four precious seconds. Your ad has lost its opportunity to say anything at all. This is why you must decide what you want readers to see first. If you don't capture their interest, they won't read anything.

Type with Movement

Setting type or a visual at an angle gives it a sense of movement. Also, placing type to one side of the page makes the reader think it "walked in" on that side. Stacking type one line over another gives it a vertical feel. And if it's stacked from the top of the page down, it appears to be moving down the page (see figure 2.6 for examples).

Repeated overlapping type, especially in different sizes, can give the text a frenetic look. It adds typographic noise and chaos. But this can be dynamic if used appropriately. For example, if a page repeated the line "You're driving me nuts!" with different-size type layered one over the other, it could motivate someone in distress to seek counseling. You can actually make the reader feel the tension in the type, as if the type is actually screaming out for help. Likewise, a headline can speak in a specific voice, all due to the font. One font, Butterfly Chromosome, has an ethereal softness like the butterfly its name depicts. This could be an

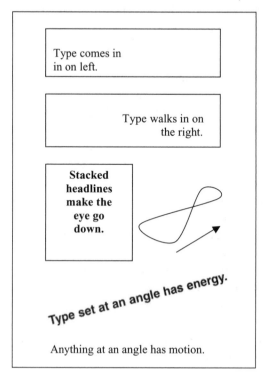

FIGURE 2.6 Examples of How Type Shows Movement

interesting font for a headline for a park, a nature and science store, or an arts and crafts store.

Type can create its own sense of rhythm. It can actually reflect the spoken voice or "sound" like an object. Look at how the type in figure 2.7 creates auditory imagery of a horse with bells around its neck strutting down the street.

Here the text is working to actually portray the meaning of the words. By manipulating the letters' weight, size, typeface, and position, type can become a rhythmic interpretation and can be used as an effective tool to communicate movement, music, sound, and more. Music album covers often use type to illustrate the music inside, such as typographically portraying lightning bolts with electrified-looking type to depict a lightning bolt.

Type can depict a state of being or an object. For instance, a sense of isolation could be shown by separating the "ed" from the rest of a word, like this: "isolat - ed." Birds in flight have been depicted with the type set in the birds' shape and tilted at an angle as if it were airborne. (More typographic meaning and manipulation will be discussed in chapter 3.)

Type can also contribute to the symmetry or asymmetry of the layout. (These are principles of design, which will be further discussed in chapter 4.) When the layout is *symmetrical*, there is an even distribution of the various components. The left side mirrors or matches (in weight, number, and placement of

FIGURE 2.7 Example of How Type Shows Rhythm

verbal and visual items) the right side, or the top reflects the bottom. There is an even distribution of the components. Typographically, you could have the same number of copy blocks and subheads on both sides. This kind of layout conveys order, organization, and serenity. In *asymmetrical* layouts, there is an uneven arrangement of the verbal and visual items. For example, you could stack the type on one side of the page and place only a small graphic on the other. The ad could appear heavier or denser on one side than on the other. This inequity often creates an edgier, less predictable, and more intriguing layout.

Another consideration with type is how larger, heavier type adds weight to the page. Type alone can make a promotional piece serious or foreboding. Set a headline with fonts in three different weights or thicknesses of type. Notice how the headline is influenced by the heaviness of the type.

Now imagine that headline twice the size in a small-space ad or a small four-inch-by-nine-inch rack brochure (one that sits in display holders). You can easily picture the impact a big, bold headline carries. That is why an *all-type ad* (an ad with no visuals, only *typography*) can be just as powerful as one with a visual. Type is such a strong communicator that it can deliver the message all by itself.

Just remember that for the type to be an integral part of the layout, it has to have energy and work in complementary units to hold together yet have some element of surprise. That element could be an unexpected placement of the type. Or the introduction of a unique typeface. Or the use of type as a shape (which we'll discuss in chapter 3). Or the combination of type sizes and fonts. Or the inclusion of *ghosted-back* (faded to appear translucent) type.

No matter how you use type, you must be able to understand how it can function on many levels as (1) a communication agent, (2) a priority gauge, (3) an emotional conduit, (4) a psychological trigger, (5) a graphic component, (6) a repeat graphic icon, (7) an image, and (8) a historical reference.

■ EXERCISE

Go on the Web and visit font sites like fonts.com, fontworld.com, philsfonts.com, coolarchive.com, larabie.com, itcfonts.com, linotype.com, renaesroom.com, chank.com, typefonts.com, and fontfoundry.com. Describe the personalities of various typefaces.

Find fonts for specific advertisers, such as lawyers, cardiac centers, pet stores, party stores, Italian restaurants, tropical resorts, computer companies, investment firms, and graphic design firms. ■

■ PROJECT

Create several ad headlines for different companies, using type to portray the firms' brand personalities (serious, whimsical, childlike, authoritative, trustworthy, established, etc.).

Try setting the headline in different places in the layout. You can use a square to represent the image, or you can go online and download a visual. Place the headline (1) above the image, (2) below the image, and (3) next to the image. Now change the size of the type for each of the ads.

Adjust the size of the visual to work better with the headline. ■

■ PROJECT–PART ONE

Create at least three different layouts by manipulating the type. You can layer the type over a part of the image. You can *ghost* the type back if you have a dark image, so the type appears to be transparent. You can rotate or stretch the type to emphasize a point.

Play with the layout. Don't worry about judging which one is best at first. Feel free to explore new fonts and various placement of the type. After you've created several different layouts, take a look at how the type changed the entire tone of the ad. For example, an Old Letter font would make it look reminiscent of another era. A funky or trendy font would make it look contemporary. A whimsical typeface would make it seem playful. If you happen to stumble upon a well-balanced layout right away, keep working. The idea is to try myriad type variations and layouts. ■

■ PROJECT–PART TWO

Now use different fonts to create headlines for an ad or article illustrating any or all of these emotional, historical, or visual effects: (1) to create a mood; (2) to take the reader back in time; (3) to depict a strong emotion like anger, hate, or fear; and (4) as a repeat graphic icon. ■

Suggested Reading

David Dabner, *Graphic Design School: A Foundation Course in the Principles and Practices of Graphic Design*, 3rd ed. (Hoboken, NJ: John Wiley & Sons, 2005).

Spencer Drate and Jutka Salavetz, *Extreme Fonts: Digital Faces of the Future* (New York: Madison Square Press, 1999).

Paul Martin Lester, *Visual Communication: Images with Messages*, 2nd ed. (Belmont, CA: Wadsworth/Thomson Learning, 2000).

Rob Walker, "Type Casting," *New York Times Magazine*, July 7, 2005: 20.

Notes

1. Wieden+Kennedy, www.wk.com (June, 28, 2005).

2. Ilene Strizver, "Font Selection Made Easy," *HOW,* February 2005: 104–7.

3. Steven Heller, "Acceptance Letter," *New York Times,* August 29, 2004: AR26.

4. Thomas Petzinger, Jr., "For a Designer Known as Chank Letters Are Art," *Wall Street Journal,* November 7, 1997: B1.

5. Kathleen Tinkel, "Taking It In," *Adobe Magazine,* March–April 1996: 40–45.

6. "Go with the Green," *Color News* 1 (1): 1–2.

7. William F. Arens, *Contemporary Advertising*, 9th ed. (Boston: McGraw-Hill Irwin, 2004), 585.

8. T. H. Nilsson, "Ensuring Color Legibility," AIC Colour 05 Poster Papers, www.upei.ca/~psych/Color.pdf (accessed August 22, 2005).

9. Jerry Greensfield, "Web Page Legibility Recommendations," September 22, 2000, www.miyazaki-mic.ac.jp/faculty/jgreenfi/Web_Legibility.html (accessed August 22, 2005).

10. Rob Carter, Ben Day, and Philip Meggs, *Typographic Design: Form and Communication*, 2nd ed. (New York: John Wiley & Sons, 1993), 43.

11. Michael Newman, *Creative Leaps* (Singapore: John Wiley & Sons, 2003), 65.

12. Tinkel, "Taking," 43.

13. Tinkel, "Taking," 43.

14. Timothy Noah, "The 1,000-Word Dash: College-Educated People Who Fret They Read Too Slow Should Relax," *Slate,* February 18, 2000, http://slate.msn.com/id/74766 (accessed August 25, 2005).

15. Alex Postman, "*Elle* Leading Women: Linda Kaplan Thaler, Advertising Innovator," *Elle,* May 2004: 150.

16. Tim Nudd, "Does Sex Really Sell?" *Adweek*, October 12, 2005: 14–17.

Embrace Type as a Design Element

Many a small thing has been made large by the right kind of advertising.

—MARK TWAIN[1]

Even with all the attention to legibility and readability of type, there are times when designers deliberately make the type barely discernable. In these cases, type is primarily used graphically to create tension, add energy, or drive the eye across the page. As we have seen in chapter 2, you can create an edginess to the page by layering the type, staggering the type lines, altering the leading from line to line, combining incompatible typefaces, varying column widths, changing the size of the characters, and setting the type at an angle.

Without a straight line of type or consistent *leading*, the eye scrolls across the page, and the reader's mind grabs the type as a visual unit first. Then it deciphers it and later deconstructs it into a verbal communication. Because these kinds of unorthodox layouts force an interaction with the reader, they're like a surprise invader: they stimulate a response and engage the audience.

Often the type is used as visual amusement and entertainment. Andy Altmann of the British graphic design firm Why Not Associates calls it "type as entertainment."[2] Rick Poynor, designer and author, talked about this kind of typographic freedom when he discussed the catalog dividers and covers created by Why Not Associates for Next, a clothing line: "The designs function decoratively as a means of engaging, amusing, persuading and no doubt sometimes infuriating the reader, rather than as vehicles for extending meaning or exploring the text."

Designers in the late 1980s and 1990s were experimenting with breaking the long-held typographic rules of proper etiquette. Soon, an atmosphere of "anything goes" led to type that was manipulated in all kinds of ways, even fractured characters broken into split lines of type and set against ink-blotter-like doodles and spider webs of rules. Many exciting examples of graphic applications of type are found in a visually rich work, *Typography Now: The Next Wave*, which Poynor coedited with Edward Booth-Clibborn. Take a look through it, if you can. Like many examples in this book, the layouts show innovative uses of type. Even the pages of the book itself, which were set by Why Not Associates designers, reveal a unique approach to book design and viewer interactivity. Pages that force the reader to actively decode the text or even read between the lines are an invitation to the reader to get involved. There are also visual examples of the deconstructionist technique used by Katherine McCoy, Allen Hori, and P. Scott Makela, which is discussed by Poynor: "The work that results is a direct challenge to its audience which must learn to 'read' these layered, allusive, open-ended image/type constructions with the same close attention that it would bring to a difficult piece of text."[3]

Exploring the visual nature of typography reveals its function, impact, and power to communicate. Typography is only one aspect of design, but it is an important one to master. As you know, it has a personality with an identifiable tone that can convey a sense of time, an emotion, a feeling, and even function as a hierarchical indicator or a singular or repetitive graphic icon. Is this section, we'll look at type as a visual component that can depict something graphically and deliver a message. When type is functioning in a denotative way, it is portraying a literal or actual meaning. With this approach, the *o* is a circle and an orange *o* is an orange circle. However, when type is implemented in a connotative manner, it projects a figurative or interpretive meaning. So, an orange-colored, filled-in *o* could be an orange ball, a setting sun, or a real orange (the citrus fruit).

First, we'll look at how type functions when it is used as a typographic treatment in a denotative manner. Then, we'll see how it can visually speak to the audience in a connotative way. The following list is designed as a quick typographic guide that you can refer to when you're developing layout ideas.

Naturally, there are other ways to manipulate type, but this will give you a solid start.

Denotative Typographic Treatment: Type That Is Representational Depicts Something

A letter can be transformed into a variety of icons.

1. *Graphic image*—Sentences can be arranged in cascading ringlets from someone's head to depict hair. Type can be set in a varying-width, curved line to depict a mustache, or grouped together to create any object, like a fence, a leaf, a martini glass, a pair of eyeglasses, a heart, or an animal. The letters can create words that spell out the name of the object. Designer Steve Timana, a graduate of the Miami Ad School, created a series of "Type Dog" ads (figures 3.1 and 3.2) using almost the whole alphabet for a typography class.

FIGURE 3.1 Afghan hound in "Type Dogs" ad, created by Steve Timana, designer, graduate of Miami Ad School. Used with permission of Miami Ad School

FIGURE 3.2 Basset hound in "Type Dogs" ad, created by Steve Timana, designer, Miami Ad School graduate. Used with permission of Miami Ad School

We had to do the alphabet. I thought of stuff that had personalities like cars. But, that was too dry. The Brembo Zoo work that I saw in *Graphis* inspired me. The artist designed different zoo animals in type. I used a different font for each. None of the type is stretched, because I was taught that a real designer doesn't expand it. He or she chooses the size and uses it. For instance, I used French Script for the Afghan hound and used different sizes of type. . . . At first, it wasn't an ad. Then, I looked to see if I could find a company in the yellow pages. I found the ABCs of Dog Training. I didn't mean to create a pun, because they're not used much anymore. It just happened. Then, I found a Web site with all the dogs facing the same way. So, I looked at the dog and thought, "This font fits this dog." I did it all in Illustrator.

Of course, other images can be created with type. For example, a face with a smile, where the word "smile" is curved like a smiling mouth. You have probably seen many images like this but just didn't notice them. For instance, the letters H-A-I-R could become the teeth of a comb, as in Woody Pirtle's logo for Mr. and Mrs. Aubrey Hair.[4]

Some graphic designers have used capital letters to create a self-portrait, with a *C* for an ear, a sidewise *L* as a nose, a pair of *O*s for the eyeglass frames connected with a sideways *I*, and rows of the same letter for a beard. Innovative artists like Herb Lubalin created the word "beard" in an ornate font with large scroll-type letters to portray a beard.[5] For a hairline, some artists have used bunched up, unintelligible letters for thicker hair; others have used rows of tall, single letters for a crew cut.

In this ad for the Peace Corps, art director Erin Robinson and copywriter Rob Lambrechts, graduates of The Creative Circus, used lines of type as a "paintbrush" to depict a woman's portrait (figure 3.3), very much in the same way that the pointillists used dots to create images. The copy read "If we can

FIGURE 3.3 "AIDS" Peace Corps print ad created by Erin Robinson, art director, and Rob Lambrechts, copywriter, graduates of The Creative Circus. Used with permission of The Creative Circus

eradicate ignorance, will AIDS follow?" To drive the point home, the tagline asked "What if . . .," leaving the question open for the reader to ponder. Clearly this typographic treatment was a complete unification of visual and copy.

2. *Symbol*—This is the arrangement of type into a specific symbol, like an arrow, a musical treble clef, a plus or number sign, a flag, a question mark, a caduceus (medical insignia), a male or female sign, or a horseshoe. Rows of colored letters can be used to depict a flag while verbally spelling out the country's name. If a question mark is needed, the question itself can be written in the form of a question mark. To create flyers for music festivals or concerts, art directors sometimes outline a treble or bass clef using letters. Other artists shape letters into one large musical composition.

Many logos use type to create recognizable symbols for the company. MTV's instantly identifiable logo, designed by Frank Olinsky of Manhattan Design, has a large *M* with *TV* superimposed (layered) over the right leg of the *M*. Its asymmetrical design is what adds to its fresh, edgy feel. Designer Paul Rand's IBM logo, first with solid black type, then with the word "IBM" in stripes, has become a known icon, reflecting IBM's history of solid product lines.

3. *Form or shape*—Using the type to outline, fill in, or create a shape is a clever and effective technique that adds importance to the visual and demands the reader's attention. Type can be set in the shape of a circle, square, triangle, cross, semicircle, star, hexagon, oval, or any other shape or form you can imagine. The type can also be set within a shape or a form, like the Texaco logo, with the capital *T* inside a square that is set inside a circle. Or the Harley Davidson logo, in which the type is set in two semicircles inside another circle. The Sheraton Hotel chain also uses a circle, but its logo incorporates a circular wreath around a large *S*. Sears has its name set in a rectangular box. But type in shapes is not restricted to logos—it is also effective as a strong graphic ingredient in a layout. In fact, type in a shape can easily become a unifying component that repeats from page to page in a brochure, newsletter, magazine, or annual report.

4. *Form combinations*—Integrating letters and forms together by blending visual and verbal icons is a technique that often forces the reader to take a second look. For instance, when an oval-shaped *O* is colored in and then given two vertical black bars in the middle, the result is an electrical outlet created from both type and form. Using a clock for the *o* in the word *clock* combines the form and the word. Integrating letters around a three-dimensional cube or using letters that look as if they're made of wood to create a ladder shows the marriage of two symbols into one unified image. One such logo for CBS Cable, designed by Jerry Kuyper and Sheila de Bretteville, used cables to construct the word

"CBS" for a subtle but inventive typographic treatment. This procedure creates a fluid union in which one sign flows effortlessly into the other without division or conflict.

> You cannot bore people into buying your product: you can only interest them in buying it.
>
> —DAVID OGILVY[6]

Connotative Typographic Treatment: Type That Is Conceptual Says Something

Type has the ability to represent meanings and articulate messages. When connotative type works as part of the *concept* (main message), it contributes to the overall idea of the promotional material. It is the combining of the verbal and visual message into one total expression. This type and graphic technique can create these and other effects:

1. *Metaphor*—A metaphor, or figure of speech, would be "the winter of your life." You could create a typographic metaphor by having the text act as one part of the comparison between two objects or between an idea and an object. So if you wanted to visually depict the world's resources being bled dry, you could use the word "drain" over the world with the letter *i* repeated in a cascading movement as if it were dripping blood. Typographic as well as visual metaphors can make strong political statements or social commentaries that are difficult to overlook.

2. *Typographic pun*—As in any pun, there is a humorous element, a play on words. Some slogans use verbal puns like 3M's "Ideas that stick." In this case, 3M makes Scotch tape and Post-It Notes, so the slogan is very memorable. When the Minnesota Zoo wanted to showcase its bugs exhibit, it used a brilliant typographic pun by drawing black insects gathered together with the white areas spelling out the word "bugs."[7] Another example would be a repair kit with the letters drawn as tools. The *r* would be a wrench, the *e* a level, the *p* a clamp, the *a* three overlapping hammers, the *i* a nail, the *k* pliers, and the *t* a screwdriver. Two other examples are (1) using Critter font for an animal shelter, which gives it a much-needed sense of warmth and welcome, and (2) choosing Remedy Double for a fun house at a fair.

3. *Message*—Christmas cards sometimes use the type stacking up to form the shape of the tree and spelling out "peace" and "joy." Christmas trees are popular icons used to promote compassion and kindness. The holiday expression "Ho! Ho! Ho!" is often depicted with holiday wreaths as the *o* to infuse the word with an instant sense of the season.

4. *Onomatopoeia*—This is where the word sounds like the object, and type echoes the sound. A beehive could be portrayed by the word "buzz" written in the shape of a hive, with yellow and black stripes to look like bees. Hail could be shown with a large dot on the *i* and repeated at different heights to imitate the sound of bouncing hail. The words "shivering cccccccold" replicate the sound of chattering teeth.

5. *Wordplay*—In this case, the typographic weight, positioning, character manipulation, and angle of the words make the point. So if you wanted to show a shattered mirror, you could have the type appear broken in the word "mirror." One way to show an object bearing down on another is to have the type reflect that by having one word crushing another. For example, in "case load," the word "case" could be pressing down and crushing the word "load." In order to verbally depict flight or a sense of freedom, the word "fly" could be set at an angle in rows, as if it were leaping off the page. To illustrate heartbreak, the words could be breaking apart.

6. *Neoplasm*—This is the inclusion of excess redundant words that are used to describe something. For example, to typographically show overabundance, a preponderance of similar words creates a neoplasm, like "a big, bulky oversized, overstuffed, high-back, fluffy, comfy armchair" or "a success-driven workaholic, type-A perfectionist, compulsive overachiever."

7. *Malapropism*—This is the obvious misuse of a word, as in "families share love and *affliction* with their relatives." The joke can be highlighted by incorporating knives for the letter *f* in "affliction." Someone could be a "*monster* of disguise," and the psychosis could be shown by a series of frightening jagged letters. Or the headline could read, "Another meeting in the *bored* room?" and the *o* could be shaped as an oval lying on its side.

8. *Analogy*—An analogy is a reasoning process that finds similarities between two dissimilar things. A few examples are (1) his hands are as warm as fresh baked bread, (2) the people at the party are as inviting as ready-to-strike porcupine quills, or (3) she is as calm as a placid lake. Just to get analogies more clearly in your mind, here are several you've probably heard many times: (1) sweet as sugar, (2) slow as molasses, and (3) fast as lightning. When using a typographic analogy, you could have the type look like the objects. So, the word "slow" could be stretched as if it were syrupy molasses.

9. *Visual substitution*—With this approach, part of a word is replaced by a visual. To show the word "eyeball," a graphic of an eye would be paired with the word "ball." Another example would be using pictures of three paintbrushes arranged to form the capital letter *A* in the word "Art." Visual substitution frees the artist's interpretative talent and allows for the elimination of part of the word and an interjection of a relevant visual.

10. *Simultaneity*—With simultaneity, a number or other icon can substitute for a letter. If this is done well, the eye recognizes and accepts the replacement without any difficulty. In the Ben & Jerry's 2-Twisted ice cream flavors, the use of simultaneity is obvious. This brand of flavors blends two imaginative preexisting flavors into one wild 2-Twisted flavor, like From Russia with Buzz (White Russian with Coffee, Buzz, Buzz, Buzz), Jerry's Jubilee (Cherry Garcia and Chocolate Fudge Brownie), and Half Baked (Chocolate Fudge Brownie and Chocolate Chip Cookie Dough). The word "2-Twisted" is read quickly and could even have a playful meaning of being too twisted, or too wild for words.

11. *Visual transformation*—In visual transformation, letters become transformed to personify people or objectify things. For example, in the word "communities," if emphasized and stylized, the *t* between the two *i*'s could look like someone holding hands with two people represented by the letter *i*.

12. *Visual correspondence*—This technique creates type that corresponds to the object or idea it is presenting. So the letters in the word "fiesta" could be set at various angles and at different heights to look as if they're dancing and having fun at a party.

13. *Visual exaggeration*—The type in this case is overstated or exaggerated to clearly and sometimes playfully express an idea. For example to show spaciousness, the type could be set with open kerning like this: w i d e   o p e n   s p a c e s. Or, if you wanted the type to show creative or flexible thinking, the type could be set with a noticeable curve, as if it were tracing a semicircle.

14. *Parallel form*—The typeface reflects the object in parallel form. So, if you wanted to show parallel bars used in gymnastic exercises, you could justify the type and use a rounded font over two parallel lines with drop shadows for a three-dimensional effect.

Other Typographic Treatments

Besides the above-mentioned approaches to working with type, there are many more ways to look at the treatment of type. First, let's consider how type works within the specific context in which the type will appear. What is the background? This is the negative space you have to consider. Where will the areas relegated to type or images be placed? This space is the positive space. Any blank area is called *white space*. This functions as a place that allows the reader to rest. Exactly how you arrange and treat type in a specific area is how you will establish visual hierarchy.

Becoming creative with type means learning as much as you can about different typographic treatments. Review this list, and imagine how you could use any of the following approaches.

1. *Geometric design*—Could you set some of the type so it creates a geometric pattern? This pattern could be used as a repeated graphic, for a dramatic effect, or as a prominent part of the overall design. You can create geometric letter patterns by using light type on a dark background next to dark type on a light background. Notice patterns wherever you are. Look at the curved lines of a seashell, the symmetry of paved brick, the patterns of skyscrapers, even the vertical and horizontal stripes of fences. You can see the sharp contrast created by positioning light and dark areas against each other. The distinctiveness between white and dark spaces is obvious whether you are placing type against type, type against an image, or type against background. Like contrast, geometric patterns add vigor to the layout.

2. *Movement and rhythm*—You can create movement in numerous ways, including by setting type at different heights and weights, by writing text in waves or at angles, and by grouping type together. When you group type and image together in patterns, you establish a rhythmic flow to the design. By using repetitive patterns to reflect movement, you can emulate flowing water, a skier going downhill, kids skipping rope, or other motion. The reader can recognize the underlying structure and easily follow along.

3. *References from nature*—Look at the shapes and forms of different organic matter: starfish, leaves, clouds, flowers, animals, and whatever else inspires you. You could introduce type over a starfish, or you could make the type become the shape of a starfish if you were creating material for a beachside resort. You could have type set as paw prints or animal tails skipping across the page or screen for the Humane Society or an animal hospital.

4. *Position and direction*—Consider whether you want the type to be horizontal, diagonal, or vertical. Should it be in the middle, to the right, on the top, or near the bottom? Thinking about the position and direction of the type will help you plan how you want to approach the rest of the space.

5. *Opposition or unity*—Think about whether you want the type to create conflict or harmony. Do you want one copy block challenging another? One line of type confronting another? One word bullying another? Or do you want all the type to look as if it is one cohesive community of friendly neighbors? Or like adversaries who must compete? Type can be boisterous and overbearing or gentle and soothing. Just like people, type can appear to be bossy and intrusive or easy going and considerate. How type reacts with its neighboring text and images will dictate the tension or harmony in the layout.

6. *Congestion or openness*—There may be times when you want a busy layout, with myriad areas dense with visual and verbal content. Other times, you may want an airy, open look with plenty of breathing space for all the components. Consider where and when you might want a congested look. What if you were trying to pass legislation for more roads? Or if you wanted to remind drivers to slow down to allow for clusters of turtle crossings? Or if you wanted to depict a busy retail event to urge shoppers to arrive early? These examples might help you understand how to use congestion appropriately.

7. *Linear or radiation*—In a linear layout the type and images are horizontal, vertical, or diagonal, but in radiation, they emanate from a central core and radiate outward in a circular motion. Picture a stone thrown into a pond. Where the stone hits is the center, and where the lines ripple out from is the circular or radiating pattern.

8. *Similarity and disparity*—Decide which areas you want to be alike and which ones you want to be different. How many different components do you want to introduce? Where do you want the layout to command the most attention? If you have all the type set small with regular leading, but one area has larger and heavier type with open leading, naturally the eye is drawn to look at what is different.

9. *Entirety and separation*—There may be occasions when you want to use a whole word and other times when you want to divide up the word and use part of it in one place and part of it in another place. You may want part of the word faded back, torn away, shredded, or ripped for a special effect. Think about when you would dissect a word for greater emphasis.

10. *Letter focus*—You may want to look at deconstructing a word and extracting one letter to use as a graphic icon. How could one letter drive the entire layout? Besides becoming a ghosted (or screened-back) pattern in the background, it could also be a dominant force in the layout. In fact, you could use the letter to create a *letter-inspired layout* (discussed in chapter 7).

There are endless ways to alter type. Part of the fun is to explore all kinds of effects. Here are some typographic alterations you might also consider adding to your repertoire:

1. *Texture*—What if you wanted the type to look like sandpaper, wood, glass, mosaic tile, water, stone, cement, cardboard, ridged paper, plastic, tweed fabric, bubble wrap, grass, pavement, wool, gravel, or any other texture? You could fill the letters with that effect or make the letters look as if they were cut out of corduroy, wood, and so on, so the edges would even take on the texture. Practice using the different filters in Photoshop to get an idea of the other textures you could create.

2. *Patterns*—You could add polka dots, stripes, or swirls by using these within the letters like the IBM logo. Or you could use the pattern on just parts of the letter or add a gradient shading in which the color gradually moves from dark to light or vice versa.

3. *Writing instruments*—Type can look as if it were produced by chalk, pencil, crayon, marker, paintbrush, highlighter, spray paint, or fountain pen (with ink blots, as in some of the new typefaces). What other writing instrument styles can you think of to try to imitate?

4. *Ransom note*—This could be a very effective style for promoting a TV crime show, movie channel, or mystery novel. Where else could you use one letter (or word) cut out at a time, placed side by side?

5. *Melting or flaming*—Making letters appear to be on fire was a strong visual effect for a billboard promoting the Heat, a Miami basketball team. The type depicted the high action on the court, making it look as if the Heat were so hot they were "firing things up."

6. *Three-dimensional stone or clay*—Sometimes animated films, like *Ice Age*, use three-dimensional letters to give the title a historic sense. You can also make the letters look as if they were made out of clay or marble or etched in stone.

7. *Interlocking letters*—Think about how fashion design house Chanel has two *c*'s interlocking to create its logo. Interlocking letters establish a sense of unity and cohesion. What other letters would work well when intertwined or locked together?

8. *Mirror letters*—If you placed two of the same letter next to each other, but in different positions like a mirrored reflection, it could create an interesting design. Work with the capital letter *L*. How many ways could you have two of them relate to each other? First have them mirror one another. Now, what else could you do? Try working with these capital letters next: *C, B, A, R, M,* and *T*. Do you see what beautiful patterns these letters can create when paired as mirror reflections?

9. *Extending letters*—A descender can be used to underline the rest of the design, so consider using the letters *g, q, y,* and *z*. Explore other ways to extend letters without descenders, like *t, l, k,* and *m*. Did you notice that many letters can be extended for a more dramatic effect? This manipulation works well with script fonts or some ornate (*novelty*) fonts.

10. *Hanging letters or words*—You can dangle letters or words on thumb tacks, ribbons, rings, clothespins, paper clips, or anything else. What kind of promotional piece would work well with hanging letters?

Practice executing different denotative and connotative techniques, as well as typographic treatments, to fully master typography.

See Type as Part of the Whole

Think of type as being a strong contributor to the overall layout, not just a way to place information into a piece. If used well, it is much more powerful than new designers often realize. This is why starting with type brings it into focus early in the design process. How clearly the material relays a message is often directly related to the art director's typographic skill. Sometimes the temptation to create an extraordinary visual as the focal point distracts designers and subtly lures them away from investing the necessary time that sophisticated typography requires. It is a good idea to look at the nature and purpose of the material you are working with. Then, see how the typography can support those objectives while enhancing the information. (We will look more deeply into message development in chapters 5 and 6.)

Great layout artists integrate typography into the *gestalt* of the layout. In other words, they consider the entire work as a totality and strive to make all the components interact harmoniously. The way the type will be set and whether it will function denotatively or connotatively or be manipulated with effects like shadows and outlines or be stretched and expanded or compressed and condensed are just a few of the considerations. With the convenience of graphic design programs, it is easy to compare different typographic arrangements on-screen before making a decision.

Become More Observant

It is helpful to look at type everywhere you see it. Notice packaging for all the products you use, including beverages, CDs, food labels, cereal boxes, and ice cream labels. The reason it is helpful to pay attention to labels is that there is such a limitation of space. If you couldn't find your favorite ice cream flavor right away, you'd probably get upset. This is why package designers are constantly faced with a difficult challenge: how to make every product label easy to read and immediately recognizable. Often, with such space restrictions, typography is the most important element and must convey all the information, as well as portray the nature of the product and the personality of the company.

Let's start with some of the foods and beverages that are very popular and probably familiar to you. Take a closer look at the package design, and most notably the typography, of everything you consume. Examine Starbucks cup sleeves, Taco Bell food wraps, Red Bull can labels, Ben & Jerry's pint-size carton designs, Kellogg's and Post cereal box designs, Nabisco and Keebler travel-size pack designs, and Campbell's and Progresso soup can labels. Just look at how much information is found on one single item. There may be a great deal of type, but it's all legible, readable, and distinctive. There is no confusing what the product is or which company created it.

Take a stroll through the grocery aisles and look at all the products lined up on the shelf. Each and every one of them is vying to catch your attention. Yet no matter how quickly you're moving through the store, you can probably read almost every label and recognize most of the brands. Notice the leading, the kerning, the choice of font, the use of reverse type, the spacing of the different lines of type, and the visual hierarchy. Which type stands out most? Probably the brand name, the product name, and then the particular flavor. It's amazing what designers can do with a small canvas.

Next look for unusual business cards. Here again, a small format presents a space dilemma. Whenever you see a dynamic business card, look at it carefully. Why does this card deliver such an impact? It may be the overall organization of the layout or possibly the use of bright color. But it may be the integration of the verbal and visual elements or just the selection and placement of type. Look at logos, package designs, and corporate identity annuals to see what can be done in a tiny area. Especially study the use of kerning, leading, and layering. Notice the choice of font, the size of the type, special effects (outline, shadows), and whether the type was used in a denotative or connotative manner. Also look at the *proximity* of the type, that is, the placement of the type in relation to other visual or verbal components. How close is it to another copy block or to the edge of the card?

Now, start looking at some print ads in magazines and newspapers. How is the type used? Is there text wrapping around objects? Is there type set at an angle? Is there tight leading so the lines of type sit atop one another? Is there type in shapes, as an image or in a form combination? Did you see any of the connotative uses of type, like a metaphor, pun, or analogy? Did you see any wordplay, visual substitution, or onomatopoeia? Now there are typographic techniques you can identify and employ in your design.

If you were going to design a brochure for adults to learn to read, think about how to communicate this message to a nonreader. Or if you wanted to create a flyer for a spa and only use type, how could you show relaxation and pampering in an all-type environment? What if you had to design a creative menu for a sandwich shop and utilize type to carry most of the message? These kinds of mental exercises will sensitize you to the many uses of type.

Working with Type

Now that you have an overview of type, how can you practice using it? First, you should be familiar with the different graphic design programs or desktop publishing packages. These include QuarkXPress, or the Adobe software programs InDesign, Photoshop, and Illustrator. Although some designers use Photoshop to design page layouts, most creative artists use QuarkXPress or InDesign for this kind of work. Photoshop is used more to fine-tune images, manipulate photographs, layer images, and create other effects. However, Illustrator and Freehand are the programs that enable you to digitally draw or illustrate images and then to import them into your page layout programs. If you are not familiar with any or all of these, you need to learn to use them so you can better express your ideas graphically.

Learning how to rotate type, write type to a path (where you can write freehand), layer it, wrap text, ghost it back, reverse it, compress or expand it, change the leading, and use drop initial caps will enable you to better showcase your creative ideas. The computer will not design for you, but it will allow you to work with myriad typefaces in much less time than if you had to hand letter each one.

Start by evaluating specific fonts for various types of industries. Remember to look at the x-height, stroke weight, and ascenders and descenders. Next, write a few lines of copy relevant to that field. It doesn't have to be accurate—just write. Then, set the copy in a typeface that would be appropriate for that industry. Try different fonts before deciding.

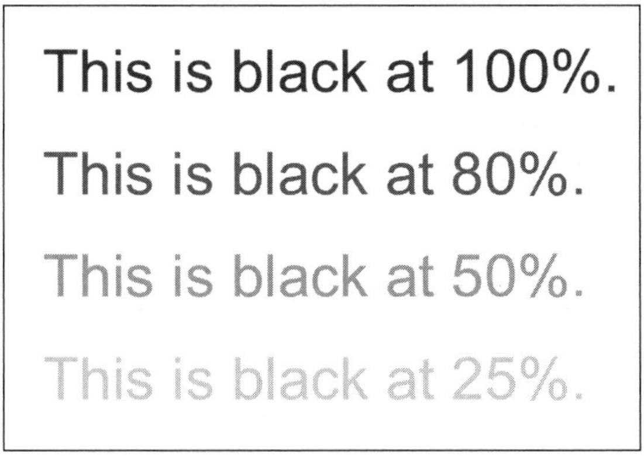

This is black at 100%.

This is black at 80%.

This is black at 50%.

This is black at 25%.

FIGURE 3.4 Example of Ghosted-Back Type

Next, layer the lines of text over each other in different fonts and different sizes. Then, *ghost back* one or more of the lines, as shown in figure 3.4. Ghosting back is reducing the percent of a color. So, if you had black type at 100 percent, you could ghost it back to 80 percent for a charcoal gray, 50 percent for a medium gray, or 25 percent for a light gray.

Then, rotate a few of the lines, just to give it some movement. After that, draw a second text box, write some copy, and add a light gray background—a *screen* (like ghosting back) of 25 percent. Add a small picture box (you don't need a visual yet), and wrap the text around the second text box. Now, draw a third text box. Make half of it white, the other half black. Write some copy, and change the color of the type on each side so it's legible on both. For example, you could use black type on a white background and white type on a black background. Or you could choose gray type, which would be visible on either white or black backgrounds.

By practicing some of the different ways to manipulate type digitally, you will begin to become comfortable working with type. You will be able to create type in shapes and form, substitute shapes for letters, choose type that corresponds with images, design wordplays, create exaggerated type, and more.

■ EXERCISE ONE

Take the initials of a company, and using type, set the initial in a distinctive way using type as a (1) symbol, (2) shape, or (3) form combination. Use a typeface appropriate for that particular industry. Refer back to the section on denotative typography. It may help if you look at a logo book (like one in the series of *The Big Book of Logos*) or go online to look for typographic logos (corporate identity marks that do not have a visual component).

When you have finished, design two more all-type logos for a different company. But this time use one of the type treatments you didn't use on the previous two logos. So, if you used a typographic symbol and a shape, now use a form combination in your design. ■

■ EXERCISE TWO

Use any of these techniques we discussed in this chapter—texture, patterns, writing instruments, ransom note, melting or flaming, three-dimensional stone or clay, interlocking letters, mirror letters, and extending and hanging letters and words—to learn to work with manipulating type. After you have created a typographic effect, apply it to one of the following: (1) a product giveaway, (2) a company logo, (3) a shopping bag, or (4) a store sign.

After completing your assignment, list three more other places where you could use this mark (letter design). ■

■ PROJECT–PART ONE

Create a lighthearted all-type invitation for an in-store retail party or fun-filled corporate fund-raiser, picnic, or party. Choose a retail store or company that would work with a whimsical approach, like a party store, a casual-dining restaurant like Chili's or T.G.I. Friday's, or a company known for its humor, like Southwest Airlines or Ben & Jerry's. Use type in any two of the following connotative manners:

1. *Typographic pun*—Try to have fun with this approach. What could you say in type that shows a little bit of humor or wit?
2. *Onomatopoeia*—Could you make the invitation mimic the sound of a party, the fizz of a soda, or the sizzle of a fajita?
3. *Wordplay*—Can you make the words interact with each other to show the fun of a celebratory event?
4. *Simultaneity*—How could you have type and a number be read together, like "Don't be L8" (late).

You can use only black and white, with screens. This way your attention is focused on type rather than on color. You can ghost back the type by using screens if you want to simulate another color. As you know, percents of black work well as various shades of gray.

After you finish, ask yourself: Does your invitation make you want to go to this event? Does it look like fun? Does it have energy and excitement? Does it intrigue you? If not, how can you make it more exciting? ■

■ PROJECT–PART TWO

Now you will create a business card for any company or service. Think about the small amount of space you have to work with and the basic information you need to include: (1) person's name and title, (2) company's name, (3) logo, (4) slogan,

(5) address, (6) phone and fax, (7) e-mail, and (8) Web site. You may use a visual in the design, but the type must be prominent. Then use type in one of the following connotative ways:

1. Analogy—What can you do verbally and visually to show a comparison like the visual that depicts "You're in good hands with Allstate"? Remember the design must use both type and graphics as a unified entity.
2. Visual substitution—Can you substitute a visual for several letters or a word in the business card? For example, you could use a flower for the *o* in "flower" for a florist.
3. Visual transformation—Does the company name or slogan allow you to use letters to represent people or objects? Could you incorporate a visual transformation that looks natural, as if it were always designed like that?
4. Visual correspondence—This technique creates type that corresponds to the object or idea it is presenting. So the letters in the word "hiccups" could be at different heights as if they actually have the hiccups.
5. Visual exaggeration—How could you show a visual exaggeration? Here's a hint: if you choose an amusement park, you could make the type look as if it's going down a roller-coaster.
6. Parallel form—How could your type mirror something related closely to the company? What could you do with a tooth or a smile for a dental clinic?

After you've completed your business card, take a close look at it. Would you go to this company? Do the type and the visual complement each other? Or are they forced together in an unnatural way? How can you refine your design to make it work as a unit? Do you need to change the font? The leading? The kerning? The visual? The spacing? The proximity of the lines of type to each other? What else can you do to make this business card generate business? ■

■ PROJECT—PART THREE

Choose one of the following typographic treatments, and apply it in a one-page flyer or an online banner ad. Select a client from one of these industries: (1) local retailer, (2) international computer company, (3) tropical resort, (4) e-store (i.e., www.amazon.com) or e-service (i.e., www.monster.com), (5) nonprofit (Red Cross, March of Dimes, Salvation Army, etc.), or (6) newspaper or magazine.

1. Geometric design	**6.** Congestion or openness
2. Movement and rhythm	**7.** Linear or radiation
3. References from nature	**8.** Similarity and disparity
4. Position and direction	**9.** Entirety and separation
5. Opposition or unity	**10.** Letter focus

After you have developed your solution, consider if this would have worked better for a different service or company. Should your flyer be a banner ad, or vice versa? Does your typeface match the client's image? Did you use type as imaginatively as you could have? Can you do anything else to enhance the type or increase the ad's "stopping power"? In what other medium (magazine, newspaper, billboards, bus sides, signs, etc.) could your solution also work? ■

Suggested Reading

Elizabeth Resnick, *Design for Communication: Conceptual Graphic Design Basics* (Hoboken, NJ: John Wiley & Sons, 2003).

Notes

1. Mark Twain, *A Connecticut Yankee in King Arthur's Court* (Mineola, NY: Dover, 2001), 121.

2. Rick Poynor and Edward Booth-Clibborn, eds., *Typography Now: The Next Wave* (London: Booth-Clibborn, 1991), 15.

3. Poynor and Booth-Clibborn, *Typography Now,* 13.

4. Philip B. Meggs, *A History of Graphic Design*, 3rd ed. (New York: John Wiley & Sons, 1998), 402–3.

5. Meggs, *A History of Graphic Design*, 360.

6. David Ogilvy, www.ogilvy.com (accessed July 22, 2005).

7. David E. Carter, *American Corporate Identity #10* (New York: Art Direction Book Company, 1995), 275.

Master the Design Elements

> Communication campaigns that actually work are never the result of "one big idea," but rather a series of ideas and continuous thinking and linking on behalf of the brand. To say that you're set once you have found that "one big idea" is silly. And irresponsible.
>
> —SHAROZ MAKARECHI[1]

Although there are many components that go into the creation of advertising and promotional materials (i.e., visuals, headlines, body copy, and graphic elements), there are two aspects of design that are the basic guidelines. These are the elements and the principles of design.

Although most designers concur that these are the two main parts of design, some disagree concerning what the subdivisions within these two categories are. In this chapter, we will examine the elements of design and look at their use. Later, in chapter 7, we will discuss the principles of design.

The Six Elements of Design

1. Format and media
2. Line
3. Shape
4. Color
5. Texture
6. Value

Some designers regard value as a separate element. Others combine it with color. Others add volume or space as elements. For practical purposes, let's settle on the above six elements, and include space within format.

1. *Format and media*—Now, let's examine them one by one. What is format and media, and why is it listed first? Many designers place line as the first element. However, the very first item to consider in any layout is how much space you have to work with. What kind of *format* is this (brochure, ad, flyer, banner ad, business card, etc.)? And, in what medium or combination of *media* will this appear (online, outdoor, print, etc.)? So, considering the format or media first will help guide your thinking and direct your focus. It is the first restriction or requirement placed on your work.

Are you developing a billboard, a print ad, a Web site, or an online or direct-mail campaign? You must know what the format is and where it will appear before you do anything else. In order to clarify the difference between format and media, think of your layout like a piece of clay. Are you creating a hanging plant pot, a flower planter, a large tree pot, or a terra-cotta vase? Will it be used to landscape the front of the house, decorate the patio, or enhance a table? The object you're creating is the format, and the place you'll be using it is the medium.

Because there are so many different types of formats, each with its own design challenge and specific purpose, you must think about how you will use the format to achieve the greatest impact. One helpful question when you're first considering the layout is to determine how close the audience is to the message. For example, with a business card or a Web site, the viewer is relatively close, but with a poster or a billboard, the reader is much farther away. This one consideration will guide your decision about type size and proportion, or how big the components will be.

Even when you're working with print ads, the shape and size of the ad will dictate the amount of information and the overall configuration of the ad. For example, a horizontal ad might work better for a panoramic photograph, and a vertical ad might showcase a stacked headline, where each line sits over another.

Besides the size of the ad, you must also look at the size of the medium or container. For instance, a tabloid paper, such as the Weekend section of the newspaper or another special section, is smaller than a broadsheet, or standard-size newspaper. So, if you're creating the same-size ad for both papers, it would appear large in the smaller tabloid paper. The same rule applies for the size of magazines. Each publication has its own page size and ad specifications. Look at *Time* magazine compared to *Vogue, National Geographic, GQ, Reader's Digest,*

Adweek, or *Advertising Age.* Can you see the size differences? A full-page ad in one may be a completely different size in another. It's also helpful to be familiar with the publications' audiences, so when you start to develop the content, you may be able to target it for those readers.

Also take a look at billboards and the new technology. Some boards can accommodate a three-dimensional component, like the MINI billboard's lifelike palm tree, which appears to be blown by the movement of the car (figure 4.1). Others can have rotating panels, while many can incorporate extensions. The point is that your billboard design may be influenced by the board's inherent flexibility.

The same guidelines apply for bus sides, bus wraps, bus shelters, and bus benches. You need to know what the restrictions are before you start designing. If the bus is going to be wrapped, what is the ultimate amount of space you have to work with? Where are the places where it bends around the bus? You will need to take those spots into account, so your image and message won't be impaired.

Whether you're designing a Web site or a brochure, you must consider the arrangement of the components, the flow of the copy, and the ease of navigation

FIGURE 4.1 "Palm Tree" MINI Cooper billboard, created by Crispin Porter + Bogusky for MINI USA. Photo courtesy of MINI USA LLC

in relation to the format. With business cards, you may want to decide if you want to use embossing (an impression on the paper) or metallic ink (gold, copper, silver, etc.) or choose unusual paper like parchment (opaque or translucent) or even a clear plastic material where the ink seems to float on an invisible background. All kinds of format-related options need to be determined before you can even begin.

2. *Line*—A dot that continues on, as if it's being pulled or stretched, becomes a line. It can be horizontal, vertical, diagonal, or free form. A line can be straight or crooked, thick or thin, connected or dotted, or open ended, or it can have a closure like an arrow. Lines create direction by going up and down, side to side, or at an angle.

The path of the line, whether it's straight or curved, is defined as the line's type, or its *attribute*. The nature of the line (whether it's skinny or chunky) is its *quality*. The position of the line, or the way it travels, like up or down, is its *direction*.

Lines are also called rules and can be used in various ways. They can underline headlines, separate blocks of copy, delineate an area, frame a picture or a page, act like a drop shadow, add depth to an image, outline type, become a graphic element, fill a space or form a *bar* (a filled-in rectangle), create stripes, and so on.

If you use a line to design a bar, you can add reverse type, widen the bar, and set it vertically like a wide stripe on the page. Or you can use reverse type in several bars to create subheads, highlight text boxes, showcase portions of the page, or establish a small banner, which you can then place at an angle at the top corner of the page.

Realize that the word "line" also refers to text and can be a headline or any line of type. You can place a line of type anywhere on the page—at the top, at the bottom (in letterhead), along the side (in a newsletter), in the middle (in a brochure or annual report cover), diagonally (in a flyer), or any other place you choose. A line of type can work to direct the eye toward an important idea or message.

Now, consider copy blocks as lines of type grouped together. They can work as one unit or as several units. These can be set straight, at an angle, along a path, around an object, or in a shape. These lines of type can create distance when they are wider at the bottom and narrower at the top. When they are curved or set at an angle, they can create movement. They can incorporate stacked lines of bold type to add solidity or they can be written in a wavy shape to add whimsy. Start noticing how graphic lines and lines of type are used in many different ways in layouts. You may want to save a few examples of ads, packages, book covers, and flyers that use rules in interesting ways for future reference.

3. *Shape*—Any shape can dominate a layout or just be a subordinate element. It can be a large square photograph of a computer or a circular illustration of a donut or the triangular-shaped image of a nutritional food pyramid. Shapes are everywhere, and they're an important graphic element.

Shapes can be two-dimensional, like an outline of an oval. These are called linear shapes. Or shapes can be three-dimensional and look lifelike. These are called representational shapes, like an ice cube that's drawn with depth, where you can see its three-dimensionality. When an illustration is made up of lines with little or no background, it's called line art. You can see what the entity is by the outline of the shape. There are many illustrations that only outline the object. One famous cartoonist, Nicholas Blechman, made this technique popular in print ads and television commercials in the 1980s and 1990s.

Some techniques that use shape in a unique way have become a style of art, for example pointillism, a French technique used by Georges Seurat and other artists in the late nineteenth century, in which small dots of paint create images, and cubism, a Parisian technique in which geometric shapes form abstract pictures, which was developed in the early twentieth century by artists such as Pablo Picasso. You can integrate these techniques or use shapes in other ways.

> I am always doing things I can't do, that's how I get to do them.
>
> —PABLO PICASSO[2]

Type can also work as shapes, as we discussed earlier. For example, if you wanted to create a classic diamond solitaire for an engagement ring ad, you could set the type in an upside-down pyramid to resemble the stone. Or you could set just the band in type and write: "Please say 'yes'" in a semicircle. You can set type in the shape of a wine bottle or as the wine being poured from the bottle into a glass. Shape and type can work beautifully together if the designer is skilled in typography.

A circular image of a romantic resort can have a soft drop shadow around it to draw the reader's eye into the center of the visual. Or a line of type can be set above or under a hammock, following its shape to entice the reader into thinking about a vacation. Or the shape of a swimming pool can be used to tempt the viewer into building or remodeling a pool.

Any object's shape can be used for a stronger graphic effect, such as a very high heel, a tall roll of carpet, a triple-scoop ice-cream cone, a cruise ship, or an exotic car. Pay more attention to shapes you see every day while you run your errands or go out for a snack. Then, see how you can use some of the shapes you see. For example, a giant overstuffed deli sandwich could create an appealing shape and enticing visual for a sandwich shop.

Shape can also guide the eye down the page. For example, arranging the text boxes and visuals with an underlying shape that may not be immediately apparent can give the layout a sense of flow. Certain letters can provide movement to the page, like *z*, *s*, and *c* (figure 4.2). Other letters give a sense of stability, like capital *X*, *L*, *T*, or *I*. Sometimes an implied free form, like using a visual to run through the layout like a sinuous letter S, helps visuals and type convey a sense of a slide that the eye figuratively rides down. Or a specific shape, such as a square, circle, or triangle, carries the eye along.

To help you think more about shapes as design elements, just look at the shapes used as icons for computer pro-

FIGURE 4.2 Examples of various shapes used in layouts

grams, for example, the feather for Photoshop, the compass for Safari, the flower for QuarkXPress, the triangle for America Online, the butterfly for InDesign, the globe for Firefox, the hat and magnifying glass for Sherlock, the free-form triangle for Acrobat, the stylized *x* for Excel, and so on.

Become more aware of the function of shapes as logos and in layouts on a regular basis. Study their use, their application, and their modifications. As you become sensitized to shapes, you will start to think of innovative uses because they will become part of your design vocabulary.

4. *Color*—This element has a strong psychological effect on the viewer and demands your full attention. We will discuss color more in chapter 8. But for now, it is important that you recognize how much power color exerts as one of the elements of design. The actual name of a color is its *hue*. The color's intensity, in other words how bright or muted it appears, is called *saturation* or *chroma*. The amount of lightness or the depth of darkness in a color is its *value*. Other words that relate to value are the color's shade, its tone, or its tint. So, when a screen like a light blue is used it's a percent or shade of the original color.

There are the basic primary colors for painting; these are red, yellow, and blue. Although these colors are not mixed, other colors are created by mixing the primary ones together. You probably remember mixing finger paints when you were a child. You discovered yellow and blue create green, red and blue produce violet (purple), and red and yellow make orange. These colors—green, violet, and orange—are the secondary colors.

However, primary colors are different for television and computer screens. They are red, green, and blue and are referred to as RGB. In these cases, the color is created by blending light. Yellow comes from mixing red and green. Magenta is formed from red and blue. Cyan, a turquoise-like blue, is created from green and blue.

When you use ink in print material, such as brochures or newsletters, the printing company creates color by using a four-color process (CMYK). This separates the inks into three colors: cyan, magenta (a raspberry-like red), and yellow. Black, represented by the K as the fourth color used in the process, is added to intensify the depth and richness of the colors.

Color adds vitality and draws attention to a page. When you look at a newspaper and most of the pages are black and white, it's impossible not to notice a full-color ad. Even a one-color ad is noticeable, because it introduces some surprise to the page. Often, when one color is added, it is used as spot color. That means the color is added only in certain places in the layout. This technique dramatizes the color, emphasizing its effect. Spot color ads are highly effective in most formats. In black-and-white newspapers, they stand out because of the one additional color. In full-color magazines, they jump out because of the punch of a black-and-white ad with a shot of one color. In chapter 8 we will talk about the meaning of specific colors, which will help you choose the best color for a one-color ad.

You may not recognize that you already have an idea of which colors are cool and which are warm. You've probably heard the expressions "ice cool blue" and "red-hot chili peppers." Well, these expressions are accurate. That is because the blues, greens, yellow-greens, and violets are considered cool colors, while the reds, oranges, orange-yellows, and red-violets are considered warm.

Complementary colors are those that are opposite each other in the traditional color wheel. The colors clockwise around the wheel with yellow as midnight are shown in figure 4.3. The complementary colors are yellow and violet, red and green, and blue and orange. There are more ways to combine colors in the wheel in groups of three and four. You can read more about that and other kinds of compatibility in the works of color specialists Johannes Itten, Josef Albers, and Farber Birren. But when you're pairing up colors, it's wise to check the color wheel, as

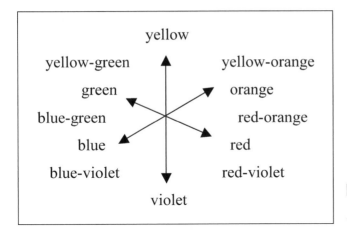

yellow

yellow-green   yellow-orange

green   orange

blue-green   red-orange

blue   red

blue-violet   red-violet

violet

FIGURE 4.3 Arrows Show Complementary Colors

well as to look at the intensity of the two colors being used. Certain bright colors seem to vibrate. These are green and red, blue and red, red and orange, pink and orange, and green and orange. Vibrating colors appear to be moving and are difficult to read. This occurs when two colors of the same intensity are set side by side. There may be times when you want the colors to bounce to show energy or even electricity. However, it's important that you know which colors can create vibrating type, so that this happens by choice, not by accident.

> Fallon is a creativity company committed to generating disproportionate results for our clients through a unique combination of rigor, relentlessness, and surprise.
>
> —FALLON[3]

5. *Texture*—Just like the use of texture with type in (discussed in chapter 3), texture in design adds the sense of touch to a layout, making it seem as if you can feel the texture. A graphic component or background can look soft like cotton, smooth like polished marble, uneven like mosaic tile, slippery like silk, plush like velvet, rough like tree bark, coarse like gravel, grainy like sand, or bumpy like cobblestone.

There are many ways to establish texture in a layout. Some are visual effects like including visuals that look like lattice or fabric. Others are three-dimensional, or tactile effects created through the use of *thermography* (raised ink, often found on quick-print business cards), embossing (an impression on the paper), pasting multi-textured items over each other, adding foil (shiny paper like gold, copper, bronze, or silver aluminum foil), layering paint to create thickness on the canvas, adding textured paper in a bound piece like a sheet of *vellum* (parchment), using a colored transparency (clear sheet), or incorporating a fabric. Some of these textures are found on brochures or book covers and inside highly designed books such as *The Blue Dog* by George Rodrigue, as well as in children's books.

Visual textures can be developed from patterns that you draw with ink, markers, chalk, watercolors, spray paint, stencils, and other writing tools. You can also create these effects on the computer with graphic programs like Photoshop and Illustrator, which simplify the process of creating repetitive designs like the ones found in gift wrapping, wallpaper, flooring, and patterned fabrics.

You can create tactile textures by becoming more observant of textures you see all the time. Look at picture frames and notice the ones with ornate, textured borders. Examine leather belts and study the etched patterns you can feel. Pay attention to the ridges in some potato chips, the roughness of corn chips, or the salt bumps on pretzels. Notice marshmallows and how pillow-like they are. Or observe the irregular contours of popcorn. There is texture everywhere, and it can be implemented into design. It only takes some imagination and skill. Just look at the innovative use of texture in the two Ossip Optometry billboards by Young & Laramore (figures 4.4 and 4.5).

6. *Value*—This refers to the integration of light and dark areas in a layout. How the light sections work next to the darker areas is called contrast. It is this contrast that gives a picture more striking detail, discernible depth, and visible

FIGURE 4.4 "Glasses" billboard, created by Young & Laramore for Ossip Optometry. Image courtesy of Young & Laramore

FIGURE 4.5 "Clock" billboard, created by Young & Laramore for Ossip Optometry. Image courtesy of Young & Laramore

texture. Images with less contrast result in a softer, more muted look. Pictures with greater contrast create a more arresting effect.

The presentation of dark against light suggests a visual dialogue among all the elements.

A conversation is created and passed from one to another. For instance, a bold line interrupts a muted background. A high-contrast image interjects its authority, dominating the discussion. And an oversized headline raises its voice to be heard above the rest.

Just look at how splitting the page into dark and light areas adds immediate contrast to the page, as in figure 4.6. Although this image only uses black and white, it still demonstrates the influence value has on the design. Notice how the second figure has a three-dimensional property because of the position and color of the gray box and the addition of three small lines. Observe how a drop shadow adds depth to the image of the square. See how a thicker line around the box makes the box look as if it could be a frame hanging on a wall.

Consider how you might use the elements of format and media (especially size), line, shape, color, texture, and value to create impossible-to-ignore layouts. What kind of message are you creating—will it appear in print, outdoor, online, in a direct-mail piece, or in a business card? Where should the eye go first? What elements should establish the page's visual hierarchy? What elements should have color? What shape should establish dominance? What color should offer contrast? Where and how heavy should the lines be? What kind of texture should be incorporated—visual, tactile, or both? Where will the light and dark areas be? Where should the conversation among the elements begin?

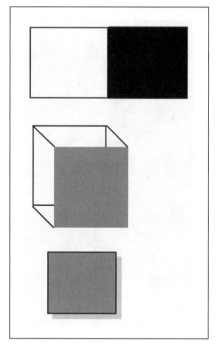

FIGURE 4.6 Example of different three-dimensional shapes

■ EXERCISE ONE

Choose one of these formats: (1) business card, (2) billboard, (3) online banner ad, or (4) print ad. Then select a company. Next, pick a texture that would reflect the company's products or services. Determine how and where the texture and shape will be used in the format you chose. Now, choose another format, a different company, and a new texture and shape. Determine why this texture and shape work better for this format and company. ■

■ EXERCISE TWO

Choose a letter to dominate a vertical ad. How can you incorporate an obvious or implied letter (like setting the type in a vertical column topped with a circular dot to suggest a lowercase *i*) into the underlying design of the ad? What letters can act as repeat graphic elements that mirror each other? ■

■ PROJECT—PART ONE

Create an ad layout only using (1) shapes to indicate pictures and graphic icons and (2) lines to indicate headlines and body copy. Create five different layouts with the same elements, namely shapes and lines, as in figure 4.7. This will help you isolate elements and work with them individually. ■

■ PROJECT—PART TWO

Create another ad layout, this time showing contrast by using dark and light areas. Using figure 4.8 as an example, develop three different layouts that show value through the use of (1) type, (2) shape, and (3) image. Use the contrasting areas to help create greater detail and depth in the layout. How else can you use value in your design? Where else can you use light and dark areas in your layout? Think about using gradient backgrounds or gradient type (colors that gradually blend from one to another like black into light gray, or orange into yellow), shadows behind visuals and text, or increasing the brightness of an image. ■

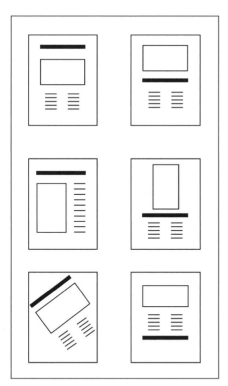

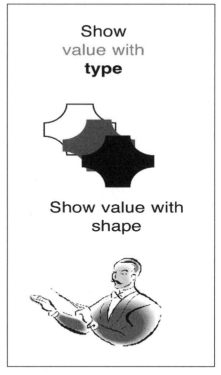

FIGURE 4.7 The use of elements in different positions in a layout

FIGURE 4.8 Examples of different shapes and values

■ PROJECT—PART THREE

Design one ad and one brochure cover that use shape as the main design element. It can be a defined or a free-form shape. Think about what object could provide the shape and serve as the focal point. In one layout, use type to highlight the shape. In the other layout, integrate type into the shape. For example, you could use type as a winding river, weaving its way through the copy. Or you could set the type around a volleyball, or in the shape of a sailboat for a lakeside park. ■

Suggested Reading

Robyn Blakeman, *The Bare Bones of Advertising Print Design* (Lanham, MD: Rowman & Littlefield, 2005).

Johannes Itten, *The Elements of Color,* trans. Ernst Van Hagen (New York: Van Nostrand Reinhold, 1970).

Robin Landa, *Graphic Design Solutions* (Albany, NY: Delmar, 1996).

Elizabeth Resnick, *Design for Communication: Conceptual Graphic Design Basics* (Hoboken, NJ: John Wiley & Sons, 2003).

Notes

1. Think Tank 3, http://thinktank3.com/ (accessed July 17, 2005).

2. Famous Quotes and Famous Sayings, 1993–2006, http://home.att.net/~quotesexchange/pablopicasso.html (accessed July 7, 2005).

3. Fallon, www.fallon.com/site_layout/about/index.aspx (accessed June 23, 2005).

5

Connect with Your Audience through Powerful Writing

> Big ideas come from the unconscious. This is true in art, in science and in advertising. But your unconscious has to be *well informed* or your idea will be irrelevant. Stuff your conscious mind with information, then unhook your rational thought process. You can help this process by going for a long walk, or taking a hot bath, or drinking half a pint of claret. Suddenly, if the telephone line from your unconscious is open, a big idea wells up within you.
>
> —DAVID OGILVY[1]

Although there is more to discuss about design, right now we need to look at your audience and the message you will develop. Later, in chapter 7, we'll examine the principles of design and the various layout formats.

Understanding who your audience is will always guide you in the right creative direction. Be specific. Find out as much as you can about those consumers. Learn how they live. How they shop. When they shop. What they buy. What brands they use. Where they live. What they earn. Whether they use coupons. And what is important to them. In other words, know what they value and what drives them to make a purchase.

One sentence should be posted on your computer to keep you focused on the target: THINK LIKE THE CONSUMER. This will make your message relevant to your audience. It will keep your campaign on target. That means your main idea will speak to consumers in their language about something important to them.

You cannot begin any design project or advertising campaign without learning to think like the consumer. The key question to ask is, What do I need to hear to take action? You must get inside the consumer's mind and internally become the consumer. Then, ask yourself this question: what would motivate me to make a purchase? If you cannot answer that question, you're not ready to begin working on a creative solution, because you don't know what the target needs to hear or what you're trying to say.

In successful creative work, the message comes before you begin designing. Knowing where the message will be seen is crucial in developing the right message for the right medium or placement. For example, if you have a small ad, you can't have a long, complicated headline, because there's no space for it. Or if you're developing a message that relies on a strong visual, they must work as a unit, with each one supporting the other. Here's where creating the main message of the ad is critical. How are you going to address your audience (tone of voice)? Who's going to be delivering the message (point of view)? What writing techniques are you going to use to make the message more memorable (*alliteration*, *ABA*, *weave*, *connectors*, *parallel construction*, *buttons*)? What tagline techniques are you going to use to make the slogan sticky (use of name, rhyme, vernacular, onomatopoeia, challenge)? In this chapter you'll see how *related word association* stimulates headline ideas. You'll discover the difference between the *benefit, feature,* and *value*.

We'll also look at examples of why breaking grammatical rules and writing in the vernacular ("Winston tastes good *like* a cigarette should," "Think *different*," "Toyota *everyday*") gives the writing more impact and functions more as a verbal logo.

Let's begin with the message. There are two basic kinds of messages: (1) the *headline,* which acts as the message of the ad and (2) the *slogan*, which serves as the message of the entire campaign. Now, let's look at them one at a time.

The Message

1. *Headline*—This functions as the main message of one advertising vehicle. So, in an ad, billboard, brochure, flyer, Web site, and or Web banner, it's the one idea you want to emphasize to the audience. To create the headline, ask yourself: what am I trying to say? Often, the headline is buried in the body copy. If you're having a problem phrasing the idea, speak out loud as if you're explaining it to someone else. This is a very helpful way to capture an idea. When you're saying it, you're in your own natural speech pattern, which makes the message more conversational and easier to grasp.

If you're developing a multimedia campaign, now is the time to look for a concept that will *spin out*, or work equally well in print, broadcast, and online. The idea should have "legs" and should be able to use one message in multiple formats with related headlines. Victoria's Secret had an angel campaign that used the visual of angel wings on models and headlines that related to angels, like "Heavenly Bodies." The angel idea was able to spin out in print ads, TV spots, and online messages.

The most important point is that your headline must have stopping power. It must interrupt the viewers' everyday activities and force them to look at the ad. It must be intrusive. There are more than 7,000 messages (and soon, a projected 10,000, as mentioned in chapter 1) that you see daily, and it's critical for yours to stand out. Knowing that the average person spends one second deciding to look at the ad and only three seconds actually reading it will help you sharpen your message-development skills. Your message has to cut through all the others and force readers to notice it and at least take a look.

2. *Slogan*—This is the short phrase that positions your product in the mind of the consumer. It acts as the core message of the campaign and changes infrequently, if at all. Think of it as the foundation of a house. You can change the windows, doors, paint color, and decor, but the foundation stays intact. Unlike the foundation of a house, however, the slogan (also called the *tagline,* theme line, or catch phrase) can be modified or changed, but not nearly as often as the headlines.

Some slogans never change, like "When it rains, it pours" (Morton Salt) or "Fill it to the rim with Brim" (Brim) or "Plop, plop, fizz, fizz. Oh, what a relief it is" (Alka-Seltzer) or "Snap! Crackle! Pop!" (Rice Krispies) or "A diamond is forever" (DeBeers) or "Chock full o' Nuts is that heavenly coffee" (Chock full o' Nuts). The longer a slogan is used, the more deeply it is imbedded in the consumer's subconscious. Look how quickly you think of the name of the candy that "Melts in your mouth, not in your hands." You know instantly it's M&M's. Or, if you were asked what food is "M'm! M'm! Good!" you'd immediately say Campbell's soup.

Some slogans are so powerful, they overshadow newer slogans and are reinstated years after they've been replaced. For example, for years Nike's slogan was "Just do it." Then, the firm unsuccessfully tried to replace it with another three-word slogan. Do you remember what it was? The line was set in a box, each word stacked above the other. Can't remember? Well, neither could anyone else. The line was "Yes you can." But, no, you couldn't (remember it).

It just wasn't sticky. It didn't have the memorability factor of the original tagline, so "Just do it" was reinstated. It's interesting to note that in 2005, Sprint adopted the slogan "Yes you can." We'll see how long it stays in use and if it works better for Sprint than it did for Nike. For Sprint the idea behind "Yes you can" highlights all the new features included with Sprint, so it may be more closely related to the product's features and the consumer's benefits.

Although creating a sticky slogan is not easy, it is helpful to recognize the common traits that successful slogans share. Being able to place slogans into their respective categories strengthens your ability to create new ones. Review the sixteen following techniques until you're completely familiar with each one. Then, refer to this handy list when you're developing slogans for current creative assignments and future clients.

Sticky Slogan Techniques

1. *Name*—Any time you can incorporate the name into the slogan, you strengthen the brand's identity. Look how these slogans have managed to stay in mind and become unforgettable, even if they are no longer in use. "For everything else, there's MasterCard." "Coke is it." "Marlboro Country." "The Pepsi generation." "Do the Dew, Mountain Dew." Although several of these taglines used other techniques (which we will identify later) they still integrated the name into the slogan. Notice also that some only consist of two or three words, and the product name is one of them.

Michael Newman emphasizes the importance of incorporating the name in his book *Creative Leaps*: "It's best if you can include the brand name in the slogan. This compression of the overall communication strategy can even eliminate the need for the logo itself to always appear. I call this marvel a sLOGOn."[2]

2. *Rhyme*—Slogans in rhyme are easy to remember, because we learn some of our earliest stories in rhyme. "Humpty Dumpty sat on a wall. Humpty Dumpty had a great fall. . . ." Of course you can finish it, because the rhyme helps you remember the rest of it. Here are a few long-running slogans written in rhyme: "Fill it to the rim with Brim." "Shout it Out." "Before you dress, Caress." "Don't get mad, get Glad." "Watch it wiggle. See it jiggle. Jell-O." Notice how every one of these also has the brand name in the slogan to reinforce the product association.

3. *Alliteration*—When alliteration is used, the repetition of several letters or sounds in the slogan makes it effortless to say. It rolls off the tongue because it is sonorous. Notice how these slogans have a repetitive first sound in adjacent words: "Gotta getta Gund." "Ruffles have ridges." "Come see the softer side of Sears."

4. *Play on words*—This technique introduces a lighthearted quality, because there is an element of fun, a twist on the message, or a double meaning in the words. For example, Polaroid's earlier slogan, "See what develops" referred to the fact that film actually got developed (as opposed to pictures from a digital camera). It also means take a picture and see what happens. This dual meaning adds impact to the phrase.

Another strong theme line that has a twist, as mentioned earlier in chapter 1, is 3M's line "Ideas that stick." The fact that 3M's products include Scotch tape and Post-it Notes makes the theme line particularly effective. One very old slogan is Morton Salt's line from 1912: "When it rains, it pours." This is a promise that the company has kept for decades. Of course, people who live in highly humid climates know to add dry rice kernels to prevent the salt from sticking. But, Morton Salt flows freely everywhere else. A more recent line from Planter's playfully states: "Relax. Go nuts." It has a sense of whimsy and a promise of pleasure.

5. *Parallel construction*—This technique makes a line sticky, because it repeats a word, phrase, or part of speech. Two notable slogans or taglines that use parallel construction are "Double the pleasure. Double the fun. Doublemint, Doublemint, Doublemint gum" and "Maybe she's born with it. Maybe it's Maybelline." The repetitive quality adds to the slogan's stickiness.

6. *Statement of use or purpose*—Here the slogan tells the audience what the product or company does, how it functions, and/or what it delivers. For example, one of the earlier Federal Express slogans stated "The world on time," promising that your deadlines were its deadlines. "Ford, where quality is job one," assures the consumer that its focus is on producing reliable vehicles. Rolaids asks, "How do you spell relief? R-O-L-A-I-D-S," guaranteeing the user will feel better.

7. *Testimonial*—In this type of tagline, the consumer enthusiastically recommends the product or raves about the benefits. Some well-known testimonial slogans are "I coulda had a V-8," "Mikey, he likes it!" "Look, ma, no cavities!" and "No more ring around the collar." If a paid celebrity makes the statement, it might be less believable than if a person who could be your neighbor says it. Some companies, however, have used celebrities to deliver the testimonial. This approach is a celebrity endorsement functioning like a testimonial, such as "L'Oréal. Because I'm worth it."

8. *Simile*—This creates a comparison by using the words "like" or "as." This differs from a metaphor, in which one object is called something else—for example, Shakespeare's famous line, "All the world's a stage." You see, there is no real comparison—the world is considered to be a stage. Here are a few slogans that are similes. "Chevy. Like a rock." "A day without orange juice is like a day without sunshine." "The soup that eats like a meal." Or the line that created controversy, because it used "like" instead of "as": "Winston tastes good like a cigarette should." (We will discuss this more later in this chapter.)

9. *Onomatopoeia*—The richness of onomatopoeia is that it stimulates one of our senses, that of sound. Here the word sounds like what it is. So, the word "buzz" sounds like the noise a bee makes, and the words "tick tock" sound like the ticking of a clock. Look at how Alka-Seltzer reminds consumers of the product's sound in the phrase: "Plop, plop. Fizz, fizz." That's exactly what two tablets of Alka-Seltzer sound like when they are dropped into a glass of water. Another powerful slogan using onomatopoeia is "Snap! Crackle! Pop!" Of course you added Rice Krispies, because nothing else sounds like that. One carbonated beverage created its own descriptive word, "Schweppervessence," from the brand's name—Schweppes.

10. *Emotional blackmail*—In slogans that use emotional blackmail, the idea is to make you feel guilty if you don't use the product. These messages force you to think about how safe you are if you don't use the product. One emotionally charged line is "Raise your hand if you're Sure." Well, maybe you were sure before you were asked. But now how sure are you that your deodorant is really working? Here's another strong line: "There's a lot riding on your tires." If you don't buy Michelin tires, maybe you're not as concerned or caring as you should be. The same is true for Hallmark's famous tagline, "When you care enough to send the very best." The underlying thought is: If you send any other type of card, maybe you don't really care very much. The phrase "Choosy moms choose Jif" suggests that if you don't choose Jif, maybe you're not selective enough.

11. *Imperative statement*—There probably isn't a stronger imperative slogan than Nike's catchy "Just do it," because it allows consumers to replace the word "it" with any activity they do. This makes the theme line applicable to everyone's level of activity. If you walk, walk. If you jog, jog. If you bike ride, bike ride. It doesn't matter what you do, *Just do it.* Other imperative slogans you may know are: Sprite's "Obey your thirst," Yellow Pages' "Let your fingers do the walking," and Greyhound's former line "Leave the driving to us."

12. *Interrogative statement*—These taglines ask a question like "Got milk?" (California Milk Processor Board) "Hungry? Why wait?" (Snickers), "Don't you look smart?" (Suave), "What's in your wallet?" (CapitalOne), and "Does she? Or doesn't she?" (Clairol). These lines make you think about something, because you begin to think about or even answer the question before you realize it.

13. *Vernacular*—This technique uses everyday language. It reflects the way your audience speaks, making the phrase automatically seem familiar. Budweiser made the phrase "Whassup?!" part of American language by using it in its national campaign. Soon, people everywhere were saying "Whassup?!" just for fun. Words like "gotta," "gonna," "wanna," and "coulda" are examples of vernacular speech. Checkers, a fast-food restaurant, reminds everyone, "You gotta eat." Twix says, "It's all in the mix," referring to different kinds of ingredients mixed together in its snack packs. Handi-Snacks tells parents, "You gotta hand it to 'em." Notice this line uses slang, or informal language, "'em" instead of "them."

14. *Reason why*—This particular type of catch phrase answers the question "why" you buy a product with a "because." For example, why do you buy a diamond? Because "a diamond is forever" (DeBeers). Why would you shop at Men's Wearhouse? Because "You're gonna like the way you look."

15. *Challenge*—When you use a challenge as a slogan you are telling the audience, "We dare you." One of the most memorable challenge slogans is from Lay's Baked Potato Chips: "Betcha can't eat just one." Of course, everyone knows that's true. How often have you heard someone refuse a potato chip and say, "No thanks, when I start, I can't stop eating them." Sara Lee's tagline, "Nobody doesn't like Sara Lee," begs you to taste one of its desserts to prove that you'll like it too. Slim Fast's challenge is "Give us a week. We'll take off the weight." The reason they can promise that is that if you do what the ads tell you, you will lose weight. Have a Slim Fast for breakfast and another for lunch. Then, have a sensible dinner. Well, if you do exactly that, you'll consume around 1,000 to 1,500 calories a day. That's less than a lot of people have for just one meal, so naturally, most people will lose weight. When Lee Iacocca said, "If you can buy a better car, buy it," his daring challenge gave Chrysler instant creditability, because he was so believable. The consumer probably thought, "Why would anyone tell you to buy another car unless he truly believed there wasn't a better-built car in the market?" It was a bold and gutsy statement that helped turn the company around.

16. *Combination*—This type of slogan combines several of the techniques together. Here are a few examples. "Can't brush? Chew on this." This combines interrogative and imperative techniques. Bounty's line, "The quicker picker upper," uses rhyme, parallel construction, and reason why. Another slogan that is a combination is the famous American Express line, "Don't leave home without it," which uses both emotional blackmail and the imperative slogan techniques.

Tone of Voice

There are many ways to speak to your audience. The message could sound informative, concerned, educational, playful, serious, authoritative, kind, warm, shocking, casual, irreverent, and so on. You must talk to your audience in an appropriate tone of voice. For instance, for financial investment vehicles, you wouldn't want to be playful, because this is a serious topic. Or for teenagers, you may not want to be authoritative, because they may shut out the message. When Mountain Dew wanted to speak to teens, it showed extreme sports and spoke in a young person's voice. The commercials made it look cool to drink this soda, and they closed with an imperative that didn't sound like a parental command, but more of a friendly suggestion: "Do the Dew. Mountain Dew."

When Cingular wanted to target teens and their parents in its TV spots, it showed text messaging and then "translated" it into standard English, as in box 5.1. This was an ingenious use of vernacular language shown in a visual way. Not only did the parents gain insight into their teen's language and lifestyle, but they were no longer outsiders looking in. Now, at least they have some idea of what their children talk about when they're text messaging each other.

> Powerful brands are built on consistency. The more times the consumer comes into contact with a brand and has the same feeling and emotional takeaway, the greater the chance they'll remember the big messages. In turn, media dollars end up working harder, with one medium reinforcing another. For big clients and small, we create brands that are consistent top to bottom.
>
> —DEUTSCH INC.[3]

Point of View

Besides developing a message that uses a specific tone of voice, you also need to consider who's speaking. This is called the point of view—whose voice is delivering the message? Is it the company's voice? The consumer's voice? Or the voice of the consumer's conscience? Here we will look at messages that use different points of view.

1. *Self-serving*—This is the voice of the company or product. It explains a feature, claim, or a promise from the company. Headlines or slogans that speak

---

BOX 5.1 CINGULAR TEXT MESSAGING TV SPOT SCRIPT

*WAZ^* (What's up?)
J/C (Just chilling.)
SWDYT re John? (So what do you think about John?)
X: (My lips are sealed.)
Y (Why?)
TIAIL (Think I am in love.)
SW:O (Say what?! gasp)
POS:6 GTG (Parents over shoulder. Bummer, got to go.)
TT4N,QT (Ta, ta, for now, Cutie.)
CUL8R :X (See you later. Big kiss.)
Closing with: *? D U ? 2 SAY?* (What do you have to say?)

Source: "Emoticon" TV spot created by BBDO New York for Cingular Wireless. Script
courtesy of Cingular Wireless.

---

from the company's point of view don't talk about the consumer. Examples are "Avis. We try harder" or "Chevy, the best built truck in America." Here are some examples of writing with a self-serving point of view: (1) "Number one in customer satisfaction for four years in a row," (2) "Your safety is our concern," and (3) "We wouldn't sell you a car we wouldn't drive ourselves."

Think of the self-serving line as one that is spoken in the first person plural, "we." That means that lines that start with "Our promise is" or "We guarantee that" or "We're the best" are self-serving. Other lines that start with a command but are spoken from the point of view of the company can also be self-serving, like "Count on us to be there." Although it addresses the consumer's needs by guaranteeing that *you* can count on the company, it is really speaking from the company's point of view ("us").

2. *Testimonial*—This is the voice of the consumer, as we discussed earlier. In this kind of statement, product users are saying what they love about the product. The phrases are in quotes to indicate someone is making a comment. Phrases like "I wouldn't go anywhere else" or "I'm glad I bought one" or "I love coming here" or "I lost thirty pounds" all exemplify the consumer's point of view, like L'Oréal's testimonial, "Because I'm worth it."

3. *Emotional blackmail*—As we discussed earlier, this type of writing makes the audience feel guilty. It reflects the point of view of the consumer's conscience: "I should do this." "I must do that." "I better choose this." It makes people feel less secure if they *don't* do it, buy it, have it. Although they come from the consumer's point of view, comments like "I coulda had a V-8" have an element of guilt implying "Oh, I really should have picked something else to drink." The slogan "Aren't you glad you use Dial? Don't you wish everyone did?" makes you feel confident about Dial. Yet at the same time, it reminds you if you don't use Dial, you might have a problem with perspiration odor as other people have.

Benefit, Feature, and Value

There are three more words that you've heard many times but may not be exactly sure what they mean in advertising messages: benefit, feature, and value. Before you read on, think about what each of these words means. Now, keep reading to see if you were right.

1. *Benefit*—Notice the *i* in benefit. The *i* means the benefit has you, the consumer, in mind. Why should I buy it? What do I get out of it? How can I benefit? You're on the receiving end asking the familiar question: what's in it for me? There is no harm in asking this question. On the contrary, the more you think like this, the more you can relate to the wants and needs of the target audience. What do they want the product to do for them? Why should they try it? What would make you go down the street, hop online, or pick up the phone to place an order? The benefit is all about you.

There are functional benefits—those that have to do with how certain characteristics of the product offer specific solutions. They may help you avoid getting lost, like a GPS (geographic positioning system) or help you transfer information from one computer to another, like jump sticks (small portable computer drives). Emotional benefits, on the other hand, are product traits that have some kind of psychological reward. They may be a designer label that makes you feel stylish, or a secluded resort that helps you relax.

2. *Feature*—A feature is a characteristic or quality of the product. Features don't relate to how the product helps consumers; instead they have to do with how the product is made—it has an eight-hour battery, an all-wood construction, a hideaway door panel, and so forth. The feature is the only word of the three with an *r* in it. Think of it as the *r* in the word "product" to help you remember it.

3. *Value*—The word value sounds like "you" at the end. Like benefit, it is consumer focused. The main point of value is this: how much are you willing to pay for the product? The key question is, what's it worth to *you*? It doesn't matter if you can get it cheaper somewhere else tomorrow, if you're willing to pay more for it today. You may knowingly spend more for a product because you want it now. There is nothing wrong with that because in this moment in time, you need that product and you don't want to wait for it. If you're willing to do that, the product has value. Some people pay more for faster delivery. They do that because it's worth it to them.

So remember benefit has an *i*, so it answers the question posed by the statement, *I* want to know what's in it for me. Feature has an *r* in it to *represent* a quality about the product. And value has the sound of "you" at the end, so it's what it's worth to *you.*

> Ideas are the currency of the future, but advertising is small change; great ideas that happen in the real world are more interesting than traditional advertising. Lesson: Ideas must be bigger than ads.
>
> —MICHAEL NEWMAN[4]

Six Basic Types of Headlines

Although most of the slogan techniques can also be used as headlines, Bendinger offers six main types of headlines in *The Copy Workshop Workbook*. These are:

1. *The one-liner*—This is a headline that says it all. It's usually catchy and short, for example, "Wanna Noah better way to fix it?" This could be for a home improvement store with a visual of Noah's ark.
2. *News*—Here the headline introduces some new fact as if it were reporting news to the audience, for instance, "New! Implants without the wait." This could be for dental implant surgery that requires shorter healing time.
3. *The spiral*—This uses writing that continues to drive home the main point because the advertiser doesn't know when the reader will stop reading. Think of the song *The Twelve Days of Christmas* as an example.
4. *The story*—This is a story about the product, the consumer, or a person in the company. Volvo had a campaign in which actual accident victims commented about how being in a Volvo saved their lives. These stories were credible because they were based on real cases of accidents.
5. *The sermon*—This approach preaches to the audience. An example is the compelling 1986 anti-drug campaign that brazenly stated, "This is your brain on drugs. Any questions?" The visual was an egg getting fried in a frying pan.
6. *The outline*—The headline prepares the reader for long copy made palatable by bold subheads that break the sections into digestible bites of information.

Instead of subheads, numbers are sometimes used in this format. An example is "Here are five reasons to wear gloves." The visual could be a hand held up, and the copy could be divided into five blocks of copy, numbered one through five, surrounding the fingers.[5]

Here are a few more:

7. *The results*—This shows the benefits of using the product. It's an especially effective headline for before-and-after results for weight-loss products, teeth whiteners, and wrinkle reduction creams. Think of it as a "Ta-dah!"

8. *The comparison*—Here a comparison of different products, like stain removers or laundry detergents, demonstrates the advantages of one over the other. It's a theirs-versus-ours approach.

9. *The celebrity endorsement*—In addition to consumer testimonials, headlines that include comments by celebrities can raise product awareness and sales. This is especially true for well-respected athletes, even those who are not very well known in popular culture. But celebrities who are controversial or involved in scandalous situations can have a negative effect on sales.

10. *How to*—Here you show the consumer how to do something, as when a product promises that it will show you "How to look years younger."

11. *The product as the star*—This technique features the product in the headline. The Absolut campaign almost always uses two-word headlines, one of them the product name, like "Absolut Houdini." (The visual in this ad was a simple ring of liquid beads, cleverly outlining the base of an absent Absolut bottle, revealing where it had once been.)

12. *Blind*—This headline is provocative, but vague. Readers have to look at the logo to determine the advertiser. Here's an example I saw: "Or you can wing it." The advertiser? A financial publication: *The Economist*.

13. *Teaser*—This campaign consists of several ads in a series but the advertiser's logo only appears in the last ad. By not knowing what the ad is for, the readers' curiosity is aroused. Here's an example. Ad #1: "It's silly." Ad #2: "It's serious." Ad #3: "It's powerful." Ad #4: It's playful." Ad #5: "It's savage." Ad #6: "It's soothing." The last ad could be, "It's the zoo!"

Writing Techniques

We have already discussed some of the following techniques for creating slogans. They're just as useful in writing strong body copy, because they make it easier to read.

1. *Alliteration*—You've heard or seen alliteration many times. That's because the use of repetitive sounds makes writing more sonorous. "Super Saturday Sale," "White Wonderland," and "Happy Holidays, Ho! Ho! Ho!" are just a few familiar examples. You probably even enjoy trying to say alliterative lines as fast as you can, like "Peter Piper picked a peck of pickled peppers" or "Sally sells sea shells by the seashore." Perhaps you've already tried to conquer this tongue twister at top speed: "Betty Botter bought some butter. But, said she, 'This butter is bitter. If I put it in my batter, it will make my batter bitter.' So she bought a bit of butter, better than the bitter butter. And it made her bitter batter better." You can see how alliteration moves the reader along.

2. *ABA*—This is a three-part process that gives the copy closure and the reader a sense of completion. The first A is the headline. B is the body copy that explains the message in the headline. The second A is the closing line, which refers back to the headline to reinforce the message. It doesn't have to be a word-for-word repetition of the headline, but a reference to the main concept. Here is an example (see figure 2.3): The headline (A) for a hard-to-find resort could be "We tried to keep it a secret." The body copy (B) could discuss the secluded area, white sand, warm ocean breezes, and soft, swaying hammocks. Then, the closing line (A) could be "Hard as we tried, we couldn't keep it a secret." Notice how the closing line wraps up the copy.

3. *Weave*—When you use weave, you create flow in your writing by taking the main idea and "weaving" it through the copy. This takes one main idea from the beginning of the ad or brochure to the end. So, if you have a headline that talks about a game that looks at the crossroads we face in making decisions, like "The *traffic* of your life," the body copy could continue that metaphor and weave driving-related words, like this: "The next time you reach a dilemma or life *intersection*, create a strategic *map* so you can *navigate* any mental *roadblocks*. Then, get behind the *wheel,* and *drive* the solution home."

4. *Connectors*—These are words that link one sentence to another to create flow. They can be conjunctions or adverbs, but it doesn't matter what they're called grammatically. What matters is how they function. Like copy glue, they create bonds that make writing seamless. Here's a short list of words that can be used to help close copy gaps.

After all	Well	The best part is
Because	Actually	More importantly
Just in case	Finally	So
And	On the other hand	The truth is
But	The fact is	

5. *Parallel construction*—Just like in slogans, the use of parallel construction is an effective way to give the copy rhythmic cadence. What that means is that like lyrics in a song, the writing has a natural flow to it. It just seems to sound right. The simple phrase "He loves me, he loves me not" is a clear example. Whenever you can use parallel construction, it makes the line more memorable. I'm sure you've heard one or both of these examples: "No salt, no sugar, no calories. No kidding!" "With a hint of lemon. Or orange. Or lime."

6. *Contraction*—Listen to the way everyone speaks. People use contractions in everyday conversations. They'll say *"We're* going to the movies," not *"We are* going to the movies." *"They're* running late," not *"They are* running late." It's more natural to use contractions, and promotional writing mirrors the spoken word.

7. *Vernacular*—Just as contractions are used in regular daily speaking, vernacular expressions are as well. We use language like "shoulda," "gotta," "yeah right," "oh sure," "no way," "veg out," and so on. Start listening to conversations in restaurants, at the gym, in bookstores, at the mall, and at the movies. Pay attention to everything you hear. It will make you a better copywriter. In *The Art of Writing Advertising: Conversations with Masters of the Craft*, Denis Higgins interviewed great copywriters. Many of their comments are as true today as they were in 1965, when the book was written. For example, David Ogilvy advises, "If you're trying to persuade people to do something, or buy something, it seems to me you should use their language, the language they use every day, the language in which they think. We try to write in the vernacular."[6] George Gribbin similarly states, "There's just nothing like pieces of the vernacular in advertising, or in any other kind of writing. It's not just using the vernacular, it's using the color of the life around you in a fresh way."[7]

8. *Break grammatical rules*—Often, copywriters deliberately use incorrect grammar because it sounds better. There are several examples of this going back as early as 1954, when the line "Winston tastes good like a cigarette should" became infamous. The correct word would have been "as" not "like," but it doesn't have any flow. So, George Gribbin broke a grammatical rule to make the copy sound more conversational. In explaining his use of "like," he said: "It's just that to a writer's ear, he knows that that phrase has more bite with the word 'like' than with the word 'as.' 'As' is grammatically correct, and I would tend to use it in conversation. But many people misuse the word in their language, so 'like' is more familiar to their ears. Therefore, use it."[8]

Many copywriters believe that the copy should sound natural. Breaking the rules and using improper English is acceptable if it fits the context and works better. Leo Burnett claimed that writers can use "ain't" if that says exactly what they want to express, or it sounds like the target audience or it adds emphasis. Leo Burnett was known to use "ain't" when it better expressed what he wanted to say. Here's a much-quoted Burnett comment using "ain't:" "A good basic selling idea, involvement and relevancy, of course, are as important as ever, but in the advertising din of today, unless you make yourself noticed and believed, you ain't got nothin'."[9]

When Apple used its "Think Different" slogan, created by Omnicom Group's TBWA\Chiat\Day, grammarians complained that "different," an adjective, should be "differently," an adverb. But Apple answered that it wanted people to think "different," because "different" was a thing, and therefore a noun, not a modifier. The word "differently" would convey a different meaning. Apple didn't want to tell people how to think, which would be "differently." It wanted people to think about something, namely something different.

When Toyota used the line "Toyota Everyday," developed by Cordiant's Saatchi & Saatchi Advertising, the big debate was that "everyday" should have been two words because it wasn't an adjective, like "everyday" schedule. The response was that "everyday" was easier to read and delivered the message faster. "Toyota Everyday" worked more like a verbal logo and was grasped as a unit by the reader.

A billboard headline for Seagram's Captain Morgan Spiced Rum was changed from "Get Spicy" to "Get Spicey." The reason for the change was that consumers thought "spicy" rum would be fiery hot like hot sauce, and the actual flavor of the rum had a touch of vanilla.

Angel Martinez, the president and chief executive of Reebok International's Rockport division, created a new word, "uncompromised," in an ad campaign. He believed that "don't compromise" or "be uncompromising" had no energy and didn't express a strong message.

By breaking grammatical rules, using words as a different part of speech, and creating new words, copywriters have breathed life into language, forcing it to express what their meaning really was. They've manipulated the language and made it more flexible, so it reflects the language of their consumers.[10]

9. *One- or two-word sentences*—I'm sure this was frowned upon in English class, but one-word sentences work perfectly in ad writing. *Why? Because. They're simple. Short. And punchy.* See what I mean? The reason this works is that it's the way we speak. We don't speak in long-winded sentences. We speak in short, quick phrases. For example, "Hi. How are ya?" We don't say, "Good afternoon. It's just lovely to see you again. Please describe how you are feeling today." It sounds unnatural, stiff, and stuffy. We just don't sound like that in our everyday chatter. So why would you write like that?

10. *Start in the middle*—You only have three seconds of the reader's time, so you have to jump right in. Think of it this way: If you were writing a play, you might just skip act one. Start in act two. Your writing will have more energy. This will help you get readers involved right from the first sentence, instead of assuming they'll wade through a slow introduction. In promotional writing there is no introduction. It just begins.

11. *Call to action*—This is a line toward the end of the copy that tells people what to do. They should call, go to a Web site, visit a store, order from a catalog, use a coupon. Sometimes, the action you want them to take is obvious. For example, when you see an ad from a car manufacturer, the underlying idea is to go visit a dealer. Or when you see a flyer for a pizza shop with a phone number, the intention is clear: Call and order a pizza.

But there may be other times when a strong call to action is necessary, especially when it comes to charitable donations.

12. *Buttons*—These are clever closing lines that do not have to refer back to the headline. They are a way of rewarding the reader with a little twist at the end and giving the copy a sense of closure. For instance, if you were writing an ad for a Mexican restaurant and wanted to emphasize its affordability, you might write a button like this: "Margaritas, Mariachis, Mexican Pizza . . . for Beans!"

13. *Read aloud*—All these techniques help make your writing sound familiar to the reader. But there's one more way to help you write in your own natural voice: read aloud. When you do this, you can instantly hear sections that sound awkward, areas that sound wordy, and parts that sound bumpy like a rock-strewn road. Don't worry about what's wrong with the writing grammatically. Think about how to make it flow. Every spot that you stumble over is a place that needs repair.

A good trick is to give your copy to other people to read out loud. If they're tripping over the lines, there's something wrong with the writing. Everyone should be able to read it without struggling. It should feel as if they're on a smoothly paved road, without a pothole in sight.

Related Word Association

Sometimes writers can't seem to get started. They're searching for a headline idea. Often copywriters create lists of words to prime the creative pump. The best way to engage the creative or right side of the brain is to shut off the analytical left side. One way to do it is by using *related word association*. Start by choosing a product or company that you want to write about. Then get a pad of paper, a flip chart, or a white board. Use anything you want to write ideas down. Now, as fast as you can, write down every word you can think of that's related to the product or company. Keep writing. Don't analyze, don't criticize, and don't satirize. Just write everything that comes into your head. Now, take a different color pen or marker for each of the following assignments. (1) Circle any words that rhyme. Now, create a headline or tagline using those words. (2) Highlight words that are alliterative (have the same first letter or sound). Write a line of copy, a headline, or a slogan using alliteration. (3) Draw a square around words that have opposite meanings. If there aren't any, add a word that is an opposite. Then, develop some copy using opposites like big/small, top/bottom, high/low, and so forth. (4) Last, draw a line connecting words that stimulate an abstract connection. If you don't see any, write in new words or phrases sparked by the words in the list.

Here are some examples of solutions for a baby store using *related word association*. Words would include toys, pacifiers, bedding, rattles, bassinettes, strollers, books, diapers, bibs, swings, cribs, mobiles, and so on.

Related Word Association Technique

1. *Rhyme*—Everything from Bibs to Cribs
2. *Alliteration*—Monitors, Mobiles, and More
3. *Opposite*—From Bonnets to Booties . . . Covered Top to Bottom!
4. *Abstract connection*—Shake, Rattle, and Stroll

This technique will help jump-start your creative engine.

Slogans with Legs

One of the most important results of well-targeted writing is the development of a timeless slogan. The creation of a phrase that is so memorable, so catchy, it becomes part of the American vernacular is something advertisers value and consumers grasp. Some of the most famous slogans have long histories and go back decades. The Marlboro Man was created in 1955 by Leo Burnett and was used on billboards for many, many years. You may not realize it, but Nike's "Just do it" slogan was developed in 1988. It's probably older than you realized. And DeBeers' line "A diamond is forever" has been around since 1948, seemingly forever. Avis has been trying harder since 1963 with its "We try harder" tagline. Maxwell House coffee has been "Good to the last drop" since 1959. Kellogg's Rice Krispies has been the "Snap! Crackle! Pop!" cereal since 1932, when the words first appeared on cereal boxes. It wasn't until the 1960s that they were used in a jingle in a television spot.

Let's look at the "Got Milk?" campaign. This theme line was so strong that it was always being stolen. It seemed people were unaware that when they stole a trademarked line, they were guilty of trademark infringement. Most companies will issue a cease-and-desist letter legally advising offenders that they can be sued if they do not stop using their slogan or jingle. What the milk producers (the members of the California Milk Processor Board) recognized early on in 1996, when Mattel asked for permission to create a Barbie doll named Got Milk Barbie, was that a reciprocal agreement was more important than a licensing or usage fee. So, the creator of the campaign, Jeff Manning, who was also the executive director of the board, allowed Mattel to use the slogan to name its new Barbie doll. Another reciprocal agreement was arranged with Nabisco to use its Oreo brand in one of the "Got Milk?" TV spots. No dollars were exchanged. Instead, Nabisco received free advertising, and the milk board got the benefit of the Oreo trademarked brand.[11]

In fact, with all this shared advertising, what happened was that "Got Milk?" became part of American vernacular as a result, and it generated free publicity.[12] However, the milk board was so amused by the theft and by the slogan's popularity that it created a poster titled "Got Ripped Off?" which lists the top one hundred rip-offs. It's available in black on white or white on black. Some of the borrowed uses are "Got a job?" "Got fleas?" "Got Freud?" "Got cookies?" "Got clients?" "Got respect?" "Got clout?" "Got munchies?" "Got tickets?" The list goes on. The campaign started in 1993, so it's "got legs." When a concept has legs, like the "Got Milk?" and the Milk Mustache campaigns, it continues on and on.

The point is that the "Got Milk?" campaign has now become a brand like Coca-Cola and McDonald's all because of a super-sticky slogan. Box 5.2 lists the top ten slogans of the century according to *Advertising Age*.[13]

Concept before Layout

To write strong copy, you need more than just techniques. You need a strong idea. Often, new creative talents just start designing long before they have a strong concept. They're thinking about the visuals and placement of the type, but they're really getting ahead of themselves. The fact is, before you start designing anything, you must determine what you're trying to say, to whom you're saying it, how you're going to say it, and who's going to say it. The message and even the medium usually drive the campaign.

BOX 5.2 *AD AGE'S* **TOP TEN SLOGANS OF THE CENTURY**

1. "A diamond is forever" (DeBeers) N. W. Ayer & Son, 1948
2. "Just do it" (Nike) Wieden+Kennedy, 1988
3. "The pause that refreshes" (Coca-Cola) D'Arcy, 1929
4. "Tastes great, less filling" (Miller Lite) McCann-Erickson Worldwide, 1974
5. "We try harder" (Avis) Doyle Dane Bernbach, 1963
6. "Good to the last drop" (Maxwell House) Ogilvy, Benson & Mather, 1959
7. "Breakfast of champions" (Wheaties) Blackett-Sample-Hummert, 1930s
8. "Does she . . . or doesn't she?" (Clairol) Foote, Cone & Belding, 1957
9. "When it rains it pours" (Morton Salt) N. W. Ayer & Son, 1912
10. "Where's the beef?" (Wendy's) Dancer-Fitzgerald-Sample, 1984

Source: "Top Ten Slogans of the Century," www.adage.com/century/slogans.html. Copyright 1999 and 2005 *Advertising Age*. Published by Crain Communications, Inc.

Occasionally, the visual is the star, and there is no slogan for the campaign. The Absolut campaign is a perfect example of that. Innovative visuals using the bottle are married to perfectly crafted headlines for a remarkable, long-running campaign, which started on April 20, 1980. "Absolut Perfection" was its first ad, and Boston was the city where the first bottle was sold. The campaign for this Swedish vodka was so compelling that in 1993 it catapulted the brand into the American Advertising Hall of Fame. Only two other brands have achieved this honor: Coca-Cola and Nike.[14]

In talking to the target market, the designers' original directive was to create advertising centered on the bottle with a modern yet timeless quality, but without showcasing any specific kind of lifestyle. The campaign's originator was Geoff Hays, a creative talent at TBWA in New York.[15] The bottle became a work of art, or "Absolut Art," in 1985, when Pop Art artist Andy Warhol, who gained global recognition for his repetitive multicolored images of soup cans and Marilyn Monroe, was asked to graphically interpret the Absolut Vodka bottle. His image gained instant attention across the world and launched Absolut as a cultural icon.[16]

The Absolut campaign first speaks to the audience visually. Then it delivers the second part of its message verbally with perfectly paired headlines, like "Absolut Houdini," "Absolut Marilyn," "Absolut L.A.," and "Absolut Britto." If you read *Absolut Book* and *Absolut Sequel*, you will discover that the ads fall into categories, like "Absolut Cities," "Absolut Cities of Europe," "Absolut Art," "Absolut Fashion," "Absolut Statehood," and even Absolut custom-tailored ads. Some of these, like "Absolut Centerfold," which ran in *Playboy* as the

centerfold, or "Absolut Index," which saluted *Harper's Index*, focus on a particular magazine.

The Starting Point

Many big ideas are powerful because of their relevance and simplicity. The "Got
Milk?" campaign focused on deprivation. It addressed what happens if you
don't have milk. You have the cookies or the cereal, but you don't have the milk.
You have the answer, but you can't say it, because you don't have milk to wash
down a mouth full of food. It showed specific situations where people absolutely
need milk. It emphasized how milk was a critical component in a perfect part-
nership and what a sense of loss is felt when one of the partners is missing. The
thinking behind the big idea is so natural, so unforced, so linked to the product
that it cannot be ignored, let alone forgotten.

The "Energizer Bunny Keeps Going" campaign with the "spokes hare"
was created in 1989. What was the thinking behind the bunny idea? How to
show the longevity of Energizer batteries. That simple idea was the heart of the
campaign concept. The bunny shows up over and over again to beat the message into the consumer's mind that these batteries can keep going and going and
going. The more people saw the bunny, the more it reminded them to choose a
battery with a longer life cycle. In other words, this is a battery that keeps going
while others conk out.

The pink bunny, decked out in black sunglasses, blue sandals, and beating a
white drum, has continued making surprise appearances in more than 115 TV
spots, including comedic parody commercials and community events and he now
even appears online. He's appeared in TV spots with famous characters like Wile
E. Coyote, Darth Vader, the Wicked Witch, and Elvis. He's made guest appearances on *Cheers* with Ted Danson, ABC's *Wide World of Sports*, *The Emmy
Awards*, *The Tonight Show* with Jay Leno, and *The David Letterman Show*. He's
even been named one of the top five advertising icons of the twentieth century.[17]

Each of the campaigns discussed in this chapter highlights one important
unique selling proposition (USP). It showcases exactly what separates this product from its competitors. "Got Milk?" emphasized milk's most popular food
partners and reminded everyone what an irreplaceable position it has in everyday life. The "Energizer Bunny Keeps Going" campaign promised consumers
that they can count on these batteries to continue working when others fail. And
the Absolut campaigns accentuate the vodka's influential "cool factor"—the
indefinable "it" ingredient that makes it more desirable, more chic, more "in"
than other vodkas.

Ad-Writing Tips from the Great Copywriters

One main theme of how to write great copy found in *The Art of Writing Advertising: Conversations with Masters of the Craft* is the importance of understanding the product's uniqueness. When Rosser Reeves met with John MacNamara, the president of M&M's candies, he realized instantly that the candy-coated shell held the main idea of the campaign's famous 1954 slogan, still used today: "M&M's. Melts in your mouth. Not in your hands." Reeves later said that within ten minutes into that discussion, he had discovered that the message was an intrinsic part of the product itself, and that was how he developed the line. Once he realized M&M's were the only candy in the country encased in a hard sugar-coated shell, Reeves decided to show two hands on the screen and have the announcer ask a simple question: "Which hand has the M&M chocolate candy in it? Not this hand that's messy, but this hand because M&M candies melt in your mouth, not in your hand."[18]

According to Bill Bernbach, David Ogilvy, Leo Burnett, and other writers, it is important to fully understand your product and find something magical to say before you start to write an ad. Bernbach said:

> Your cleverness, your provocativeness and imagination and inventiveness must stem from knowledge of the product. I think the worst thing that's happening today is this juggling of a page of graphics—it's not hard for anybody to get ideas—the important thing is to recognize when the idea is good. You must have imagination, you must have inventiveness, but it must be disciplined. Everything you write, everything on a page, every word, every graphic symbol, every shadow, should further the message you're trying to convey.[19]

But Bernbach did not consider an ad successful unless it accomplished one thing: clearly stating the intended message. Although Leo Burnett had been a newspaper reporter, he discovered writing ad copy required a totally different set of skills. It is not at all like writing an article. He said of the experience, "I learned a lot from newspapers (as a reporter) as to how to communicate and how to put color into copy. But finding the magic things to say about a product that would interest people and lead them by the hand to the conclusion that they should buy something—that was another art, really."[20]

Finding a way to make the product sexy or appealing is easier than it appears. Just making the layout dynamic is not enough to sell the product. The product itself must be exciting. It must be the star. Reeves explained one of the first lessons in training a copywriter as follows: "You must make the product interesting, not just make the ad different. And that's what too many of the copywriters in the U.S. today don't yet understand."[21]

Creative Problem Solving

Before you even begin *brainstorming* (thinking up and writing down every idea you can think of, without judging any of them) for a big idea, you need to have an understanding of a basic five-step creative problem-solving process.

1. *Insight*—It is important that you gain insight into the problem you are solving before you begin to think about solving it. Be sure to have a clear picture of what needs to be accomplished. You must fully understand exactly what you are trying to solve.
2. *Preparation*—During this phase, you gather research and collect information about the assignment. You learn all you can about a company, service, or product. You become fully familiar with its audience and the beliefs that the audience presently holds about the company, service, or product you are trying to sell. You gain a deep understanding of its competitors and their current and past marketing campaigns. The more information you pour into your head, the better armed you are to come up with an effective solution.
3. *Incubation*—This is what I like to call the mental marination™ stage. It's the time period when you just let the ideas stew in the back of your mind and soak in the information gathered in step two.
4. *Eureka*—This is the "ah-ha" moment when the idea comes to you in a flash, usually when you're not even thinking about the problem. Because a lot of people get ideas in the shower, there are now waterproof pads and pens you can use to jot down ideas as soon as you think them up. The reason you have the thunderbolt is that your mind has temporarily forgotten the problem. It was put on the back burner and allowed to simmer. Once the mind is relieved of the pressure to solve the problem, it is able to subconsciously formulate, or cook up, a solution.
5. *Verification*—It is in this final phase when you double check or confirm that you solved the correct problem. You may have come up with a terrific idea, but it might not address the problem you started with. If you still haven't solved the problem, you need to go back to step one and gain a clearer understanding about precisely what it is you were trying to solve.

■ EXERCISE ONE

Look for examples of ABA in magazine articles, movie titles, films, newspaper ads, Web sites, and brochures. If you're observant, you'll see that ABA is often used in literature and film to give a sense of completion to the work. For example, the sheer red veil that appears at the beginning of the film *What Dreams May Come* reappears at the end, like the recurring feather in *Forrest Gump*. Where else have you noticed this construction? ■

■ EXERCISE TWO

Work in teams of four, or if you're alone, you can complete this exercise by yourself. Type up the lyrics to your favorite song. If you're working in a group, make copies for everyone. Have one person bring in a CD player. Distribute copies of the lyrics. Play the song. Now, work as a team to write a jingle for a product using *the exact same rhyme* that is used in the song's chorus. Play the song a few more times. Analyze the rhythm of each line. Does the line use a short-short-long pattern? Long-short-long? Long-long-short? Sing or chant (with the music playing in the background) each group's solution.

Repeat this exercise with another song. Write another jingle for the same or a different company. It will probably be easier the second time, because now you're thinking in the rhythm of the song.

The reason this is an effective exercise is that it teaches you to edit other writers' copy. You will learn to write in someone else's rhythm so the changes work seamlessly. This is helpful if you're in a recording studio and need to rewrite copy at the last minute or if you're filling in and editing other people's copy because they're not available. You may need to match the original writer's writing style if the client shows up with some changes that need to be made immediately. ■

■ EXERCISE THREE

Write a nonrhyming poem with a specific number of syllables per line about a product or company. For example, you can use haiku as your format. It consists of three lines with five syllables in the first line, seven syllables in the second line, and five syllables in the last line. After you have written it, consider how it could work as a jingle. If it doesn't flow, edit it. Think about some jingles you already know. Now, write catchy lyrics about your product. And remember, you want to create something that's rhythmic and easy to set to music. ■

■ PROJECT—PART ONE

Select an ad, jingle, or Web page. Now rewrite it by (1) changing the headline and (2) using at least two of the writing techniques we discussed (alliteration, ABA, weave, connectors, parallel construction, onomatopoeia, or buttons). After you've used two techniques, change your focus, choose a different audience, rewrite the message, and use two other techniques. ■

■ PROJECT—PART TWO

Choose a company or product and create a new slogan for it using one of the sixteen sticky slogan types we discussed in this chapter—name, rhyme, alliteration, play on words, parallel construction, statement of use or purpose, testimonial, simile, onomatopoeia, emotional blackmail, imperative, interrogative, vernacular, reason why, challenge, and combination.

Now create a second slogan for the same client using a different technique. Which one would speak to the widest audience? Which one delivers a stronger benefit? Which one would work for myriad headlines? Which one do you think is stickier? Why? ■

Suggested Reading

Margo Berman, "In Advertising, Don't Write Copy. Compose a Sonata," *Journal of Advertising Education* 3, no. 2 (Fall 1999): 57–59.

Margo Berman, "Tips for Developing Sticky Taglines," *Journal of Advertising Education* 6, no. 1 (Spring 2002): 54–57.

Robert W. Bly, *The Copywriter's Handbook*, updated ed. (New York: Henry Holt, 1990).

Courtland L. Bovée, John V. Thill, George P. Dovel, and Marian Burk Wood, *Advertising Excellence* (New York: McGraw-Hill, 1995), 220–47.

Erica Levy Klein, *Write Great Ads* (New York: John Wiley & Sons, 1990), 35, 74–75, 127.

Richard W. Lewis, *Absolut Book* (Boston: Journey Editions, 1996).

Yumiko Ono, "Some Times Ad Agencies Mangle English Deliberately," *Wall Street Journal* 4 Nov. 1997, 1(B).

Notes

1. David Ogilvy, *Ogilvy on Advertising* (New York: Vintage Books, 1985), 16.

2. Michael Newman, *Creative Leaps* (Singapore: John Wiley & Sons, 2003), 232.

3. Deutsch, www.deutschinc.com (accessed August 3, 2005).

4. Newman, *Creative Leaps,* 315.

5. Bruce Bendinger, *The Copy Workshop Workbook*, 3rd ed. (Chicago: The Copy Workshop, 2002), 226–63.

6. Denis Higgins, *The Art of Writing Advertising: Conversations with Masters of the Craft* (Chicago: NTC Business Books, 1965), 93

7. Higgins, *Art of Writing,* 64.

8. Higgins, *Art of Writing,* 65.

9. Brainy Quote, www.brainyquote.com/quotes/authors/l/leo_burnett.html (accessed May 5, 2006).

10. Margo Berman, "Teaching Grammar through Lyrics, Film and Literary Quotes: The Grammar Controversy," *American Society of Business and Behavioral Sciences* 10 (February 1998): 67–73.

11. "Milk: 'Got Milk?' Article," *UC Davis Innovator,* Spring 1999, www.milk.com/value/innovator-spring99.html (accessed September 20, 2005).

12. "Milk: 'Got Milk?' Article."

13. *Ad Age Advertising Century*, "Top 10 Slogans of the Century," 2005, www.adage.com/century/slogans (accessed July 23, 2005).

14. "Absolut Vodka Turns 25 Tomorrow," April 19, 2004, www.vsgroup.com/417_633.html (accessed September 20, 2005).

15. Absolut, "About Absolut: The Confessions of an Adman," 1996–2003, www.absolutad.com/absolut_about/history/advertising/#the_confessions html (accessed September 20, 2005).

16. "From Palate to Palette," 1996–2003, www.absolutad.com/absolut_about/history/advertising/#the_confessions html (accessed September 20, 2005).

17. Energizer, "History of the Energizer Bunny," 2005, www.energizer.com/bunny/historyofbunny.asp (accessed September 20, 2005).

18. Higgins, *Art of Writing,* 98–99.

19. Higgins, *Art of Writing*, 17.

20. Higgins, *Art of Writing*, 28.

21. Higgins, *Art of Writing,* 125.

Spark the Creative Process for Focused Campaign Strategies

To begin any creative assignment, you must understand the company's needs and be able to interpret the needs of its audience. Determine what you would say to shoppers to convince them there's a benefit, or W-I-I-F-M (What's in it for me?), as we discussed in chapter 5. Decide what features support this benefit and should be showcased to give consumers a reason to buy this product. Consider the consumers' needs (what features solve specific problems) and their emotional benefits (what features satisfy them on an emotional level). Conduct research about the company, and focus on everything from A to Z.

a. What do the current buyers think, and how do you want to change their perspective?

b. Who are the product's or company's competitors, and what are they offering in their advertising messages and images?

c. What separates your product from the competition? What is its USP (unique selling proposition)?

d. What is the one main idea you want to convey to the audience?

e. What kind of *shell* (basic layout that is used throughout the campaign) would create instant recognition for this product?

f. What is the appropriate tone of voice? Should the vernacular be used? Would more formal language be preferable? Would *corporate speak* (business lingo) work better?[2] Here are a few examples of corporate speak and their translations: Due diligence means to completely research the issue. Emotional intelligence means how well the person handles criticism. And needing a reality check means you're not right.

g. What new concerns does your audience face, and are you addressing them?

h. What big idea can you develop that will spin out and be applicable in several media?

i. Can the product become an icon for the campaign (like the Absolut bottle and the milk mustache)?

j. What are the best ways to reach your audience—online, in print, in broadcast, outdoors, in transit, on CD, through word of mouth?

k. How can you modify a medium to make it more compelling? An example we discussed earlier in chapter 1 is using live people dangling from ropes on a billboard as TBWA\Japan did for Adidas, when it used live soccer players tethered to a billboard in Japan (figure 6.1).

l. How can you work with another company in a *cross-promotion* to reduce costs and gain exposure?

m. Would a new icon, like the Aflac duck created by The Kaplan Thaler Group, increase brand recognition?

n. Does the slogan need modification, or should it remain exactly as it is?

o. Would a non-celebrity spokesperson add credibility to the product, as Jared Fogle did for Subway when he lost 245 pounds in less than one year by eating two sub sandwiches a day?

p. Should a celebrity deliver the message, as Kirstie Alley did when she lost weight by following the Jenny Craig program?

q. Should the name be the focus of the campaign, as in "With a name like Smucker's, it's got to be good"?

r. Can the company "own" a word, as Volvo owns "safety" and Pepsi owns "generation"? Or even two words, like McDonald's "happy meals"?

s. Can a unique characteristic (feature) about the product become an identifying factor, like the wiggle and jiggle of Jell-O and the "plop, plop, fizz, fizz" of Alka-Seltzer?

t. Can the cool factor revive the popularity of a product, as the "California Dancing Raisin" campaign did in 1984 when Claymation figures of raisins boogied to Marvin Gaye's hit song "I Heard It through the Grapevine"?

FIGURE 6.1 Live people tethered on "Soccer" billboard created by TBWA\ Japan for Adidas

u. Can you create a new use for a medium as Crispin Porter + Bogusky did for Burger King with the Subservient Chicken Web site, in which a person dressed up in a chicken outfit and followed the commands of online viewers?

v. Can you create a new way to raise awareness, as Think Tank 3 did by drawing custom stencils on New York City streets in the exact place where pedestrians had been killed to draw attention to the importance of pedestrian safety?

w. Can you integrate the product in a TV program, a Broadway show, or a film, as Federal Express did in *Castaway*, starring Tom Hanks?

x. Should you consider a promotion that would gain national attention, like Oscar Mayer Wieners' jingle campaign, in which the Wienermobile traveled the country so children could audition to sing the "Oh I wish I were an Oscar Mayer Wiener" theme song in TV commercials?

y. Can you change the target audience by redirecting the advertising message, as Cadillac did with its high-energy and youthful "Breakthrough" campaign and Mountain Dew did with its "Do the Dew, Mountain Dew" TV commercials, which showed teens involved in extreme sports?

z. Can you demonstrate what product deprivation would mean to the audience, as the "Got Milk?" campaign did by highlighting how milk is an unrivaled partner for popular foods like cereal and cookies?

To learn how to create an advertising buzz, the real question is, exactly how do creative teams in ad agencies and graphic design firms develop their creative solutions? Whether they're for campaigns, logos, package designs, billboards, or interactive online campaigns, the process involves the creative problem-solving steps outlined in chapter 5.

But before we discuss steps to develop effective solutions, we need to understand what a creative *brief* is and how it is used to outline the campaign *strategy*, or basic goal.

The creative strategy is a simple formula that explains the broad direction of the campaign. Just fill in the following blanks: The brand is advertising to say something to _____ (VERB—persuade, convince, inform, educate) the audience (SPECIFIC CONSUMERS) that this _____ (PRODUCT, SERVICE, OR BRAND) will _____ (STATE THE BENEFIT) because _____ (FEATURES THAT EXPLAIN WHY AUDIENCE SHOULD BELIEVE IT. THIS ACTS AS A SUPPORT STATEMENT). Once you have outlined your strategy, you can develop the creative *brief* by answering these critical questions:

The Creative Brief

1. What is the brand's character or personality?
2. Why does the brand want to advertise?
3. Who is the audience?
4. What do they (your audience) currently think?
5. What do you want them to think?
6. Why should they buy this product/service?
7. What is the big message you want them to know?
8. What kinds of tactics do you want to use? For example, do you want to use viral marketing, interactive online components, outdoor or print ads, transit advertising (buses, subways, taxis, etc.), new media, direct mail, floor talkers, or other vehicles?

> "First, they [creative talents] should understand that they'll have plenty of bad ideas for every good one. The key is understanding how to evaluate the ideas so that they can sort out the good from the bad. For instance, we always start with respecting the intelligence of the audience."
>
> —TOM DENARI[3]

The Power of the Brand

You'll notice the first question is, what is the personality of the brand? But let's first look at what a brand is. It's more than just an instantly identifiable name like Coke. A brand is something the audience claims as its own. There's a relationship between a brand and the consumer. This is why people will pay more for a brand. Why they'll look for a specific brand. Why they won't settle for anything other than that brand. There's a commitment and sense of trust that's created, much like a friendship. When brands can be customized to perfectly fit buyers' needs, consumers actually begin to identify and personally connect with the brand, which deepens the relationship.

Certain brands stand out immediately when you think of consumer loyalty—these include Saturn, MINI Cooper, Nike, and Apple. Consumers who are repeat buyers feel the brand fulfills needs that are important to them. It could be the product's facility of use, its reliability, dependability, durability, portability, or even its cool factor. Many people like to look or feel cool, and they gravitate to products that they believe deliver that look or feeling.

Getting inside the consumers' minds and understanding what drives their buying decisions gives you the unique ability to fully understand the symbiotic marriage between the brand and the buyer. Agencies that understand this—like the strategists at Crispin Porter + Bogusky—are able to reach audiences in unexpected ways, because they know what will resonate with the target audience. They know what will deliver a "wow" impact and create a universal stir. In short, they know how to win the battle of the buzz.

According to Norm Grey, the executive creative director at The Creative Circus (a portfolio school in Atlanta), the CP+B creative teams are futurists:

> Crispin Porter + Bogusky is the agency of the year by any measure, because they're on the leading edge of where advertising is going. Sometimes it's not about being on TV or on a billboard. It's about putting a MINI on a Ford Expedition and driving it around town. Or creating a kiddy ride outside a store and the ride being a MINI that costs $16,900 [see figure 6.2]. Those are not TV commercials. It's like when CP+B got Burger King to change all their doors and there are 18,000 doors. Instead of it saying "push" on one side and "pull" on the other, now it says, "Push or pull, have it your way."[4]

The Five-Step Creative Process

Now, let's get back to the five-step process that guides the creative process in creative firms and agencies and graphic design shops.

FIGURE 6.2 The kiddy "MINI Ride" MINI Cooper created by Crispin Porter + Bogusky for MINI USA. Photo courtesy of MINI USA LLC

1. *The assignment*—This is the beginning stage when the agency gains insight into the client and seeks clarification of the corporation's identity and overall message. Client input is outlined and recorded as meeting notes. Then, a creative brief is developed to guide the strategic planning.

2. *The preparation*—Here the agency compiles a creative brief by conducting research, gathering ideas, and identifying the audience. This brief is referred to throughout the conceptualization process to ensure that the creative work is on strategy. What "on strategy" means is that the creative solution matches the strategy that was developed by the agency.

3. *The creative process*—After the agency's creative teams become informed about the objectives and audience, they begin their creative exploration to search for the appropriate answer through brainstorming sessions. During these sessions, all ideas are heard, considered, and embraced, no matter how far-fetched or wild they may be. Some of the craziest ideas are the catalysts for the best solutions.

4. *The solution: Eureka!*—The creative teams have an idea and move forward to develop several campaign solutions. They select the best one to present to the client. Often they have backup solutions ready in case the client doesn't approve their selected campaign.

5. *The verification*—Creative solutions must always be evaluated to determine if they (1) solved the correct problem, (2) targeted the correct audience,

(3) remained on strategy, (4) used the appropriate tone of voice, and (5) delivered a relevant and believable message with a needs-driven benefit.

More Insights into the Creative Process

When asked "How do you come up with the ideas?" Linda Kaplan Thaler, CEO and chief creative officer of The Kaplan Thaler Group, answered:

> Actually, ideas are simple, but we're just not always aware of them because we tend to live in the past or the future, rather than in the enticing present, where all action is. Creative sparks are all around us, but you have to live in the "now" in order for them to reach your consciousness. . . . The biggest challenge is not coming up with ideas, but where to place them. Everyone's trying to get heard in this noisy world and it's more difficult with the plethora of entertainment media to choose from. How do I reach that elusive eighteen-year-old male when he is, at any given moment, either using his cell phone, entering a chat room or grazing through 600 cable channels?[5]

Kaplan Thaler further explains how her agency focuses on developing a message that can work equally well in all media in order to reach her target audience:

> To begin with, an eighteen-year-old male is probably not watching network TV. So why spend a billion bucks on expensive channels he's not even watching? At least not much of the time. This is why, since you don't know from one moment to the next what people are watching or doing, you need to create an idea that makes such an impact it can work in any medium. So if you have the Aflac duck quacking, that iconic representation of the brand can easily be re-created in a ringtone, on a banner, on Monday-night football, or in a radio ad.

Work at Your Own Pace

Just as with all tasks, some people work faster than others when they are designing creative advertising campaigns. Some get ideas in a flash, and others labor over their solutions. In fact, David Ogilvy, a celebrated copywriter and agency head, complained about his own struggles with writing: "I know other writers who are much more fluent, and facile, and surer-footed, and can write their stuff down, and that's the way it runs. I'm not that good. I'm awfully slow. I've done as many as 19 drafts on a single piece of copy before I've presented it to anyone to edit. I wrote 37 headlines for Sears Roebuck last week and I think three that I thought were good enough to submit to other people for their comment. So, you see, the writing business is not easy for me."[6]

Although advertising is a deadline-driven business, some ideas take longer and must be allowed the proper time to percolate. It is better to have an on-strategy solution than to have a weak campaign that isn't well thought out.

On Target and On Strategy

Not only must the campaign be on strategy, but the advertising must clearly focus on the main objective, accurately explain the benefits, and specifically highlight why consumers should buy that product. In addition, it must also be on target. This means that appropriate language should be used so that it speaks in the correct tone of voice to the audience. For example, if you're targeting investors, you wouldn't want a chatty or casual manner of speech. Instead, you'd want the copy to sound serious and sophisticated so that it projects intelligence and insight while commanding the reader's attention.

The information must be delivered in a way that is intrusive and interruptive. It must stop the audience and make the reader say, "That's what I needed to know." Or "Wow, that sounds like my life." Or "That's exactly how I feel." The message must sound natural and believable, so the targeted audience internally nods its approval. It must also make an emotional connection with the audience.

This is why the 2005 Dove "Campaign for Real Beauty" seemed so honest when it used women of various sizes, not bone-thin supermodels, in its print ads, billboards, and TV commercials. The women in the campaign looked like members of its target audience—real women. This followed Nike's campaign directed at average-size women (sizes twelve and fourteen), which carried a headline that proudly stated, "I Have Thunder Thighs." There was some criticism that the women in the Nike ads were athletically built, unlike many women. But the question is, why shouldn't they be physically active? The stereotypical attitude might have been that heavier people don't work out, and obviously, that's not true. People of all sizes and shapes can be involved in sports. The point Dove and Nike were making was that their products are for all women, not just people who look like models.

Both the Dove and Nike campaigns are reminiscent of a 2002 movie, *Real Women Have Curves*, a story of Mexican American women and their struggle for survival, independence, and success. But a secondary message also encouraged women to celebrate their bodies, regardless of size. The stars cast for the film, including America Ferrera, Lupe Ontiveros, and Ingrid Oliu, were full-figured women who were aware that they didn't have perfect figures and weren't a size two.

Like the movie, the Dove campaign tapped into the idea of what it means to be a woman who doesn't look like the ones in so many fashion ads. According to trend specialist Faith Popcorn, president of the New York-based firm Brain Reserve, advertising wasn't the catalyst for this trend. "It started when we started to celebrate the black and Hispanic culture[s]. In those cultures you can be a little 'butty' and even have a little mustache, too, and it's considered cool and attractive. Now these white girls are looking at themselves and saying, 'I don't want to be a stick, I want to be natural.'"[7]

More and more advertisers are realizing that they need to speak to consumers in a way that makes the audience believe they are understood and valued. Visuals and messages are becoming more straightforward, more relevant, and more realistic. As Linda Kaplan Thaler told *Elle* magazine in May 2004: "For an idea to get noticed, it has to be disruptive. But the disruption has to be based in truth. For Clairol Herbal Essences, women in focus groups would say, 'I'm not that interested in washing my hair,' but when you'd press them they'd say, 'When I really think about it, it's the only time of day that my kids aren't screaming at me. It's very cleansing, and it's actually very sensual.' Somebody in the room made a joke about that restaurant scene in *When Harry Met Sally.* We all stopped and said, 'That's it.' So is it disruptive? Yes. Is it polarizing? Absolutely. Are women dying to shampoo their hair? You bet. And Herbal Essences is now sold all over the world."[8]

On Strategy and On Target: Speaking Clearly to the Audience

A few examples of on-strategy and on-target advertising will demonstrate how skillfully these messages are delivered, like arrows hitting the target. One print and TV campaign created by Young & Laramore for Stanley Steemer comes to mind: "Living Brings It In. We Take It Out" (figures 6.3 and 6.4). When asked how the concept was developed, Tom Denari explains that part of the success was due to the ad's ability to change how consumers thought about carpet cleaning. "Over the years, carpet cleaning advertising has trained people to only clean their carpet when they see a stain. Currently, only 9 percent clean their carpets at least once a year. Ninety-one percent don't. Instead of simply talking to the 9 percent, we appealed to the 91 percent who don't. We shifted the thinking of carpet cleaning to a maintenance strategy, not just stain removal."[9]

"BACKPACK" :15 TELEVISION

This spot follows a boy heading home from school one day, highlighting the "journey" his backpack takes as he drags it alongside. Going through the school cafeteria, playground and a few stops along the way, an announcer and super hint, "Maybe having your carpet cleaned once a year isn't enough." This is where Stanley Steemer comes in. Cutting back to the boy as he simply continues his path into the house and up the stairs, the announcer and super drive home the campaign idea, **LIVING BRINGS IT IN. WE TAKE IT OUT.**™

FIGURE 6.3 "Backpack" TV storyboard, created by Young & Laramore for Stanley Steemer. Image courtesy of Young & Laramore

By changing how people looked at getting their carpets cleaned, the advertising was able to make consumers rethink their beliefs. It actually created a paradigm shift. "In other words, we're saying, 'Look, you're living your life. You're bringing in a lot of stuff. We'll help you take care of it.' Understanding that women didn't need more guilt inflicted upon them, we didn't want to be heavy handed." Now people realized that carpets get dirty from everyday activities and that they needed to be cleaned more frequently, not just to remove stains. The slice-of-life yet lighthearted approach made consumers aware of the assault carpets endure from regular daily traffic. Our purpose is to prove that our mixture

LIVING BRINGS IT IN. WE TAKE IT OUT.™

MAYBE HAVING YOUR CARPET CLEANED ONCE A YEAR ISN'T ENOUGH.

STANLEY STEEMER

FIGURE 6.4 "Doggie Door" print ad, created by Young & Laramore for Stanley Steemer. Image courtesy of Young & Laramore

of applied intuition, radical common sense, and solid judgment will result in truthful, beautiful, and relevant ideas every time.

Targeting Specific Audiences

As we've already discussed, it is essential to know what to say and how to talk to your audience. Sometimes the product needs to be repackaged to become more useful to the user. In 2004, Procter & Gamble combined fabric softener with its detergent and introduced Tide with Touch of Downy. This formula helped increase its market share by 0.4 points, moving it above its 40-percent share of the detergent category's $3.31 billion market. Recognizing the importance of answering consumers' needs, in January 2005, Tide introduced Tide Coldwater, a formulation designed to be more effective in cold water, which resulted in an even greater market share, and an increase of more than one point. It is interesting to note that neither of these products or similar products negatively affected the sales of fabric softeners.[10]

Song, a Delta Air Lines subsidiary, recognized that women were its primary target after research showed that women consisted of 62 percent of its leisure passengers, 75 percent of those doing the bookings, and 90 percent of those handling family travel. To speak to this audience, Song focused on providing special features to appeal to this market, including healthier foods and beverages, organic foods for youngsters and infants, and specially named cocktails like Song Cosmo and the Song Appletini.[11] It's obvious that reaching a specific audience goes beyond just the advertising message and must also embrace the packaging and amenities.[12]

Song is not the only advertiser noticing the importance of the female market. Electronic retailers are now courting women as managers and are focusing on how employees speak to their female customers. Companies like Best Buy, Office Depot, and Radio Shack are now targeting women, who represent 46 percent of household electronics purchasing decision makers. Furthermore, 50 percent of all households with women possess large-screen color televisions, DVD players, computers, color printers, Internet connections, cell phones, and boom boxes. Office Depot found out that 80 percent of its shoppers are females who owned home-based businesses.

To make Best Buy more appealing to women, it has introduced Jill concept stores, which have "Just for Kids" areas where children can play with store products and toys. Research had shown that women were spoken to in a condescending manner and their questions were left unanswered. To counteract this, Best Buy has instructed its staff to ask simpler, nontechnological questions like "What kinds of pictures do you like to take?" instead of questions that require a specific brand-driven answer like "What digital camera brand were you interested in?"[13]

Women have also emerged as the majority of online browsers, climbing to 52 percent of online shoppers. By 2003, they accounted for 60 percent of online dollars spent. Between 2003 and 2004, sales in female product categories showed the most growth, with jewelry and watches rising 68 percent and furniture and appliances escalating to 58 percent.[14]

When the milk industry wanted to pitch its product in Asia, it realized the big drawback was milk's nondescript flavor. So, to be more appealing to this market, it created a sweeter taste and introduced ginger- and rose-flavored milk, reflecting flavors familiar to this audience. Another cultural difference is that the Asian market appreciates scientifically enhanced products, as opposed to Americans, who are looking for natural products. Knowing this, the milk producers added extras like vitamin B and fatty acid DHA, based on fish oil, which are thought to enhance cognitive function in children.[15]

In 2004, major airlines also started targeting pet owners by introducing programs like United Airlines' United Pet Class, which rewards flyers with 1,200 miles for taking their pets along. Virgin Airlines offers frequent flyer points to pet owners and free giveaways for pets after their first flight, including T-shirts and shiny tags for dogs, toy mice for cats, and limited edition flying jackets for ferrets. Once they arrive in London, pets receive complimentary food and grooming at the "pet reception center."[16]

With the growing number of people who are either diabetic (17 million) or those who have high blood-sugar levels (16 million), sugar-free products are now the focus of Hershey, Kellogg's, Coke, and other food and beverage products. Hershey's now promises to give chocolate back without the sugar, but with all the taste to those who have to cut their sugar intake. One of the ads in 2005 reminded consumers how having chocolate back in their lives brought them happiness. Notice how the message delivered a real benefit to the consumer. This on-strategy ad demonstrated an understanding of the sense of loss and deprivation sugar-free diets create. It focused on what was new about these chocolate products. The campaign ran in mainstream magazines such as *People* and *Prevention*, as well as publications that targeted diabetics, like *Diabetes Forecast* from the American Diabetic Association.[17]

To target teens in a relevant way, the American Legacy Foundation® turned to two agencies: Crispin Porter + Bogusky and Arnold Worldwide. The foundation wanted to help reduce the number of teen smokers. So, how exactly do you talk to an audience that doesn't want to be told what to do or lectured and convince them to give up a habit that they consider a personal statement of freedom and an outright display of rebellion? According to the foundation, CP+B, and Arnold Worldwide, they decided to speak in teens' language—defiance—and to "tell teens the truth in a rebellious manner and respect their decision-making ability."[18]

How did they go about doing this? What was the step-by-step creative process that led to the creative solution? Here's how the creative teams explained their creative approach:

> First of all, we looked at the current anti-smoking messaging and asked ourselves why it wasn't working. One thing we continually saw in the work was the word "Don't." The minute you tell someone "don't," they automatically want to do it. Also, teens don't want to be told what to do in the first place. This lead to the idea of "What if we just told teens the truth and not really make a judgment call on it or tell them what to do with the message? Let teens come up with their own conclusions."[19]

As brands, stores, and companies continue to target specific audiences, the advertising message reinforces the changes delivered in the marketplace, including the language used in one-on-one, in-store contact with consumers, the product displays and stores' organization, and the specific media vehicles used to reach the audience, as well as the visuals included in advertising to more closely reflect the audience's physical attributes.

Other Ways to Communicate with the Target Audience

Today ads, billboards, direct mail, and TV commercials are only a few ways to reach consumers. Podcasts (radio shows that can be downloaded and played on a computer or other media players like an MP3 player) as well as blogs (online diaries or daily personal logs or commentary) and vlogs (online video logs) have also become significant communication tools for individuals, small businesses, political parties, and corporate entities. In fact, more than 30 percent of all Americans visited blogs during the first quarter of 2005, according to a comScore Networks study. After evaluating the 400 largest blogs, the study found that the most popular ones were political blogs, then those focusing on lifestyle and technology and blogs written by women.[20]

One blog, "Go Fug Yourself" (www.gofugyourself.com), which started as some fun, catty remarks among friends about celebrity clothing disasters, became an instant hit, attracting more than 126,000 visitors a day. Based on traffic alone, it was ranked number six out of 18 million blogs tracked, and ranked eighty-third in the one hundred largest blogs. The two young women who created the site, Jessica Morgan and Heather Cocks, both work in reality TV. Just due to their entertaining commentaries, MSNBC invited them to moderate an exciting red-carpet parade of stars for the Oscars. In addition, the blog attracted online sponsors like Random House and Viacom, both of which run their ads on the site.[21]

Many blogs become reference points for marketers trying to gain insight into specific audiences. For example, putting the proverbial pulse on what's cool has long been an elusive but important find. Blogs that focus on the latest trends, like photo flirting, in which teens send photos to each other on their mobile phones, and hair graffiti, which combines shaved and dyed hair sections to create messages, can be insightful resources. A few blogs that have been "cool trackers" that focus on cool businesses, trends, and news are PSFK (www.psfk.com), Cool Hunting (www.coolhunting.com), and Ypulse (www.ypulse.com).

Written by Piers Fawkes, a brand consultant, and Simon King, a creative director, the PSFK Web site spots trends and invites readers to send in photos of what they consider cool. Cool Hunting was created by a former Motorola user-interface designer and reveals what brands, gadgets, products, and T-shirts get cool kids' approval. Ypulse, developed by cable channel Current's viewer-driven content manager Anastasia Goodstein, showcases what teens think is cool, with the firsthand input of her two teenage daughters and their friends.[22]

Teens being addressed by advertising immediately sense the message's authenticity. Blogs that provide accurate insight can help guide strategists to develop on-target campaigns.

In late August 2005, the *Wall Street Journal* reported that there were 12.5 million blogs, while the *San Jose Mercury News* estimated there were 70 million blogs across the world, and other firms that track blogs, like IceRocket, estimated 18 million blogs after showing 3 million more over a four-month period.[23] Some companies are abusing the use of blogs and are using them as spam, the main purpose of which is the creation of "splogs" that post links to their Web sites.

Because of new technology, now advertising can send customized messages not just on the tops of taxicabs, as discussed in chapter 1, but also in magazines and newspapers. Instead of creating one ad and sending it to all the print media, companies can digitally create new messages that speak to different audiences. So, an ad in a fashion magazine can talk about a new look, and the same ad in a sports magazine can address fitness and health.[24]

Online, consumers' blasé attitudes toward banners have sparked an evolution of another medium, the RSS (really simple syndication). Now news feeds can single out particular audiences by offering links to news relevant to the audience. So, Diet Coke could run an Internet ad with upbeat headlines like the promise that eating cereal for breakfast might help consumers win the battle of the bulge, thus showing dieters a new way to watch their weight. Ads on NYTimes.com or other online newspapers could present news on politics or world events.[25]

Another change that has occurred is that TV spots have become shorter and shorter. Some earlier spots like some of the emotionally charged Hallmark spots, were as long as one or two minutes. Then commercials became thirty and fifteen seconds long. They were then reduced to ten-second spots. Now, a breath-refreshing gel called One Second is being advertised in a one-second spot. The commercial consists of a young girl putting a tiny bit of gel under her tongue and showing a close-up of the product, while a voice whispers, "One Second." With the advent of TiVo and DVRs, thirty-second spots can no longer exact the higher prices of yesterday, because consumers can so easily skip them altogether. So, shorter spots at lower costs can be more appealing.[26]

It's Not Just about the Media

Everything needs to work together to support the strategy: the media, the message, the visual, the tone of voice, the shell, and all other aspects of the ad. That is why developing any advertising or promotional materials before a clear strategy is established is premature. When Tide added fabric softener and Hershey's chocolate removed sugar, the ads focused on what was different and how that benefited the consumer. Granted, the ads may have been straightforward, but they delivered an intelligible and relevant message that persuaded the target audience to buy the product. And it is wise to remember that this is the fundamental purpose of advertising.

Some ads appear to be creative, but all you remember is the ad, not the advertiser. The goal is to do both: (1) to create excitement by using a medium in an unexpected way, like the live soccer players on the Adidas billboard or the MINI Cooper's kiddy ride in front of retail stores, and (2) to emphasize the company or brand. In both of these examples, there is no confusion about the name of the product. People remembered the buzz created by the Adidas board and the MINI Cooper ride. They didn't walk away saying, "Great idea, but what was it for?"

■ EXERCISE ONE

Scrutinize unique print ads, billboards, TV spots, and interesting package design (food and health-care products, CD albums, and DVD covers). Determine who the audience is and what the strategy may have been. Now, decide which ones you think are on strategy and on target. Go to the company's Web site to see if there is any information on the campaign. Seek out the name of the agency that developed the work. Can you find any information about the campaign strategy on agency Web sites or magazines like *Adweek* or *Advertising Age?* ■

■ EXERCISE TWO

Collect exciting examples of typography, copywriting, or new media uses. If you find an entertaining interactive Web site, jot it down. If you find an online ad that drove you to a link, note it. If you found a blog that kept you reading for more than two minutes, write it down. The more references you have, the more examples you have to stimulate your imagination. ■

■ PROJECT

If you are able to, work in teams. First select a product most of you use frequently. The objective is to think up a new place to advertise your message to your peers. First, write a creative brief. Remember the audience is people like you. Explain what you're trying to say that will prompt them to take action. Be sure to answer these questions:

- What are you trying to say?
- To whom are you saying it?
- How do you want to say it (tone of voice)?
- What do these consumers currently believe?
- What do you want them to believe?
- What are the competitors saying?
- What is the W-I-I-F-M? (What's in it for me?)
- What product features will convince the audience to buy and support the benefit?
- What would you need to hear to take action?

Be sure you focus on staying on strategy during the creative brainstorming session. Then, double-check that your solution also stayed on strategy.

Now, if you're working in teams, each team should present its solution, one at a time. When you've all presented, decide which team had the most imaginative idea that targeted the right audience and remained on strategy. ■

Suggested Reading

Bruce Bendinger, *The Copy Workshop Workbook*, 3rd ed. (Chicago: The Copy Workshop, 2002).

Rob Walker, "Social Lubricant: How a Marketing Campaign Became the Catalyst for a Societal Debate," *New York Times*, 3 Sept. 2005, 24.

Notes

1. David Ogilvy, www.ogilvy.com (accessed July 22, 2005).
2. Gregg Fields, "Mastering Corporatespeak," *Miami Herald*, August 18, 2005: G28.
3. Tom Denari, personal communication, July 20, 2005.
4. Norm Grey, personal communication, September 26, 2005.
5. Linda Kaplan Thaler, personal communication, January 4, 2006.

6. Denis Higgins, *Art of Writing Advertising: Conversations with Masters of the Craft* (Chicago: NTC Business Books, 1965), 93.

7. Rich Thomaselli, "Beauty's New, ER Face," *Advertising Age,* August 15, 2005: 1, 21.

8. Alex Postman, "*Elle* Leading Women Linda Kaplan Thaler, Advertising Innovator," *Elle,* May 2004: 150.

9. Tom Denari, personal communication, July 20, 2005.

10. Jack Neff, "Laundry Lines Find New 'Touch' Points," *Advertising Age,* June 27, 2005: S8.

11. Tom Denari, personal communication, July 20, 2005.

12. Rich Thomaselli, "Cruising on High Brand Awareness, Exec Turns Attention to Expansion," *Advertising Age,* June 27, 2005: 48

13. Beth Snyder Bulik, "Electronics Retailers Woo Women," *Advertising Age,* November 15, 2004: 16.

14. Kris Oser, "Women Wear the Pants Online Also," *Advertising Age,* April 25, 2005: 45.

15. Chris Prystay, "Milk Industry's Pitch in Asia: Try the Ginger or Rose Flavor," *Wall Street Journal,* August 9, 2005: B1, 8.

16. Hannah Karp, "Airlines Want Your Pets Aboard," *Miami Herald*, August 8, 2005: 23.

17. Stephanie Thomson, "Marketers Target Growing Diabetic Population," *Advertising Age,* March 17, 2003, 4: 32.

18. Sarah Howard, personal communication, December 14, 2005.

19. Sarah Howard, personal communication, December 14, 2005.

20. "Bloggers Are Younger, Wealthier and High Speed Connected," *Research Brief,* 2005, www.centerformediaresearch.com/cfmr_brief.cfm?fnl=050829.html (accessed August 29, 2005).

21. Brooks Barnes, "Fashion Trash Talk Is a Big Blog Hit for the 'Fug Girls,'" *Wall Street Journal*, September 28, 2005: A1, 8.

22. Jena McGregor, "Cool Runnings," *Fast Company,* October 2005: 40.

23. Minute@mediapost.com, www.mediapost.com (accessed August 23, 2005).

24. Brian Steinberg, "Speaking Up through Bespoke Ads," *Wall Street Journal*, February 11, 2005: B5.

25. Brian Morrissey, "Advertisers Fight Banner Blindness with News Feeds," *Adweek*, September 19, 2005: 10.

26. Kasy Wehrum, "And Now a Syllable from Our Sponsor," *Inc.*, August 2005: 22.

Take Charge of the Design Principles

Ideas can come from anywhere.

—SAATCHI & SAATCHI[1]

Now that we have discussed copywriting and strategy, it's time to get back to the fundamental components of design. In chapter 4, we discussed the six elements of design: (1) format and media, (2) line, (3) shape, (4) color, (5) texture, and (6) value. Now we will examine the principles of design and see how carefully crafted layouts effectively integrate the six elements with the five design principles. These are:

1. balance
2. emphasis
3. rhythm

4. unity
5. proportion

As we did with the elements of design, we'll examine these principles one at a time.

1. *Balance*—When different design elements look out of place they create an off-balance impression and give a feeling of instability to the layout. You can

immediately sense if a layout is balanced or not. Does it look lopsided, off kilter, out of sorts? Does it look top heavy? Does it look like it's about to topple over? Does it make you feel like the tilted room in the fun house at an amusement park?

On the other hand, when all the elements are appropriately positioned, the layout gives an impression of flow and balance. When flow is created, each element leads gracefully to the next. There is a natural quality about the entire design that looks right to the eye and imperceptibly leads the reader along.

It's usually easier to start by creating a formal, or *symmetrical,* design, in which both halves of the layout mirror each other. This projects an unmistakable sense of serenity, organization, and balance. An informal, or *asymmetrical,* design, in which the components on either side don't match each another, is a little trickier. In these layouts, although one side can have more type or larger pictures or more white space than the other, both sides must work together to create a balanced and harmonious layout. Basically, what gives a layout balance is an even division of weight, regardless of how many components are on each side. If the weight seems proportionally distributed, the layout looks balanced.

Another important aspect of visual weight is that although the different items in the layout are sitting on a one-dimensional surface, they seem to actually have three-dimensional weight to them. Dark areas; large visuals; and big, bold type have a heaviness to them, whereas small, light type; thin rules; and small graphics have a lightness and airiness to them.

2. *Proportion*—This principle addresses how all the components in the layout work in relation to each other. Those that are more important proportionally take up more space, even if they're smaller. For instance, if the headline is important, it could be tiny but set in a wide expanse of open space, thereby commanding more physical presence and more attention. The difference between positive and negative space also needs to be considered in proportion to each other.

In a photograph, *positive space* is the main visual. *Negative space* is the background, or whatever appears behind the photographic subject. In an ad, the primary graphic or headline is the positive space. Those areas that serve in supporting roles are the negative space. Blank areas are also called *white space.* These are places where the eye can rest, providing visual silence for the reader. All space that appears unused or open needs to be as carefully designed as the areas that carry visual and verbal messages.

In addition to visual weight, different aspects of the layout can be arranged to give the illusion of distance or depth, offering perspective in the layout. You can achieve this by creating a vanishing point, like a horizon line, so objects in the foreground (front) seem closer than those in the background, which seem farther away. Picture yourself driving your car and looking down the road ahead. The white lines on the side of the road appear wider right in the front of the car. Then the lines seem to move toward each other, getting closer together farther ahead to form the letter *V*. The wide part of the *V* looks closer to you, and the narrower area appears to be down the road, in the distance.

3. *Emphasis*—What is featured or prominent is what is most important. Visuals or headlines that are prominent force the readers' attention to focus on them, naturally creating visual hierarchy. You can accomplish this by using a larger-size type or visual, a darker area, more white space, an unusual shape, color, rules, boxes, and so on. Creating emphasis establishes a focal point, or a principal place of reference.

Secondary areas that stop the reader are called visual accents. So, the headline might be the main focal point, but bold subheads punctuating the body copy could serve as accents. Think of them as road signs pointing the way.

4. *Rhythm*—This is created by repetition of an element that establishes a visible pattern that gives a feeling of movement to the layout. In the same way that a refrain punctuates a song with repetitive sections, patterns add rhythmic regularity like the cadence (rise and fall) of the spoken voice. Patterns can be formed in many ways. For instance, if the visual or type radiates out from the center, it has a circular pattern, like the rays of the sun. If it moves back and forth across the page, it creates a transitional layout, like a sinuous snake in motion. If visuals move from small images to larger ones or vice versa, they develop a pattern of gradation, like Russian stacking dolls.

Sometimes the eye can recognize a pattern, regardless of how subtle it is, like screened-back repeat patterns that act as a background, almost like a soft blanket, over which the other items are gently placed. Patterns can be created with light and dark areas or icons that create a visual beat, like a rhythmic graphic phrase.

5. *Unity*—This occurs when everything works together as a singular cohesive unit. In multiple-page layouts like brochures, repeat typographic elements, borders around each page, rules separating copy blocks, screened-back boxes, or recurring visual icons can create correspondence or relationship between the elements, resulting in continuity as well as unity in the layout. Sometimes an underlying grid serves as the unifying device. Other times, the alignment of the visuals, headlines, or copy blocks can create a consistency in the design. Layouts with too much open space or a poor arrangement of typographic and visual elements can look disorganized or loose.

Cohesive and unified layouts don't usually happen quickly. Often, they require multiple revisions. Just as good writing is the result of editing, great design emerges from a series of refinements or tweaks.

There's something that comes out of the intuition, or the heart or the inspiration in an individual that defies all the logic of science and focus groups, and committee meetings and all that other stuff. That somehow people are suddenly talking to other people and sharing something that's important to them. And, that's a really cool thing.

It's fun to do. It's fun to hear. It's fun to be part of. And, at the end of the day it builds some of the most powerful brands in the world. Because people have a relationship with an honest-to-god emotion coming from honest-to-god people that are real.

—DAN WIEDEN[2]

Campaign Shells

Most strong ad campaigns show layout unity from one ad to another by using a *shell*. This consistency of the placement and use of elements establishes a recognizable identity for the company or product. Memorable campaigns often have an intriguing visual that commands the reader's full attention. One example is the print campaign for Monsoon Audio Systems by Young & Laramore (figures 7.1 and 7.2). Notice how in the first ad the Eiffel Tower corresponds to the electrical towers, and how in the second ad the palm trees connect to the telephone poles. The reader has to take a second look, because this technique of illusion, *trompe l'oeil*, tricks the eye and requires further examination.

When asked what the thinking was behind the visuals in the Monsoon Audio Systems ads, Tom Denari answers, "With the Monsoon idea, what we found was how they listen to music in their car changes how they look at things. You feel like you're in a cocoon. You can make the music as loud as you want. It can change a boring drive and can put you in a completely different place."[3]

A Library of Layout Formats

As we just saw, ingenious campaigns have a unique aspect yet fit into a format or shell. The following list of layouts will help give you a reference of some of

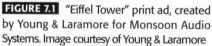

FIGURE 7.1 "Eiffel Tower" print ad, created by Young & Laramore for Monsoon Audio Systems. Image courtesy of Young & Laramore

FIGURE 7.2 "Palm Tree" print ad, created by Young & Laramore for Monsoon Audio Systems. Image courtesy of Young & Laramore

the basic ad formats. You can also use some of these page layouts for brochures, annual reports, and magazine articles.

1. *Picture window*—A large picture dominates the layout, much like a picture window, often in the front of a house.
2. *Multipanel*—This layout consists of equal-size boxes and is useful for showing several items at a time.
3. *Split*—This type of layout looks as if the page were divided up into sections. It can be split vertically, horizontally, or diagonally and can be broken into two or more sections.
4. *Frame*—When a layout has a border, it's called a frame ad. The border can be a thick or thin rule, a visual, or type that runs around the layout.
5. *Circus*—This is a layout that can look disorganized. Although designers usually detest circus ads, they are often used for supermarkets, electronic retailers, automotive dealerships, garden nurseries, and tire stores and can be very effective. People looking for a car, for example, want to see that the dealership has a big selection. Therefore, when they see an abundance of cars, potential buyers think they have a better chance of finding what they

want. So for circus ads, the busier the layouts, the better they seem to sell their product.

6. *Rebus*—When a layout includes pictures that substitute for words, it's called a rebus ad. If the ad were for a pizza shop, the ad could read like this: "Do you love [picture of a slice of pizza]? With lots and lots of [picture of cheese]? Then, it's [clock's face for the word "time"] to try our cheesiest [picture of pizza with tons of cheese] ever!"

7. *Mondrian*—When you have different-size objects to show in a layout, using various sizes of rectangles can unify the design. Named after the style of Dutch painter Piet Mondrian, the Mondrian offers a sound way to showcase unrelated objects in an organized way.

8. *Picture caption*—Here images are accompanied by a little bit of copy. This format makes it easy for the reader to quickly grasp the image and product information as one unit.

9. *Cartoon*—Any layout that uses cartoon illustration as a visual is considered a cartoon format.

10. *Comic strip*—Just like the comics in the newspaper, the comic strip format has several boxes of cartoons that continue the message from one to the next.

11. *All type*—This format uses no visual. Often, the headline is so strong, or set in such interesting or unusual type, that a visual would weaken the communication (see figures 7.3, 7.4, and 7.5) Art directors who are typographic connoisseurs can design imposing messages. These powerful messages were designed to run as pump headers at gas stations to remind car owners each

FIGURE 7.3 Example of sticker designed to be placed on gas pumps. "Petrol Donate" was created by Think Tank 3 for Citystreets. Image courtesy of Think Tank 3

FIGURE 7.4 Example of sticker designed to be placed on gas pumps. "Petrol Support" was created by Think Tank 3 for Citystreets. Image courtesy of Think Tank 3

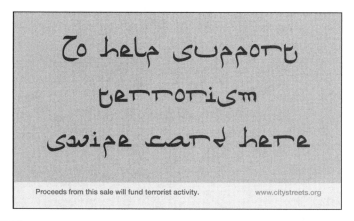

FIGURE 7.5 Example of sticker designed to be placed on gas pumps. "Petrol Swipe" was created by Think Tank 3 for Citystreets. Image courtesy of Think Tank 3

time they filled up who was ultimately receiving their gasoline dollars. The imaginative use of type only added to the signs' impact. According to Sharoz Makarechi, creative director of Think Tank 3, the agency that designed these stickers, the message was further explained on the reverse side: "Printed on the back of the stickers were an explanation of the message, a bit about the organization, instructions and a list of gas stations that import oil from the Middle East, and a list of those that do not. Useful information for people who care about such matters."[4]

12. *No Type*—Many fashion designers, perfume companies, and clothing lines use large visuals with only the logo in their ads. This format has no copy in it. The brands are so well known that no explanation is needed for the product shown.

13. *Letter inspired*—You've probably seen layouts in which you can instantly spot a letter as an important part of the design. As we saw in chapter 3, type can be used as a design element. It can also be used as the main format for a layout. For instance, the copy blocks can be set in the shape of a letter, one large letter can dominate the page, or the visuals can be text wrapped to suggest a letter.

14. *Silhouette*—This format has a visual with no background. Sometimes furniture stores use silhouettes of sofas, dressers, and chairs. The furniture appears as if it were cut out, so that all you focus on is the one object. Other times, furniture stores will show the furniture as part of a whole room. In these cases, the furniture is set against a background and is not shown as a silhouette.

15. *Big type*—Many retail sale ads use gigantic type to make sure you don't miss seeing them. Other times, large headlines are included for their stopping power.

16. *Spot color*—Some layouts are black and white with just a touch of another color in certain spots. For example, a florist could be showcasing red roses by using red just for the roses in a black-and-white ad.

17. *Special effects*—Layouts that look as if the corners were burnt or as if someone took a bite out of the side are examples of special effects. Sometimes an ad will depict a visual metaphor like a man with his head buried in the sand or someone in a backbend. What these visuals are saying is "Don't bury your head in the sand" or "We'll bend over backwards" to deliver excellent service. Visuals that are obvious exaggerations or have been manipulated to create an effect are also considered special-effects layouts.

18. *Strip (vertical or horizontal)*—Ads that are narrow and tall or wide and short are called strip ads, because they take up a vertical or horizontal strip of a page. This format is useful for objects that stack well in one direction or the other. For example, if you wanted to show a four-scoop ice-cream cone, a vertical strip ad would be ideal.

19. *Double truck*—When a layout goes across two pages, it's called a spread or a double truck. At least one graphic or typographic component travels across both pages, unifying the layout. Usually spreads are seen as magazine articles or newspaper ads. These layouts do not have to take up the entire page. They can also be half-page designs that go across two pages.

20. *Small ads in a series*—Usually small ads in a series appear in the same newspaper section or magazine issue as punctuation marks reminding the reader about the product or service. Functioning like a mini-campaign in one medium, a series of ads might appear on several pages of the same section suggesting you use the paper to advertise. In that case, the advertiser is the newspaper. Or you might find a series of ads for the same hotel over several consecutive or nearby pages in a leisure travel magazine.

Three Ways to Present Layouts

There are three ways to show your design ideas to a professor, client, or creative director. These are as a (1) *thumbnail*, (2) *rough,* or (3) *comp*. *Thumbnails* are miniature rough layouts that reduce the design down to about a fourth of its size or less for easy viewing. They can be sketched by hand or computer generated. If you were designing a 9-by-12-inch brochure, your thumbnail might be as small as 2-by-3.5 inches or even 1.5-by-2 inches.

Roughs are actual-size layouts that usually include hand-drawn visuals. They also used to include hand-lettered headlines, but since so many fonts are now available digitally, most headlines today are set on the computer. Roughs are not completed layouts but rather provide an idea of the concept and composition of the elements.

Comps or comprehensive layouts are virtually exact replicas of the final design. These usually give the client a precise idea of what the ad, brochure, flyer, newsletter, annual report, or billboard will look like.

Today graphic designers can create promotional materials and send them digitally for placement to publications or other media.

Going from Roughs to Comps

Often small changes are all that are needed to finalize a layout. Sometimes just the type needs to be refined or the placement of a visual needs to be realigned or one component needs to be shifted for a clearer visual hierarchy. New creative teams can improve their creative judgment by making suggested revisions. These changes may be recommended by another creative talent, a professor, or a client. Learning to absorb criticism and become less sensitive to it helps talented art directors and copywriters grow creatively. Creative talents who defend their work and dig their heels in to protect their "creative baby" only develop inflexibility, which makes them difficult for others to work with. However, new creative talents who are willing to make changes and see the differences small changes can make usually develop a greater understanding of what makes a stronger layout.

> "Use the medium" has always been great advice, so in an age where media are metamorphosing on a daily basis, don't just be in it or on it, embody, extend, expand, and explode it. Don't just color in within the edges.
>
> —MICHAEL NEWMAN[5]

The Elements of a Layout

Ads have specific elements. Some of them are common to other layouts. Others are found mostly in ads. Here are the main ad elements for easy reference.

1. *Headline*—Just as in all layouts, the headline delivers the main message of the ad. Headlines that have a benefit to the consumer deliver an immediate reason for the ad to be read.
2. *Subhead*—This is a line of type that supports the headline. It reinforces the main idea and motivates the consumer to continue reading.
3. *Body copy*—Here is where the user benefits and product features are highlighted. Writing in an easy-to-read style helps keep your readers' interest and should take them from the first line to the last without any break.
4. *Visual*—The image chosen should be so closely related to the main idea that together they are absorbed as one cohesive unified message. In addition to photographs, cartoons, illustrations, charts, graphs, and other images like infographics (visuals that depict statistics or deliver facts in boxes), there are two other visual components you could consider including: lines and repeat graphic elements.
   a. *Rules*—Lines that separate copy blocks, create a frame, or serve as a thick stripe or bar can add structure to a layout.
   b. *Repeat graphic elements*—Any visuals that are used in repetition can create a unifying pattern that helps coordinate the design.
5. *Logo*—This is an unforgettable element. If the ad does not have a logo, how will readers know who ran the ad?
6. *Slogan*—Although most campaigns have a slogan, there are a few that do not. Absolut is one example of an instantly recognizable, long-running print campaign without a slogan. Each of the ads has a short two- or three-word

headline like "Absolut Attraction," "Absolut Marilyn," "Absolut St. Louis," and "Absolut Les Bains." But none has a slogan.

7. *Typeface*—The choice and placement of type can add immeasurable character and unique identity to the ad. Designers who master the art of typography are in command of a critical communication device.

8. *Color*—As we will see in the next chapter, colors have specific psychological effects on viewers. Understanding the personality of color is vital when you're developing ads and logos. When adding one color to a black-and-white ad, the positioning of color should help direct the audience's attention and the choice of color should be appropriate for the product or company.

9. *White space*—Every layout must have visual silence, an oasis where the blank space serves as a respite.

10. *Emphasis*—The most important information must be seen first. It is highlighted so that it immediately draws the reader's attention. This, as we have seen, is done through weight, size, color, and placement to establish a focal point.

11. *Balance*—When all the elements work together, they create harmony.

12. *Unity*—This is achieved when everything in the ad is seen as an integrated whole, not as separate pieces of a disassembled puzzle.

13. *Proportion*—The relationship of one element to another dictates its place in the communication hierarchy. Think of it this way: when enormous furniture is stuffed into a tiny room, it is out of proportion for the given space. Just like a room, layouts need components that work together within the framework.

14. *Call to action*—Unless your audience knows exactly where to buy this product, it is important to inform them with a call to action. This tells them whether to call, go to a store, or go online to make a purchase. Many products, like bread, eggs, or orange juice, are widely distributed and obviously don't require this.

15. *Signature*—Including the "sig," or advertiser's contact information—address, phone, e-mail, Web site—is vital if you want your target audience to be able to communicate with or purchase from the company.

When you're developing ads, remember they are communication vehicles that must reach a specific audience with a relevant message based on a predetermined creative strategy.

Examples of Work in Progress

Now let's talk more about the importance of revisions. Sometimes, just a change in the background color from gray (see figure 7.6) to black (see figure 7.7) adds

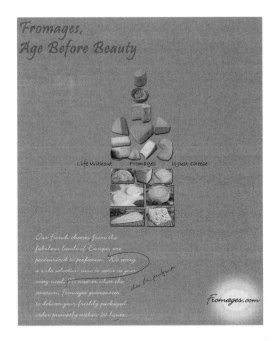

FIGURE 7.6 "Age Before Beauty," created by Jennifer Camille and Jennifer Otero, graduates of Florida International University, for Fromages. com. Used with permission of the School of Journalism and Mass Communication, Florida International University

FIGURE 7.7 "Age Before Beauty Revised," created by Jennifer Camille and Jennifer Otero, graduates of Florida International University, for Fromages.com. Used with permission of the School of Journalism and Mass Communication, Florida International University

strength to the layout. The mosaic cheese image pops against the solid black background but just rests stagnantly on the drab gray carpet-like background. The change in font from script to a serif font like Times New Roman makes the type more legible. In addition, the modification from white type on gray to yellow type on black makes a bolder, more legible statement. Also, although the headline fonts are similar, the choice of yellow for the font set against the black background delivers greater impact.

Keeping with the mosaic visual and the black background, the campaign continues with the second ad, "Aged to Perfection" (figure 7.8). This is a good example of continuity with the same style of visual, the same use of color, and the same application of type. Notice how the subhead interrupts the visual in both ads.

In these ads for Fromages.com (figures 7.9 and 7.10), the meaning of the first headline, "Fromagin' Temptation," is unclear. The word *fromage* is not part of everyday American speech and would easily be mispronounced and misunderstood. In addition, the visual of bread, wine, and cheese—although selected to clarify the message—does little to explain it. In the revision, "To Slice or Not to Slice," a word play on a famous Shakespearean quote cleverly invites the viewer to think about the age-old question of whether to tear the bread or slice it. This ad engages readers' imaginations and makes them consider the dilemma. The simplicity of the headline and the visual adds to the overall effect.

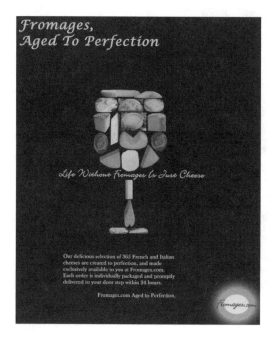

FIGURE 7.8 "Aged to Perfection," created by Jennifer Camille and Jennifer Otero, graduates of Florida International University, for Fromages. com. Used with permission of the School of Journalism and Mass Communication, Florida International University

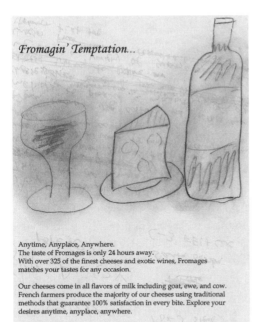

Fromagin' Temptation...

Anytime, Anyplace, Anywhere.
The taste of Fromages is only 24 hours away.
With over 325 of the finest cheeses and exotic wines, Fromages matches your tastes for any occasion.

Our cheeses come in all flavors of milk including goat, ewe, and cow. French farmers produce the majority of our cheeses using traditional methods that guarantee 100% satisfaction in every bite. Explore your desires anytime, anyplace, anywhere.

Fromages
Pleasure in every slice.

FIGURE 7.9 "Fromagin' Temptation," created by Joshua Levine and Mariana Segura, graduates of Florida International University, for Fromages.com. Used with permission of the School of Journalism and Mass Communication, Florida International University

To slice or not to slice...

That is the question. All we can do is help you find your passion. The cheese is up to you. Just think, more than 325 choices are only a click away. Luscious and exotic cheeses perfectly created with century-old secrets by generations of French farmers.

Discover la crème de la crème of flavors from cow to goat and even ewe. All paired up with the prefect wine to match. Now the question is to slice or not to slice?

www.fromages.com
Pleasure in every slice

FIGURE 7.10 "To Slice or Not to Slice," created by Joshua Levine and Mariana Segura, graduates of Florida International University, for Fromages.com. Used with permission of the School of Journalism and Mass Communication, Florida International University

Revision Enhances Creative Growth

Just like great writers, great designers revise over and over. Even the very first Absolut ad, which featured a halo over the bottle and the headline "Absolut Perfection," started as "Absolut. It's the Perfect Vodka." It happened very quickly. Art director Geoff Hayes came up with the idea of putting a halo over the bottle and added the headline "Absolut. It's the Perfect Vodka." The next morning he showed the rough to his copywriter partner Graham Turner. He simply suggested to Hayes that they shorten the headline. With that one suggestion and easy revision, the creative team at TBWA in New York launched one of the most recognizable campaigns of the century.

If Hayes had resisted revisions, the campaign would never have had the impact it had. That's why learning to make revisions and carefully observing how those changes affect the layout are crucial in creative growth. It's always a good idea to consider different fonts, to try alternative sizes of copy blocks, and to contemplate various graphic approaches. It's clear that even the smallest change can make a big difference.

The best way to learn what works is to learn what doesn't. You must look at each ad element separately and then how it relates to the other elements on the page. If you have an area of weakness and have heard criticism about your use of typography, study graphic annuals for examples of great uses of type. Ask yourself exactly what is it about these typographic examples that enhances the communication. Likewise, if your visuals are predictable and lack freshness, closely examine advertising materials that showcase exciting visuals. Then, analyze them and ask, why are they so exciting and unexpected?

So, before making a final design decision, manipulate the elements. Play with the type. Move the headline into different positions. Try it above the visual. Then next to the headline. Under the headline. By moving each element around the page, you can see where the emphasis lies. Always remember to keep the reader in mind and create layouts that guide the reader's eyes.

A Word about the Projects

The projects in this chapter deliberately avoid having you use the computer for any typesetting or visuals. This prevents you from using the computer as a design partner to help you find unique fonts and interesting graphics. Instead, it forces you to find fonts and visuals in complementary colors by cutting them out and placing them side by side. By removing the computer from the layout process, you are forced to work only with the elements. Rearranging them in several positions before deciding where they should be placed helps develop the critical skills necessary for excellent design. You can learn to establish visual hierarchy by deciding what is most important. Then, change the placement of the elements. Move them around the layout until they are sitting in an appropriate position for maximum emphasis, balance, contrast, and overall communication.

■ EXERCISE ONE

Collect several issues of the same magazine or several brochures from the same company. Next, gather a few more magazines in the same industry (fashion, sports, fitness, etc.) or promotional materials from the same firm. For instance, if you selected *Business Week*, you'd also select several other issues of that publication, as well as *Time*, *Newsweek,* and other news magazines. For print collateral, you might have several brochures, flyers, mailers, or annual reports from any one company, such as Norwegian Cruise Line, AT&T, MasterCard, Bank of America, or Disney. You can choose a local firm, if you prefer.

Now, examine each magazine cover. Do you see a relationship between them? For instance, did you notice the red border around each *Time* magazine cover and the placement of the magazine's title? Are there any elements that are layered in front of or behind the name? Does the layering technique repeat in several issues or brochures?

By examining several issues of the same publication, or several print examples from the same company, you're training yourself to identify and recognize common patterns on each of the covers. You're seeing a template, a shell that establishes immediate product or company recognition and awareness. You're also developing your ability to recognize various design techniques and critique the selection and arrangement of myriad components, including fonts, visuals, color, and rules. ■

■ PROJECT ONE

Develop two different cut-and-paste layouts, one for the cover and another for the inside spread (a two-page layout for a magazine or facing inside panels for a brochure). Do not use the computer. Cut out all your headlines, subheads, body copy, visuals, and graphic icons (illustrations, cartoons, photographs, charts, design elements) from the magazines. Don't worry about what the type says. Use all typography as a graphic element. It doesn't have to make sense. It only has to work from a visual perspective. Examine the color, size, and placement of the type, not the content.

First, create a magazine or brochure cover. On a blank 8.5-by-11-inch sheet of paper, arrange the elements in several ways. Analyze the impact of the placement of the elements. In which position do they:

1. Grab the reader's attention?
2. Emphasize the main idea?
3. Organize the information?
4. Exhibit balance?
5. Deliver the strongest message?
6. Speak directly to the audience?

Lastly, use a glue stick (preferably removable) to glue down your design. Then, create a two-page magazine spread, or design the three inside panels of a brochure. Tape two 8.5-by-11-inch sheets of paper together horizontally so that they are side by side. Look for a large graphic element and/or headline that can stretch across the two pages to unify the layout. Be careful not to have small blocks of copy or tiny visuals in the *gutter* (the space between the two pages). It will cause a problem in alignment where the two pages meet.

Use one 8.5-by-11-inch sheet of paper and create three columns with *margins* around and between each one. Be sure to allow breathing space around graphics, pictures, and text boxes. How can you make the three columns balanced yet eye-catching? ∎

∎ EXERCISE TWO

Collect several examples of graphic design, such as ads, brochures, flyers, and door hangers. Which ones engage your interest? Which ones make you want to take action? Which ones communicate a compelling message?

1. Select one example.
2. Make at least three photocopies.
3. Keep the original example intact.
4. Cut apart one of the photocopies.
5. Rearrange the elements.
6. Change the size of some of the elements to add emphasis. (You can use a copy machine to enlarge or create rough sketches of the elements.)
7. Create a new layout using all the elements.
8. Cut apart another photocopy.
9. Create another layout.

10. Layer some of the elements.
11. Cut apart the third copy.
12. Create a totally different layout.
13. Rotate the type or a visual to add movement.

Now, look at all three layouts. Which one has the greatest impact? Why? ∎

■ PROJECT TWO–PART ONE

Now, take your favorite layout from the previous exercise and add new elements to improve the layout. Do you need a better subhead? A different visual? A repeat graphic element? A different typeface? What else can you change to strengthen the communication of the message? ∎

■ PROJECT TWO–PART TWO

Gather a group together, or work alone. Brainstorm a new frozen coffee product. Don't limit yourself to frozen cappuccinos or coffee ice cream. Dream up something exciting and tantalizing. Now name it, give it a delectable tagline, and create a layout. Use the same process as in the above exercise and project, thinking through the various components. This time use the computer for any part of the process AFTER YOU ROUGH SOMETHING OUT ON PAPER. Starting with a layout rather than designing first at the computer will give you a greater sense of creative control.

The second part of the project stimulates the right brain and engages your creativity. It challenges you to come up with a new product idea, so you won't be influenced by existing ads, commercials, and promotional materials. New products often spark new creative approaches. Let yourself go, and see where you end up! ∎

Suggested Reading

Edd Applegate, *Strategic Copywriting: How to Create Effective Advertising* (Lanham, MD: Rowman & Littlefield, 2005).
Robyn Blakeman, *The Bare Bones of Advertising Print Design* (Lanham, MD: Rowman & Littlefield, 2005).
Robin Landa, *Graphic Design Solutions* (Albany, NY: Delmar, 1996).

Notes

1. Saatchi & Saatchi, 2004, www.saatchi.com/worldwide (accessed November 29, 2005).

2. Wieden+Kennedy, www.wk.com (accessed June 28, 2005).

3. Tom Denari, personal communication, July 20, 2005.

4. Sharoz Makarechi, personal communication, January 4, 2006.

5. Michael Newman, *Creative Leaps* (Singapore: John Wiley & Sons, 2003), 324.

8

Explore the Power of Color Psychology

> People should experience your idea at once, when they see it.
>
> —MICHAEL NEWMAN[1]

Just as you need to have an intimate knowledge of typography, as a line element, you should also have a mastery of another important element: color. This is because colors (1) have specific meanings, (2) create a psychological impact, and (3) can cause a physiological change. Certain colors have a calming effect. Light pink, for example, is the color used in certain rooms in prisons across the country, because it quiets down violent prisoners. After about fifteen minutes in the "pink room," aggressive prisoners start to relax, making it safer for guards to handle them.

Take a moment to guess the answers to these questions. You may instinctively pick the right colors.

1. Which colors raise your pulse?
2. Which color makes you hungry?
3. Which color is the happiest color?
4. Which color is the most popular in the United States?

5. Which color represents dependability?

6. Which color is used most often in one-color logos?

7. What color, when added, makes other colors appear sweeter?

See if you guessed right. Here are the answers. (1) Two colors—red and yellow—actually raise your pulse. (2) Red, in fact, has the greatest effect psychologically. It causes a faster pulse rate than yellow, raises the energy level, and actually increases the appetite. It's known as the color with the highest energy quotient, meaning it generates the most action. (3) Yellow is the color of happiness. (4) Blue is America's most popular color and is most often used in one-color logos. (5) Brown represents dependability. (6) And white, when combined with most other colors, makes them appear sweeter. So dark red becomes pink with the addition of white. The lighter the pink, the sweeter the color. Notice how light blue, which has a high concentration of white, is used on sweet products like Yoplait yogurt and Equal.

Colors, which also reflect climate and culture, are grouped together that way: warm, tropical colors are the reds and yellows, and the cool, wintry tones are the blues and greens.

The Meaning of Colors in the United States

Now let's look at the colors one by one. Most of the colors reflect specific meanings, which vary from author to author. However, some meanings have been generally accepted.

1. *Red*—It's the color of love, passion, and romance. Red roses are sent to sweethearts to show love. Valentines are red, as are the many greeting cards that express love. Red, as we just learned, has the most energy. It also affects you physically by raising your pulse, increasing your blood pressure, hastening your breathing, stimulating perspiration, and raising your heart rate. Notice that the stop signs on the road are red to attract your attention as you're approaching them. One interesting rumor is that red sports-car drivers are pulled over more often and given more traffic tickets than other drivers. That's where the expression "arrest red" came from in sports-car circles.

Red also stimulates the appetite in a variety of ways. Did you ever wonder why you might eat more at an Italian restaurant, aside from the fact that the food tastes so good? Well, look at all the red in the restaurant. Probably the menus are red, the walls may be red, the chairs or booths may be upholstered in red, the wine may be red, and the food may be topped with red marinara or meat sauce.

The waiter may even have on a red jacket, and the table may be dressed with a red-and-white checkered tablecloth. No wonder you have such a hearty appetite at Italian restaurants. Once you realize red affects your appetite, you might want to limit the use of red in your kitchen and dining areas if you're battling a weight problem.

Red is daring, expressive, competitive, and aggressive. In fact, red is so strong that some professional wardrobe consultants suggest not wearing red in an interview, because it might overpower the person making the hiring decision. A small amount of red, like a tie, seems to be acceptable, but image experts generally concur that for women, a red jacket or suit may make too strong a statement.

2. *Yellow*—This sunny color represents joy and happiness. Bright yellow, like red, raises the pulse, but not to the same extent. Yellow demands attention; and products packaged with yellow are often noticed first on store shelves. When it's a bold yellow, it's cheery and energetic. Pale, soft, or creamy yellows are soothing and sophisticated. Yellow is often paired with black in packaging. This combination delivers a "wow" because of the contrast. Picture bumblebees. You know how they can sting, and their eye-catching yellow-and-black stripes act as a warning sign.

3. *Blue*—Dark blue symbolizes stability, reliability, establishment, trust, confidence, constancy, and truth. This is why many financial institutions use blue in their logos. Look at IBM. It has been known as "Big Blue" for many years. Now Pepsi is focusing on the color blue, claiming it as its own, just as United Parcel Service "owns" the color brown. Pepsi trucks have even been painted with a phrase that directs people to "break out" the blue, referring to the blue on Pepsi cans.

Blue also signifies tranquility, serenity, and peace. It reminds us of powder blue skies and rich blue seas. It represents two ever-present elements, air and water, reflecting a calm, enduring constancy. Blue has a quieting, restful effect on the psyche. It's often chosen for hospital attire and decor because of its soothing nature.

The darker the blue, the more power and presence it has. As mentioned before, the lighter the blue, the sweeter it is, like the robin's egg blue used for baby boys. Although you don't necessarily think blue would be appetizing when it comes to food (even though blue ketchup might be appealing to little kids), blue Jell-O, blue M&M's, and blue Hypnotiq liqueur are considered exciting and fun to consume.

There are many shades of blue with varying meanings. Brilliant blues are vibrant, alive, and almost electric. Floral periwinkle, a delightfully warm, purplish blue, is found in beautiful clothing and home furnishings. Rich cobalt blue is found in glassware used at upscale restaurants. Navy blues are credible. That's why navy blue suits are so well received in business. Navy uniforms, like the ones worn by police officers and firefighters, convey trustworthiness.

According to the Pantone Color Institute, blue is still the favorite color in the United States, and denim is the still number one fabric in fashion.[2]

4. *Orange*—Orange is the color of harvest and is one of the most edible colors. Think about carrots, cantaloupes, pumpkins, sweet potatoes, and oranges. But it also has a nervous, agitating quality to it. Because of that characteristic, you might wonder why it's chosen as the color for prison inmates. It could be because it's highly visible outdoors, in case of an attempted prison escape. Orange is used for traffic cones and on vests for workers repairing roads, specifically for its attention-grabbing personality. Like red, orange stimulates the appetite. It's also an energizing color and has its own vitality and exuberance. Outgoing and capricious, orange has a youthful appeal, which everyone from six year olds and preteens to young adults enjoys. Because of these qualities, it's not a color to choose for marketing investment vehicles or other serious services. However, it's often used for products with a Hispanic flair or Indian foods like curry.[3]

Orange also represents knowledge and civilization. It's also the color of warmth, energy, force, and gaiety. Lately, it's come to convey cleanliness. You'll find it on cleansers and detergents, like the orange in Tide's logo.[4]

Pale or pastel orange has a fruity and luscious quality that brings to mind peaches, melons, and apricots. It appeals to a high-end audience and is often chosen for home decor because it adds a soft, comforting warmth.

5. *Green*—Green depicts nature, freshness, and health. It's the color of trees, grass, plants, flora, and many vegetables. It immediately reminds you of the fresh outdoors and is often used in beauty and skin care products. It connotes a natural cleanliness found in soaps and cleansers, like Irish Spring soap and Cascade dishwashing detergent.

Darker greens represent wealth and status. Financial establishments sometimes use green to instill fiscal confidence and to suggest that the institution is secure and well funded.

6. *Purple*—This majestic and mysterious color denotes royalty, nobility, spirituality, mysticism, and sensuality. It has also been known to depict loneliness.[5] During the Middle Ages, purple was the most costly dye, which made it affordable only for the richest people in society. In fact, for many years only nobility were permitted to wear this regal color, and commoners were banned from and punished for wearing it.

A highly spiritual color, purple is connected to New Age thinking and Eastern philosophies. It is also chosen for products indicative of innovative technology, new trends, and creative vision. Individualistic and free spirited, purple stands out for its own uniqueness. Purple is also a color loved by many children and people in the creative arts. In addition, this color is highly favored by women, which is why many products that target women use purple in their packaging. Because of its presence in fashion, purple has become more accepted by a wider audience.

Light purple, or lavender, is reminiscent of spring. The addition of white, to create lavender, adds to its sweetness. It reminds people of naturally sweet berries and the heavenly aromas of lilacs and lavenders.

7. *Black*—Although black can denote nothingness, nighttime, and evil; gloom, depression, death, and mourning; or the darker side of life, it's most often the color of choice for high-end, sophisticated products targeting an upscale market. That's because black is formal, elegant, rich, polished, powerful, and magical. It's a color associated with high status and class, such as sleek black limousines and luxurious granite.

When you think of being "dressed to the nines," black is the color that comes to mind. Black makes a strong statement and delivers a message that is distinguished, cultured, and refined. Dignified and chic, black is always fashionable and in vogue. It's the perfect color for most occasions, whether they are professional or social events.

Because of its power, weight, and definitive presence, black works well with most lighter shades, offering a bold contrast to them—white and black, yellow and black, light blue and black, pink and black. All of these are beautiful combinations and clear examples of the harmony created between light and dark. Black, in fact, carries so much weight that it is avoided in vehicles that require buoyancy and lift, like boats and aircraft. These types of vehicles usually use white as the background color because of the color's light and clean effect.

8. *Brown*—Brown is known for dependability and durability, and so it makes sense that UPS chose brown as its color. Then they drove the point home by using brown in its slogan: "What can brown do for you?" This color generates feelings of home and hearth. Its comforting hominess conveys a message of safety and shelter. Brown also connects to the outdoors, with its earthy, woodsy, and rustic tones.

Today, all shades of brown, from chocolate browns to taupes, are in fashion and are often used by designers to create sophisticated home decor. Rich brown leathers add depth and comfort, lending a protective cavernous or den-like ambiance to any room. Browns also conjure up the aroma of dark, robust coffee and luscious chocolates, all of which are soothing elixirs, relaxing rewards, and comforting escapes from the frantic pace of contemporary life.

9. *White*—The color of purity, cleanliness, innocence, and simplicity, white embodies everything that is pristine, from unblemished snow and unspoiled beaches to untouched naïveté. For products trying to project purity, no color portrays this better than white. Ivory soap was positioned as 99 percent pure, and the white color supported that claim. White wedding dresses in the United States were designed to represent the bride's purity and innocence.

10. *Gold*—Although it is close to yellow, gold has a totally different meaning. Long associated with riches and great wealth, gold projects a luxurious lifestyle. Used in the home, gold's warm tone reflects the owner's sophisticated taste. When paired with black or purple in packaging, it enhances the product's opulence.

11. *Pink*—Known as a feminine color, today it is worn by both sexes and used in myriad settings, from homes to shops. Soft pink depicts young love, sweet romance, and the youthful exuberance of a sweet sixteen party. It is a romantic and sentimental color, yet it reminds us of the innocence of a newborn baby girl.

Darker pinks, like hot pink and fuchsia, have more intensity, drama, and power, while dusty rose pinks convey a turn-of-the-century softness and romanticism.

Pink foods and beverages, like strawberry smoothies, raspberry yogurt, watermelon slices, cotton candy, and bubblegum ice cream have sweet, tantalizing flavors. Products that pamper, like perfumes, bath gels, and skin creams, are soothing remedies both visually and sensually. The color of bubblegum, pink has young and fun qualities.

12. *Neutrals*—Colors like beige, creams, pale taupes, and grays blend with all colors and don't presume to have any particular personality. They are totally neutral in their approach to any other color. Timeless and classic, neutral tones do not go in and out of fashion, because they are always considered chic and well mannered. They work as well in fashion as they do in other products. They're as comfortable in interior design as they are in package design.

The Power of Color

Color not only evokes an emotional response, but when used in promotional messages, it also captures the viewer's attention, holds it longer, and significantly increases impact and retention. The fact is, color increases an ad's attention and recall power.[6] Color ads are fifteen times more effective than black-and-white ones.[7] In addition, color adds memorability to packaging. People often shop looking for the "yellow box" or the "red one." They also recognize brands by colors: red is Coke, and blue is Pepsi. Also, when testing people with different shapes in various colors, Faber Birren noted that they recalled the colors more readily than they did the shapes.[8]

According to Suzanne Raitt, vice president of marketing for the Canadian Newspaper Association, the association determined that the power of color has increased over the last five years. This was ascertained after averaging the results from many studies around the world, Today, the use of color is credited with a 36 percent higher impact than that achieved with black and white. The Newspaper Association of America reported that four-color ads are seen 20 percent more often than black-and-white ads, and 13 percent more frequently than two-color ads.[9]

Designers like Jan White recognize that the purpose of color is to enlighten, not dazzle, the audience. Designers should use color logically and creatively to clarify the message for the reader. White states that color can provide the reader with additional information, establish relationships among graphic components, create identity, and energize the message.[10]

Color Expressions

As you learn more about color, notice how some everyday expressions reflect the cultural associations attached to colors. Each culture has its own expressions using colors, like the Spanish expression *viejo verde*, which is slang for "dirty old man." The word *verde* means green, and *viejo* means old. Today, this expression has two contradictory meanings: (1) an older man who lusts after someone youthful, and (2) an elderly person who is robust and healthy looking. Box 8.1 lists some popular American expressions using colors. It is helpful to be aware of any negative connotations a color may have when you are choosing colors.

Color Trends over the Past Decades

Colors reflect trends of the times. Bright, wild, psychedelic colors are reminis- cent of the free-spirited 1960s. Kitchens decorated in avocado green or harvest gold signal the passion for earth tones of the 1970s. The 1980s demonstrated a return to vibrant colors. Bright red, for example, was former first lady Nancy Reagan's signature color because she wore it so often. At that time, earth tones were replaced by mauve as the popular choice for home decor. In the 1990s, qui- eter, more neutral colors came into vogue, while unexpected colors like lime green and chartreuse suddenly took center stage. Soft neutrals and lighter brown tones were fashionable at the beginning of the new millennium.[11]

BOX 8.1 EXPRESSIONS THAT USE COLORS

Green with envy—Very jealous
Green-eyed monster—Someone who is jealous
To have a green thumb—To be a talented gardener
Green movement—Organizations and activities focused on protecting the environment
The grass is greener on the other side—Something's always better somewhere else
Greenhouse—A room for growing plants
Green belt—An area of gardens or parks surrounding a city
He's green behind the ears—Someone who is inexperienced
Give someone the green light—Give someone the go ahead, or the okay to move forward
Lily white—Virginal
White-collar and blue-collar workers—Professional workers and manual laborers
White-glove test—Checking that all the details were completed perfectly
White elephant—Something of value but too expensive to maintain
White space—Blank areas that allow viewers a visual rest
To whitewash something—To hide negative facts and give them a positive spin
Don't fire until you see the whites of their eyes—Don't anticipate, wait for the right moment
Pitch black—As dark as possible
Black-tie event—A formal event, such as a gala or an elegant wedding
Black eye—A bad reputation
Blackout—No electricity
Black belt—Highly skilled in an area, like physical combat
Black widow—A cruel person
In the black—Profitable
Yellow-bellied coward—Someone who has no courage
There's a yellow stripe up your back—You are a coward
Mellow yellow—Relaxed
Old blue eyes—At one time it was Frank Sinatra's nickname, also used for anyone with particularly noticeable blue eyes
True blue—Honest and loyal
Once in a blue moon—Very rarely
Blue blood—To come from an aristocratic or very wealthy family
Got the blues—To be depressed
Golden rule—Do unto others as you want them to do unto you
Gold brick—To trick people, for instance, to sell them a gold brick, but give them an ordinary one
Paint the town red—Go out and have fun
Red-letter day—A lucky day
Red herring—To send someone off course

Red tape—A lot of bureaucratic steps resulting in excessive busywork
So mad you see red—Very angry
Red with anger—So mad your face and neck turn red
Hot-tempered redhead—Quick to anger
It's red hot—Extremely hot in temperature or appeal
You don't have a red cent—Broke
In the red—Losing money
Red-carpet treatment—Treated like a celebrity
Beet red—Flush with embarrassment
In the pink—Everything is wonderful
Looking at life through rose-colored glasses—Overly optimistic
A rosy complexion—Beautiful skin with pink tones
What a brown noser—Placate someone or "butter 'em up"
Brownie points—To gain someone's trust through false flattery or going out of
   your way to look good, but with a lack of sincerity
Brown out—Partial loss of electrical power, inconsistent power
Brown-bag lunch—Usually a meeting over lunch to which people bring their
   own food (often in brown bags)
You have a brown thumb—Someone who cannot grow any plants or flowers
Born with a silver spoon in your mouth—Privileged
Every cloud has a silver lining—There's always something positive in a negative
   experience
Passed with flying colors—Great success
A rainbow of happiness—Very joyous

The Meaning of Colors across the Globe

Colors have strong psychological and cultural impact, and that impact can vary from country to country. Although here in the United States yellow is a color that increases blood pressure and radiates joy and happiness, in Mexico it denotes death or disrespect,[12] and in Asia and Europe it is considered a sacred color.[13] White, which usually represents purity in Western cultures, is used for mourning in some Asian countries.[14] And whereas red represents passion and love in many parts of the world, it is the color of wedding gowns and other celebratory events in China and India.

One interesting reaction to color is the Scandinavian people's belief that blue is evil, because of a blue demon that supposedly tortured the dead. In fact, in the fairy tale *Little Red Riding Hood*, the heroine's cloak is blue instead of red. In Finland, "being blue" is a slang expression for being financially broke.[15] Also in Scandinavia, yellow represents a germ-free or sterile environment.[16] Gray, a color usually used for stately fashion and subtlety in North America and

Western Europe, means strength in Spain and Portugal and is the color of the Rock of Gibraltar.

In Islamic countries, gold has a mystical quality, but it also triggers greed.[17] Red represents blood; however, in Africa it also means death. In Africa yellow symbolizes high rank. Green means fertility. Black depicts spirituality and maturity. Gold means continuous life. And white depicts victory, as well as the commonly accepted meaning of purity.[18]

Green bottles in the United Kingdom promise a high-quality product inside, while in Spain and Portugal, they represent cheap and low-end contents.[19] Although gold represents fine objects in Israel, it warns against objects of desire.

In both Portugal and Brazil, purple is the color of mourning. It shows respect for God's power over life and death.[20] In Israel, it connotes divinity.[21]

Vibrating Colors and Other Problematic Combinations

Some color combinations create vibrating type. This means the colors seem to be electrified or animated. This happens when certain colors of the same intensity appear side by side. One of the colors seems to be vibrating or bouncing. Vibrating colors should only be used to create an effect like the frenetic colors in *Wired* magazine or to deliberately obscure a message. For example, if the word "advertisement" needed to be prominently displayed in red, but you wanted to minimize its readability, you could set the word in bright red against a bright blue background. If the right red and blue were chosen, the word "advertisement" would be harder to read even though it was prominently showcased because it would be vibrating.

Here are some of the combinations that can vibrate with certain hues. These are all bright, vibrant colors.

1. Red and orange
2. Red and neon green
3. Red and bright blue
4. Orange and hot pink
5. Orange and lime green

Colors that are too similar in their shade (hue) and in their intensity (value) do not work well together, because they are too much alike. Dark blue and dark green is a poor combination with little contrast, but yellow and purple is an interesting pair with strong contrast.

Yellow and neutral colors are practically invisible on white backgrounds. It is better to use them as soft graphic components rather than type. Yellow type on a white background is almost impossible to see. That is why when yellow is the second color in a two-color piece, you must be careful how you use it. It can work well as a headline if the type is set in reverse, as in yellow type on a dark background. But using yellow as the body copy on a white or cream background would result in illegible or barely visible type.

Birren also showed how equal-sized colored squares appear larger or smaller depending on the background color on which they appear. For example, a bright yellow square appears larger on a white background than on a black one. But a bright red square appears larger on a black background than on a white one.[22]

Color Combinations

More important than the impact and meaning of color is the combining of colors. There are many helpful charts that have been created as guides for color harmony and compatibility. Birren's twelve-hue color circle (figure 8.1), often used by artists such as Eugène Delacroix as a handy reference mounted on a studio wall, shows complementary colors on diametrically opposite sides.[23] Harmonious colors sit side by side. The outer circle is divided into twelve equal parts, consisting of the primary colors (yellow, red, blue) and the secondary colors (orange,

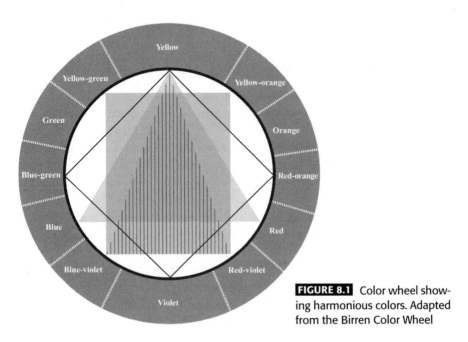

FIGURE 8.1 Color wheel showing harmonious colors. Adapted from the Birren Color Wheel

green, violet). A set of six colors, or the tertiary colors, is created when one primary and one secondary color are combined. So, yellow and orange create yellow-orange, red and orange become red-orange, red and violet make red-violet, blue and violet create blue-violet, blue and green result in blue-green, and yellow plus green make yellow-green. All together they represent the sequence of the spectrum of the rainbow.[24] Here are the colors around the circle from the top going in a clockwise direction: (1) yellow, (2) yellow-orange, (3) orange, (4) red-orange, (5) red, (6) red-violet, (7) violet, (8) blue-violet, (9) blue, (10) blue-green, (11) green, and (12) yellow-green.

Birren shows that harmonious colors are easy to find, because they create triangles (equilateral or isosceles), squares, or rectangles.[25] The equilateral triangle contains the three harmonious primary colors: red, blue, and yellow. The rectangle of compatible colors is yellow-green, yellow-orange, blue-violet, and red-violet. The square of complementary colors is yellow, red-orange, violet, and blue-green. The isosceles triangle is a combination of yellow, red-violet, and blue-violet. Birren states that the artist sees these twelve hues as clearly as a musician hears the twelve notes of the chromatic scale.[26]

> The world is but a canvas to the imagination.
>
> —HENRY DAVID THOREAU[27]

Useful Color References

L. K. Peterson and Cheryl Dangel Cullen's book *Global Graphics: Color—Designing with Color for an International Market* will help you further understand the use of color in international markets. There are many useful examples and explanations of product packaging, which may serve as excellent references. The Global Color Chart (figure 8.2) provides an overview of international color meanings based on the principles from this work.

Another wonderful reference book on the meaning of colors and their effects when used in combinations is Leatrice Eiseman's *Pantone Guide to Communicating with Color*. Besides describing each color, one at a time, this book also devotes four beautifully designed pages to each color. Then, every color is used in several well-paired color combinations and includes two complementary Pantone swatches, in case readers want to use those colors in their designs. (The Pantone Matching System, PMS, is the universally accepted reference guide that assigns every color a Pantone number and the

GLOBAL MEANINGS OF COLOR

	North America	South America Latin America	Western Europe	England Scotland Wales/Ireland	France	Germany Austria Switzerland	Spain Portugal	Italy	China	India
RED	exciting sexy lust				love passion lust	assertiveness daring creativity	aggression	charity	good fortune fertility, joy celebration	birth fertility new phase
YELLOW	cowardice happy warm	caution pliability	magical sexy	power authority	flowers summer joy		Inquisition treason shame	cowardice treachery	earth	sun power festivity
GREEN	refreshing nature healing	Rainforest	fertility nature health	forests quality performance health	nature freshness health	help support	racy jokes	faith, rebirth immortality contemplation	birth youth exuberance	plants crops
BLUE	trust durability authority	freedom infinity blessings	fidelity sincerity reliability	dignified tranquil refinement	calm soothing upscale	reliability neutrality		hope, heaven religious virtue judgmental	sky water	heaven/love truth mercy
BLACK	elegant mourning upscale sophisticated	quality product	mourning luxury nobility	mourning dignified	luxury rich		death power	death humility	water truth, life stability	laziness anger indolence
PURPLE	regal spiritual sensual mysterious	mourning (in Brazil)	royalty rich	royalty			mourning (in Portugal)	royalty nobility		
GOLD	luxury wealth	wealth social standing	mystical quality	royalty	luxury preciousness value	wealth	wealth value	priceless treasure	prestige wealth status	
WHITE	clean purity pristine	accomplishment aspiration	purity	peace upper class				high virtue and status	knowledge death mourning	light serenity
BROWN	dependable earthy strong	nature earth/soil	earthy practical strong	honesty manual work				earthy fine leather goods		
PINK	sweet, young romantic	sensitivity feeling								

FIGURE 8.2 Global Color Chart, adapted from L. K. Peterson and Cheryl Dangel Cullen, *Global Graphics: Color— Designing with Color for an International Market*

exact formula, identifying the percent of each color needed to create that particular color.)

In addition, Eiseman's guide to color communication shows how different combinations of hues of colors create specific moods when they are assembled as color palettes. Then, on the opposite page, there are several examples using those colors.[28]

Max Lüscher's early works on color are worth reviewing (although some may be out of print). These include *The Lüscher Color Test, The 4-Color Person,* and *Personality Signs.* Even though these are psychological profiles of the impact of color on individuals, rather than on cultures, they are interesting reads.

Several books can serve as guides when you're determining general color combinations and their usage in Web design. Although there are some very comprehensive studies out there, three excellent sources are *Design for Interaction* by Lisa Baggerman, *Color Harmony for the Web* by Cailin Boyle, and *Web Site Graphics Color: The Best Work from the Web* by Jeff Carlson, Toby Malina, and Glenn Fleishman.

It's interesting to note that Boyle mentions that metallic inks change online. So gold turns to yellow, silver to gray, and so on. This is an important point if your logo uses bronzes or other metallic inks. It's even more important for you to know that there is a standard of 216 Web-safe colors set by Netscape Explorer and Microsoft Internet. Although digital technology allows for 16.7 million colors, and the computer screen can display 256 colors at one time, only 216 of them are included in the Browser-Safe Palette. Those not included in the Browser-Safe Palette will visibly change colors online.[29]

How do you know which colors are Web-safe? Web designer Fabio Storti, founder of Doghaus Design, offers an easy answer.[30] In each of the three main design programs—Photoshop, Illustrator, and InDesign—there are windows that indicate which colors are safe for the Web. Here's how to find them when designing. Or you can go to http://en.wikipedia.org/wiki/Web colors to see the actual color samples.

How to Find Web-Safe Colors in a Design Program

1. *Photoshop*—Go to the Color Picker (the two overlapping squares in the tool box). Click on Only Web Colors on the left side under the large color box.
2. *Illustrator*—Go to Window at the top of your screen. Scroll down toward the bottom. Click on Swatch Libraries. Hold the mouse down, and scroll across to the next window. Scroll down to Web.
3. *InDesign*—Go to Window, again at the top of your screen. Scroll down to Swatches. Click on the little arrow button in the upper left corner of

Swatches. Scroll down to Swatch Options. Click on Color Mode and scroll down to Web.

In *Blue Is Hot Red Is Cool*—an excellent listing of logos grouped by color—David E. Carter mentions that blue is often the color selected for corporate logos. In fact, 60 percent of all one-color logos are blue.[31] Also significant is the fact that blue is a universally embraced color with few negative connotations.[32] Although red is seldom used for one-color logos, it is most likely to be chosen for two-color designs.[33] Carter says he only offers suggestions, not laws, for creating logos.[34]

> There are no "rules" about color. Only guidelines.
>
> —DAVID E. CARTER[35]

The *Color Index* by Jim Krause is a handy reference that pairs colors together in thumbnail designs, so you can see how well they combine. It can serve as a guide when you're considering your color palette. The book is organized into sections that group colors together in various ways, including by energy, intensity, and era. There are chapters on primary colors, deep muted tones, and quiet tones; on urban chic- and fashion-inspired combinations; and on active, quiet, and progressive colors. It is helpful to see the colors used in patterned designs.

The Pervasive Influence of Color

According to Boyle, preteens and members of generations X and Y like dark colors such as black, dark browns, and grays with splashes of brighter colors. But the older generation is just the opposite, preferring lighter, less severe colors. In the same way that more older adults are enjoying more active lives, they are also appreciating brighter colors.[36]

Just as there has been a trend to add vibrant colors to basic household products like toasters and can openers, colors for standard office supplies, like staplers, staple removers, and pencil holders have also moved away from boring colors. Reflecting this trend are the new colors of iMacs, iPods, cell phones, and other electronic devices. Now almost anything you look at can be redesigned in fashion colors or selected in a color to reflect your personality.

Likewise, the colors used in Web sites are selected to evoke an emotional response, to depict a certain era, to create or reflect an environment, or to create other reactions. For example, to create a sense of nostalgia, the Absinthe restaurant used colors and images from the late 1800s, the period known as the belle epoque.[37]

Designers developing a Web site or other integrated materials for a zoo, botanical garden, or park would gravitate to greens and browns because they conjure up a natural, earthy ambiance. Look at the Starbucks colors. They are comforting, soothing, and inviting in their greens and rich browns, which evoke lush foliage where luscious coffee beans grow.

Designers choose Web colors to work with all the company's colors, as well as to speak directly to the viewer. Boyle divides Web sites into different categories, such as fresh, earthy, lively, romantic, energetic, calming, vibrant, and so on. Color palettes are included, as well as Web page examples reflecting the site's tone. This is a very handy guide for creating visually well thought out, interactive sites.

Become Observant When Online

Get into the habit of being an active observer of trends all around you. Notice the colors used in fashion. The fabrics currently in vogue. The changing styles of furniture. Then, look at recently introduced products. Do they reflect a trend? Do you see that some of the same new colors in fashion also appear in packaging? Today, there are bright orange and hot lime green colors being used in clothing as well as hair product package designs.

Now, to see how observant you've been, or how much you've absorbed about online design, answer the following questions.

A Short Quiz

1. Where are the drop-down windows located on many Web sites?
2. Which colors are most often used for news and financial Web sites?
3. Which colors are chosen for entertainment Web sites?
4. Which colors are selected for travel Web sites?
5. Which background color offers the best legibility?
6. Which colors change online?

The answer to these questions are as follows: (1) Drop-down windows usually appear across the top of the page. (2) Red and blue are frequently selected for news and financial Web sites. (3) Bright colors like reds, yellows, purples, blues, oranges, and hot pinks are often found on entertainment sites. You'll also find more reverse color used on these sites with dark black backgrounds in order to generate greater excitement. (4) Travel sites, like news and financial sites, use a lot of dark blue and red. (5) White is now the most common background color. Years ago, black backgrounds were used, but now they are used mostly in the entertainment industry. (6) Metallic colors like gold, copper, silver, and bronze lose their reflective properties and appear flat. So, gold looks like yellow, and silver looks like gray, as we mentioned earlier.

Study trends in advertising as well. When you surf the Web, look at sites within the same industry. Then, see if you notice any similarities in the graphic design, the choice of fonts, the use of colors, and the overall navigation.

■ EXERCISE ONE

Choose an existing brochure, ad, magazine cover, or logo. Determine why the colors in the advertising materials, magazine cover, or logo were chosen. Do you agree with the color choices? Choose other colors to use instead. Get several sheets of clear plastic. Place one over the layout. Use highlighters to change the colors. Create a different version on each transparency sheet. You can also use the computer to create headlines and visuals. Print them on transparency sheets. Cut the elements apart, and place them over the existing layout to see how the changes affect the layouts. Or you can create several versions on the computer, then print them out and compare them. Which colors work better and why? ■

■ EXERCISE TWO

Choose two colors to create a brochure for a tropical resort. What colors might you use for a ski resort? ■

■ PROJECT

Using the computer and only two colors, create an all-type billboard for an optical center. Which color combinations would be most legible? Now re-create the same billboard using two different colors. ■

Notes

1. Michael Newman, *Creative Leaps* (Singapore: John Wiley & Sons, 2003), 113.
2. "Go with the Green," *Color News,* Summer 1993: 1–2.
3. Leatrice Eiseman, *Pantone Guide to Communicating with Color* (Cincinnati, OH: Grafix Press, 2000), 26–29.

4. David E. Carter, ed., *Blue Is Hot Red Is Cool* (New York: HBI, 2001), 72.

5. Roy Paul Nelson, *The Design of Advertising*, 7th ed. (Madison, WI: WCB Brown & Benchmark, 1994), 225.

6. Matthew D. Shank and Raymond LaGarce, "Study: Color Makes Any Message More Effective," *Marketing News,* August 6, 1990: 12.

7. Nelson, *The Design*, 212.

8. Nelson, *The Design*, 213.

9. Newspaper Association of America, 2006, www.naa.org/utilartpage.cfm?TID= NR&AID=1386 (accessed November 16, 2005).

10. Jan White, "Using Color to Carry the Message," *Folio,* April 1, 1991: 86.

11. Pantone, "40 Years of Color," 2003, www.pantone.com/products/products. asp?idArticle=541&idArea=1&idSubArea=0 (accessed October 21, 2005).

12. Courtland L. Bovée and John V. Thill, *Marketing* (New York: McGraw-Hill, 1992), 265.

13. Nelson, *The Design*, 225.

14. Nelson, *The Design*, 225.

15. L. K. Peterson and Cheryl Dangel Cullen, *Global Graphics: Color—Designing with Color for an International Market* (Gloucester, MA: Rockport, 2000), 100.

16. Peterson and Cullen, *Global Graphics*, 100

17. Peterson and Cullen, *Global Graphics*, 131, 138.

18. Peterson and Cullen, *Global Graphics*, 142–43.

19. Peterson and Cullen, *Global Graphics*, 66, 106.

20. Peterson and Cullen, *Global Graphics*, 58.

21. Peterson and Cullen, *Global Graphics*, 131.

22. Faber Birren, ed., *The Elements of Color: A Treatise on the Color System of Johannes Itten,* trans. Ernst Van Hagen (New York: Van Nostrand Reinhold, 1970), 87.

23. Birren, *The Elements of Color.*

24. Birren, *The Elements of Color,* 29–30.

25. Birren, *The Elements of Color,* 21.

26. Birren, *The Elements of Color,* 30.

27. Henry David Thoreau, *Walden and Civil Disobedience* (Boston: Houghton Mifflin, 1960), 72.

28. Eiseman, *Pantone Guide,* 92–93.

29. Cailin Boyle, *Color Harmony for the Web* (Gloucester, MA: Rockport, 2001), 19.

30. Fabio Storti, personal communication, November 23, 2005.

31. Carter, *Blue Is Hot*, 3.

32. Carter, *Blue Is Hot*, 6.

33. Carter, *Blue Is Hot*, 3.

34. Carter, *Blue Is Hot*, 3.

35. Carter, *Blue Is Hot*, 3.

36. Boyle, *Color Harmony*, 4.

37. Boyle, *Color Harmony*, 26.

Discover Exciting Strategy-Based Ads and Campaigns

> Powerful brands are built on consistency. The more times the consumer comes into contact with a brand and has the same feeling and emotional takeaway, the greater the chance they'll remember the message. In turn, dollars end up working harder, with one medium reinforcing another. For big clients and small, we create brands that are consistent from top to bottom.
>
> —DEUTSCH INC.[1]

We have seen how great creative work is not just innovative, but it's also clearly on strategy. It follows through on the basic objective that was strategically designed for the product or company. It addresses the right audience, uses the proper tone of voice, incorporates suitable typography and graphics, then delivers a relevant message. In this chapter, we'll examine more excellent examples of strategy-based ads and campaigns.

Most importantly, the message is developed before the medium. In other words, what you're trying to say normally comes first, then deciding where to say it comes next. By developing the message first, you are sure to create a well-focused communication. This little mantra might help: remember, message before format.

There are times, however, when the message is media driven. That means the medium is so important, it actually directs the development of the message. This can occur when you're constructing a Web site, an interactive campaign, or even a billboard.

Tom Denari used a billboard to establish a local icon for Ossip, an optical center (see figures 4.4 and 4.5). The objective was to draw attention to Ossip's desirable location by creating a strategically placed, eye-catching billboard. Denari explains it this way: "Fifteen years ago, Ossip had one location in the most hip district of the city. It was known as the most progressive optical center with the coolest frames. We [Young & Laramore] proposed a landmark billboard that would generate attention and solidify their position as the coolest place to find glasses. We proposed a fine art sculpture of glasses made of junk. It has in fact become a landmark that has now existed for about fifteen years."[2]

How Agencies Arrive at the Campaign Strategy

The manner at which the creative strategy is reached differs slightly according to the problem-solving approach of each creative team. Every agency has its own process that it finds most effective. Reading through some of the painstakingly systematic procedures can serve as a guide when you're developing your own strategies. Linda Kaplan Thaler explains how her agency goes from the creative brief to execution as follows:

> In developing a creative brief, we get most of the information from the client. Then, we do our own investigative research in a very nontraditional way. Instead of a focus group, which is a very forced environment, we will very often give people video cameras. Then, we ask them to film themselves in their own home environment using the products or services we're going to be advertising. . . . This is how we gain insight into the consumer and understand how the product is really being used. Then, we bounce the brief off the creative team to see how they react to it. And hopefully, it will spark their creative juices.[3]

When asked how The Kaplan Thaler Group uses the creative brief in designing campaigns, Kaplan Thaler says:

> The creative brief is really our guidepost because if you're trying to create a Big Bang—that is, an advertising campaign that is going to explode onto the

marketplace and take over the cultural universe—then you have to make sure you're going to create an explosion in the right universe. . . . For example, if you do a phenomenal campaign for a new cereal and it's absolutely a home run for children, but in fact, the people you have to talk to are mothers, then you've just wasted the client's money. So you first have to know who you're talking to. Woody Allen once said that 80 percent of life is just showing up. So if the right target isn't watching you, what's the point?

So, how does The Kaplan Thaler Group come up with solutions for different clients, like Aflac? She states, "For every client, the needs are different. In the case of Aflac, they had a low recall of their actual name. For another client, like Coca-Cola for example, I certainly wouldn't be sweating about name recall. I'd have a very different set of criteria I need to put out there."

Tom Denari explains the process his agency uses to arrive at creative solutions this way:

> It's not as much about the creative process as it is about the strategic process, which helps to define the communication objective. This is critical to developing a solid campaign. Surprisingly, the more the subject matter is narrowed and focused, the more powerful the creative solution will be. Once the strategy is agreed upon, the creative team develops a number of solutions until the entire account team settles on a recommendation. . . . There's less of a process in the idea-generation stage. Most of the process is up front in understanding the mindset and connecting to that mindset. If the creative team has a deep insight into the target audience and a clear understanding of the product or service, the ideas should easily flow.

Students Learn Early about Strategy

Just like agency teams, students at The Creative Circus must first establish their strategy before working on concepts for their ads. When asked how his students learn to develop a creative strategy, executive creative director Norm Grey explains:

> Basically, nobody can present anything until they present a strategy. They have to explain what they're trying to do. How do we go about doing that? We tell them a headline isn't a strategy. It comes out of a strategy. . . . We have account classes, so the first thing a student does is explain the strategy. For example, if they wanted to send someone a greeting card that said, "Happy Birthday, Ma," the creative piece can't say, "Sorry your cat died."

That's not what they wanted to say and we'll tell them that. We'll remind then that their work didn't stay on strategy and wish someone a happy birthday. . . . Or, if they say they're creating a message for senior citizen housing, they may need to be reminded that what they created wasn't talking to the senior, but to the senior's children. They must first tell us what they're trying to say.[4]

This type of cognitive discipline forces creative teams to think strategically before they start brainstorming for solutions. By doing this, they are better armed to produce on-strategy and on-target work.

The Use of Humor

Humor is used effectively in many campaigns. But in order for it to work, it has to be relevant to the product and must also showcase the product's benefit to the consumer. Linda Kaplan Thaler says, "Humor is the great connecting rod between human beings. The important thing is to remember, however, is that the humor must sell the product or service. If the reason you're funny doesn't in some way enhance the product benefit, you've created a very expensive piece of entertainment that sells nothing to anyone."

The Stanley Steemer campaign also used a light touch and asked the audience to rethink its usual carpet-cleaning schedules with the tagline "Living Brings It In. We Take It Out." The idea was that no matter how often you vacuum and how clean your home is, your carpets get dirty from everyday living. Tom Denari describes the use of humor in the print ads and TV commercials this way.

> So often people think they need to use humor to break through. But if the humor is not relevant to the product, it can actually get in the way of the communication. We've all heard people talk about great commercials they've seen but can never remember the product. The humor must be used to help communicate a specific message and make it more engaging and memorable. . . . Sometimes the humor is simply an acknowledgment that a company understands its customer. To do this, you need to get to know your audience well enough to be empathetic. The communication has to demonstrate an understanding of the audience: Who are these people? What are they going through? The ad needs to connect with you on a human level before it tries to sell them. . . . The best headlines might not be particularly funny. Instead, they are simply insightful. Like the *Seinfeld*

episodes. They might point out what people haven't thought about before, like double dipping a chip. Say what hasn't been said before. Or state the obvious in a way people haven't heard before.

Using humor sometimes shows a great deal of courage. In a campaign that advertised against anti-Semitism, Think Tank 3 came up with a humorous way to promote *Heeb Magazine* and its "Anti Anti-Semite" campaign. Sharoz Makarechi, the agency's creative director, gives insight into the thinking behind the potentially controversial humor (figures 9.1 and 9.2). "The magazine takes a potshot at itself. Some think "Heeb" is a derogatory term, [a] bad name for a magazine, but it's not. It shows a sense of humor, and we call it before you can call it. 'Regularly $4.95, but for you $4.94.' We acknowledge that it's out there. It's about your ability to take potshots, [to] take a chance and tell a story. It's a magazine with a sense of humor and the campaign to promote it should be a reflection of that."[5]

The campaign exemplifies how well the agency understood the target audience, because the magazine was able to laugh at itself without offending its readers.

FIGURE 9.1 "$4.94" poster, created by Think Tank 3 for *Heeb Magazine.* Image courtesy of Think Tank 3

FIGURE 9.2 "Conspiracy" poster, created by Think Tank 3 for *Heeb Magazine.* Image courtesy of Think Tank 3

Having a deep understanding of the audience is critical to developing on-strategy and on-target solutions. When asked how Young & Laramore obtains that kind of audience insight, Denari answers:

> We do a lot of secondary research, but we also do a lot of one-on-one interviews with our target audience. It's not a quantitative survey, but it really helps us to understand how they talk about things and what are their attitudes about particular issues. . . . One-on-ones give us much better human depth. The people are much more comfortable than in a focus group. They can be themselves and let down any apprehensions they might have. On a few occasions we've had respondents break down into tears. When that happens, you really know you're reaching them.

The result of all that research is clearly seen in the following Elasta QP "Good Hair/Bad Hair" TV commercial (figure 9.3). It's common knowledge that many people wrestle with their hair each day. If it's curly, they want it straight. If it's straight, they want it wavy. Realizing this, Elasta QP didn't make a judgment as to what was good hair or bad hair. It just said there are two types of hair: yours and everyone else's. Immediately it drew in the entire audience. In this nonjudgmental approach, viewers with different hair types could relate to the product's message, which promised to make all types of hair easier to handle.

Altoids is another campaign that used humor to show it understood its audience (see figure 9.4). When Noel Haan and G. Andrew Meyer of Leo Burnett USA were asked if the

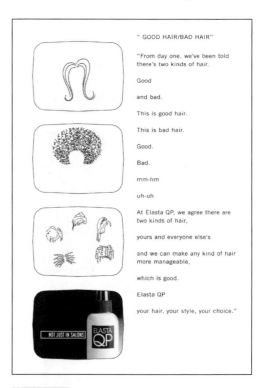

FIGURE 9.3 "Good Hair/Bad Hair" TV storyboard, created by Young & Laramore for Elasta QP. Image courtesy of Young & Laramore

campaign strategy was based on the creative brief, Haan, executive vice president/ group creative head, explained, "I'd like to think that it's not strategy driven. The creative brief, or the strategy, comes from the tin. Right on the tin, it says, 'The Original Celebrated Curiously Strong Mint.' So, that's that, then. 'The Curiously Strong Mints.'"[6]

Meyer, also an executive vice president/group creative head, discusses how campaigns capture the core essence of the product's appeal: "The best campaigns dramatize the inherent value of the product. It's nice when you don't have to make something up. Just take what's inherently interesting and manifest it in unexpected ways." But as discussion of the underlying strategy continues, he clarifies that this particular campaign was really free of a strategy. "In terms of strategy, there really isn't one. It's just about pulling out what's inherently interesting from the product, building metaphors around that. So that's our big secret strategy, which is really no secret at all."

The product itself actually became the campaign. The creative team looked at the actual tin and read the words "Curiously Strong Mints," and the message on the tin inspired the creative direction. Meyer states:

We figured there was no need to change something that's inherently brilliant. The line didn't need any additional help. We play with the notions of "curious" and "strong." If it was just "strong," it wouldn't be as interesting. The "curious" side lets us insert a bit of randomness, so sometimes the ads don't necessarily complete the circle. The ads are like a joke. An inside joke. It's only funny to the inside crowd. But the Altoids crowd is a wide group. Altoids has a cult following, but it's also mass-market. So the trick is letting that wide audience feel "inside."

In regard to the use of quirky and inside-joke humor, Haan shares

FIGURE 9.4 Visual of the "Nice Altoids" print ad created by Noel Haan and G. Andrew Meyer, from Leo Burnett USA for Wrigley. Image courtesy of Leo Burnett USA

that they weren't afraid to make fun of their audience, because they were part of it. "We like to use a lot of dry, flat humor. Making fun of people is our favorite thing to do. Some ads could be considered offensive to some people. We poke fun at people." Meyer adds this funny, insightful look at how they make fun of people in their ads, while poking fun at themselves: "Yeah, but we're equal opportunity offenders. We poke fun at everybody. We make fun of people like ourselves. There's nerdiness to the campaign. That's Noel [Haan]. There's an extreme nerdiness about him. We're both kind of geeks in our own way. . . . Like *Napoleon Dynamite*, you know the film. It's that kind of spirit. A celebration of dorkiness. It's what's out there in the real world."

In being able to joke with their audience, they also showed how common interests could be cross-generational. They're careful not to specifically target one age group or demographic, because it's not the audience that's important, it's the universality of a shared, fun experience. Meyer shares these insights:

> We try not to pander to an audience. We try not to patronize. We just dramatize curious strength. We look for things that are universally interesting. We don't think about what an eighteen-year-old would like—you run the risk of getting it wrong. There are some things that are intrinsically interesting. In every generation, there are kids who discover bands like Led Zeppelin. Because something they said speaks universally to a mind-set. My younger cousin listens to a lot of Ramones, and that makes me smile. That was my music at his age. Twenty-year-old music that's still relevant to a fifteen-year-old kid. We convey a mind-set, and it's not an age-based message.

The Altoids campaign is not based on a demographic—it's based on a youthful attitude. According to Haan: "Yeah, it's mediocrity resistant. We try to put things out there that if you're young at heart—sixteen or sixty—you'll get the wink and the smile of it." When asked what if the audience doesn't "get" the joke, G. Andrew answers: "Sometimes we look at things part of the audience might not get. The implication is that if you don't get it, well, there must be some gap in your knowledge. So Altoids is cooler than I am? Altoids gets things that I don't get? We have the luxury of doing that. Most brands don't."

As new flavors were added to the campaign, each one had to be created using the same tone of voice. Meyer says, "Everything has to answer back to 'Curiously Strong.'"

Haan has noticed there has been a change in the category and that there are more "me-too" products of even stronger mints in the market. Then he states, "But, if we're doing our job correctly, people still think it's the strongest."

Sometimes a product enters the market at just the right time. When people are willing to spend money for small luxuries, like a latte, it might be a perfect time for people to consider mints a worthwhile indulgence as well. Haan confirms that the timing was right for Altoids: "We also knew there was a trend in Seattle, where people were spending $3.50 for a coffee or a micro-brewed beer. So, people would spend money for mints as well. It was a timing issue. We were coming on the scene at the right time."

The public was so taken with the campaign, Haan says, that "people were ripping the ads off the bus shelters and hanging them on their doors." The agency was forced to replace them. This shows how the campaign clearly connected with its target audience.

> A Big Bang disrupts. At its core, a Big Bang is about taking the spotlight. It is about ideas that are simply too outrageous, too different, too polarizing to go unnoticed.
>
> —LINDA KAPLAN THALER[7]

Affecting the Audience: Finding the Sweet Spot

One of the most successful ways to ensure you're reaching your specific audience in an appropriate tone of voice and in a relevant medium is to conduct anthropological or observational research. This type of research gathers a truer picture of the target than do studies like focus groups, because it involves observing people in their natural habitats, that is, in their own homes. Often people in focus groups inadvertently misrepresent themselves. Therefore, by going into their subjects' homes, researchers can make more accurate assessments. People might say they like to have formal dinners, but if researchers find mismatched or chipped plates, they notice a disparity between what they were told and what they observe.

This is how Deutsch learned so much about its primary audience of thirty- to forty-nine-year-old educated, professional males with above-average household incomes. It was also the way it was able to create a sharply focused psychographic profile for its "Are You a Mitchum Man" campaign. Researchers learned that the Mitchum Man now is doing many of the same things he once enjoyed, but in a new cool way (figure 9.5).

Jeffrey Wolf, partner/director of account planning at Deutsch NY, explains how the planners became so familiar with the target audience:

Used to do		Is now doing
Going to movies	⟶	Renting movies
Going out to dinner	⟶	Ordering in or cooking
Playing sports	⟶	Watching sports, going to games
Going out partying	⟶	Going out for a beer
Getting first car	⟶	Having nicer cars, getting new cars
Hanging with friends	⟶	Playing with the kids

FIGURE 9.5 Mitchum—What Is Cool Now

First thing we do is research and dig really deep to find out what's really going on with them. We did anthropological research. You can do it yourself or use an anthropologist. Instead of a focus group, where people don't always tell the truth, you observe them in their own surroundings. . . . We went into people's homes. You see what is in the medicine cabinets. They can say they're down to earth, but you may find expensive products that say they're really not that down to earth. Observational research is taking in natural environments and taking cues from how they live. . . . The other piece instead of just talking to them to find out what kind of guys they were is we talked to their wives, friends, or girlfriends and got another perspective as well. So, that's one way of going out and learning more about their lives. Demographics only tell you so much—you've got to get to psychographics.[8]

In looking to target the "sweet spot"—that critical place where consumer insight and brand insight meet[9]—Deutsch looked for shared values between the target and the brand. Wolf explains how Deutsch used this approach in the "Are You a Mitchum Man" campaign in this way.

One of the tricks of the trade we're into is exploring the values that a brand shares with its consumers. Here's why we worked that way. Basically, when you think about values, they are what underlie our attitudes and drive our behavior. The reason we have to position brands on shared values is, if you position only a functional product attribute alone, like "whiter whites" or "works faster," in today's marketplace, someone else is going to trump you and give consumers "even whiter whites" or "works even faster." . . . So, what we look to do is differentiate a brand and find an intersection between the target and the product. When you position that way— guyness—you can build a brand and differentiate it, so you own that positioning. That's why we focus on value-based branding.

In analyzing both the target and the brand, Deutsch carefully developed a list of four specific shared values. These were: (1) maximum effort, (2) endurance, (3) cool, and (4) maleness (figures 9.6 and 9.7).

What it discovered was that the final two shared values—cool and maleness— were the most important to use in the campaign. The reason Deutsch selected these two, according to Wolf, was that those two could most effectively target

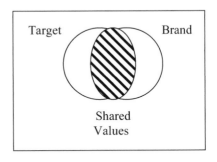

FIGURE 9.6 Mitchum—Shared Values between the Target and Brand

the audience. He clarified that choice as follows: "Really, we decided to execute against guyness. That was the creative idea within that decision. Giving it your all and lasting longer or giving maximum effort would have been more difficult. It would have been more typical—'for the man who gives it his all, we give you it all.' That was about product as hero. It had been done already. It was very expected. We were looking for a way in. The maleness was the most fertile territory."

Deutsch then applied a technique it used expertly: media intersection. The "Are You a Mitchum Man" campaign exemplifies one of the most brilliant articulations of an on-strategy message with an on-target emotional connection.

Target	Shared Values	Brand
Giving it their all	→ Maximum effort ←	Most ingredients
Hard work	→ Endurance ←	Lasts all day
A new sense of cool	→ Cool ←	Keeps you dry
Being a guy	→ Male-ness ←	Engineered for men

FIGURE 9.7 Mitchum—Finding the Sweet Spot

Armed with in-depth, one-on-one observational research, the Mitchum Man spoke to its mostly overlooked target of metrosexual males in their everyday haunts: in bars, at gyms, on the road, on the golf course, in subways and train stations, in their living rooms, online, and, yes, even in restrooms. It spoke to this target, which treasured its guyness. The message was delivered to the audience wherever he was enjoying his "guy time." Not only was the language appropriate for the target; it was also media specific.

Ads that ran in car magazines had auto-related headlines like "If you downshift in a skid, you're a Mitchum Man" and "If you ever talked your way out of a ticket, you're a Mitchum Man." Ads that ran in magazines with a mainly male readership like *Maxim* featured racy headlines like "If ménage à trois is the only French term you know, you're a Mitchum Man." One ad showed a close-up of a well-endowed woman's cleavage, with the headline "If they look real enough to you, you're a Mitchum Man" (figure 9.8).

Ads, as well as coasters and matchbooks in bars, directly addressed a favorite interest of a Mitchum Man: women. Witty headlines on coasters read "If you can see the inner beauty of the girl dancing on the bar, you're a Mitchum Man" and "If you let your buddy have the hot one, you're a Mitchum Man." (Fig. 9.9) One of the matchbooks teased, "If you're writing a phone number in here, you're a Mitchum Man." (Fig. 9.10)

FIGURE 9.8 "Real Enough" print ad created by Deutsch NY for Mitchum. Image courtesy of Deutsch Inc.

Other ads highlighted the Mitchum Man's hobbies, lifestyle, attitudes, and pet peeves. Here are a few examples of the commercials, ads, posters, supermarket floor talkers, online banner ads, and golf cart billboards geared toward the Mitchum Man.

Media-Specific Headlines

If you never left a game early to beat traffic, you're a Mitchum Man. (TV ESPN SportsCenter spot)

If you've never written "hugsz" on an e-mail, you're a Mitchum Man. (online banner ad)

If you've never worn a fanny pack, you're a Mitchum Man. (posters wrapping a construction site)

If you have no idea how to pick a melon, you're a Mitchum Man. (floor talker)

If you're here at 7 AM with a hangover, you're a Mitchum Man. (ad with close-up of large barbell)

If karaoke makes your skin crawl, you're a Mitchum Man. (bar coaster)

If you're personally offended by bad parallel parking, you're a Mitchum Man. (billboard)

What was the result of this boundless creativity? Following the campaign's launch, Mitchum experienced a quick increase in sales of more than 13 percent. In addition, its Web site, www.mitchumman.com, received almost 1,000,000 visits during the first six weeks of the campaign.

> Now more than ever ideas must transcend media—literally melt away borders. Ideas can't hide behind budgets and prevalent media placement anymore—they either stand out on their own or they don't. If you're an agency this changes things, and if you're an advertiser this changes things.
>
> —SHAROZ MAKARECHI[11]

Audience Intersection Catches Them Off Guard

With the frantic pace of many people's lives, advertisers need to reach consumers, as Mitchum did, while they're going about their daily lives. Placing a product message in front of people when they don't expect it, although interruptive, should not be offensively intrusive. Two creative teams, while students at The Creative Circus, developed two different campaigns that intersected their audiences.

To increase awareness and donations for the Salvation Army, art director L. Scott Callendar and copywriter Scott Hayes used ordinary yet unexpected vehicles to speak to their audience. For example, they placed a Salvation Army selection button as one of the choices at a vending machine, right alongside the selection buttons for sodas. The button had a one-dollar price tag and read, "Someone, somewhere is thirstier than you." The idea was for the consumer to select the Salvation Army and make a dollar donation (figure 9.11). They also placed an ad on a newspaper dispenser just under the newspaper window. It read, "It's easy to read about what's wrong with the world, it's easier to do something about it." It stated, "Thank you for your donation" under the logo and two fifty-cent signs.

The campaign for Factoryfarm.org emphasized, in a shocking way with disturbing visuals, the size of the cages in which factory farm animals actually live. Art director Miranda Gerlock, along with copywriters Jason Miller and Jeremiah Follett, posted ads on standard apartment-size mailboxes (figure 9.12). The headline read, "This Is Not a Mailbox." The copy explained, "This box represents the space a factory farm chicken is forced to live in. And sleep in. And eat in. And go to the bathroom in. We're not saying chicken is bad, just the fac-

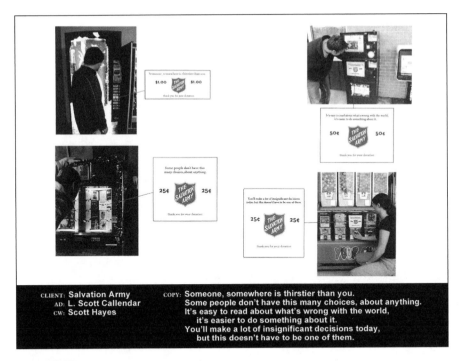

FIGURE 9.11 Ads designed to be placed on vending machines. "Vending" was created by L. Scott Callendar and Scott Hayes, graduates of The Creative Circus, for the Salvation Army. Used with permission of The Creative Circus

FIGURE 9.12 Ads designed to be placed on mailboxes. "Mailbox" was created by Miranda Gerlock, Jason Miller, and Jeremiah Follett, graduates of The Creative Circus, for Factoryfarm.org. Used with permission of The Creative Circus

tory farms that house them." The call to action suggested how the reader could take action: "To find out how you can put an end to factory farms visit our website." The Web site's address was given, and the ad closed with copy to further drive the point home: "Stop Factory Farms. Now You Know. Support Local Farmers."

Other ads were created to run on hand-held shopping baskets. These carried a similarly powerful headline: "This Is Not a Basket." The copy continued, "This is the actual size of a cage that TWO chickens are forced to live in at factory farms. They can't turn around. They never see the light of day. They have no idea what's happening, but now you do. We're not telling you to stop eating chicken. We're just asking you to get it from the right place."

More On-Target, On-Strategy Campaigns

When Volvo wanted to reposition itself as a more stylish high-performance vehicle, Euro RSCG created the "Revolvolution" campaign (figure 9.13). The intention was for the audience to see Volvo in a new light. Ron Berger, CEO and chief creative officer at RSCG Worldwide, New York and San Francisco, offers the following details.

FIGURE 9.13 "Revolvolution—Lust and Logic" print ad created by Euro RSCG for Volvo. Image courtesy of Euro RSCG

The thinking behind it was that Volvo is a strong brand and people think they know what it is. If you woke people up in the middle of the night and asked them what Volvo was, they would say the word "safety." We wanted something that signaled more: a better-looking car that was more fun to drive. . . . And we wanted a company that was going to do business in a very different way. Not a revolutionary way, which is too dramatic, or an evolutionary way, which is too incremental. But, in a Revolvolutionary way. . . . Revolvolution is a branding cry. It's a Volvo revolution with smarts. Volvo was building a car in a new way: as a Revolvolution. Everything had to be looked at in a new way.[12]

To change Volvo's image, the campaign needed to use a new medium—the Internet—not the standard television spots most often used by the car industry (figure 9.14). Berger continues: "Our idea was to drive people to a Web site to win a car. That was a revolutionary idea in content and delivery at that time. . . . We came up with the NCAA totally integrated campaign and introduced it through the Internet, interactive television and messages on BlackBerrys and

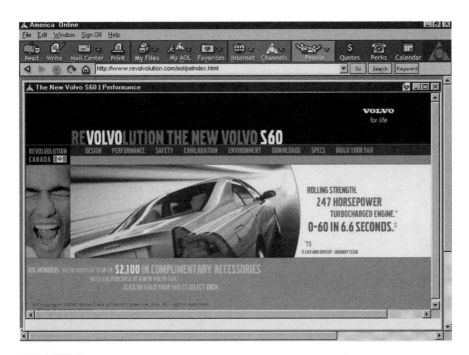

FIGURE 9.14 "Revolvolution" Web site created by Euro RSCG for Volvo. Image courtesy of Euro RSCG

phones. The call to action was to go to the Web site to win a S60 T5, which was a more aggressive, higher-performance S60 Volvo."

The result of this campaign, which strategically targeted the Volvo audience, was that 62,000 people entered the sweepstakes. Berger's explanation as to why there was such a strong response to the campaign reveals an intimate knowledge of the target:

> Volvo customers are Internet savvy, more so than any other brand I know. We knew this going in, so if we gave them a chance to participate in this dialogue, they would. They couldn't do that in a traditional monologue like television. Because there's an integrity to Volvo, we had 20,500 "opt-ins," which showed Volvo is respectful of their customers. Because they believe the brand has honesty and integrity, people were willing to give up personal information. That's because they knew they would receive something valuable back.

To communicate effectively with any audience, you must see your product from their perspective. Knowing how intimidating applying to art school might be to prospective students, Young & Laramore wanted to make its client, The Atelier Art School, more approachable and less frightening. To accomplish this, it created

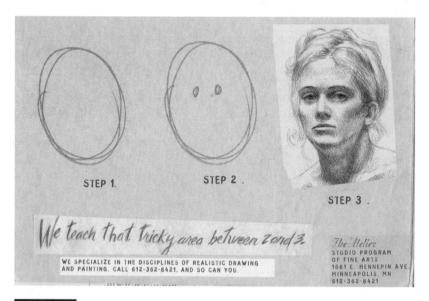

FIGURE 9.15 "Tricky Part" print ad created by Young & Laramore for the Atelier Art School. Image courtesy of Young & Laramore

a print campaign, in which one of the ads showed three drawings (figure 9.15). "Step one" shows an empty oval. "Step two" shows an oval and two small circles for eyes. "Step three" shows a finished work of art. The headline, which read "We teach the tricky area between 2 and 3," defused any formality or stuffiness and spoke directly to the needs of the prospective student. It said in a creative way: "You want to draw. We can teach you how." Young & Laramore's Tom Denari states, "We were trying to bring it down to a more human level, by not feeling too lofty or exclusive. Instead, it's speaking to you like a real person—not pretentious or putting you off."

After the 9/11 terrorist attack, Riverkeeper, an environmental protection organization that safeguards the Hudson River, wanted to focus on the danger of having Indian Point, a too-close-for-comfort nuclear power plant, just twenty-two miles outside Manhattan. Keeping in mind the goal of speaking directly to New York City residents, Think Tank 3 created a high-charged print, outdoor, direct-mail, and online campaign for Riverkeeper. The campaign brought to light the fact that terrorist attacks could threaten security right at home. Posters appeared outside phone booths, messages were sent out in postcards, ads that spoke to the public ran in the *Wall Street Journal* and *Barron's* (figure 9.16), and a haunting commercial, in streaming video, ran on Riverkeeper's Web site.

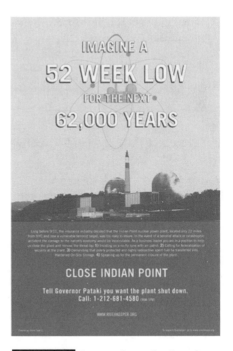

The headlines and visuals are gripping and spoke in the most electrifying language of the moment: "weapons of mass destruction." Just asking the question "What Exactly Do Weapons of Mass Destruction Look Like?" makes anyone reading it stop and wonder, "Yeah, what?" And presenting this unimaginable idea—"Imagine a 52 week low for the next 62,000 years"—is equally disturbing. There is no way a reader wouldn't be slightly shaken by such riveting headlines.

Another Think Tank 3 campaign that was on strategy was the Citystreets

FIGURE 9.16 "52 Week Low" print ad created by Think Tank 3 for Riverkeeper. Image courtesy of Think Tank 3

Stencil Project (discussed in chapter 6). This campaign focused on pedestrian safety by presenting custom stencils in the street in the exact spots where people had been killed by a vehicle. After the agency conducted careful research through the police department's records, the victims' names and the dates of their deaths were stenciled in as well. Also stenciled in was a Web address where people could access information.

How did they arrive at this idea? Sharoz Makarechi explains, "The same way we get to everything else, really. Our work is about media and relevance." She continues:

> Harris Silver led the way conceptually and personally put down the first of many of the subsequent stencils during the first year of the campaign. . . . The idea came from a real genuine place. Where we put down stencils was where blood had been spilled and then largely ignored. It is a memorial, but it's intended for the living. For those of us who use the street, it's a reminder that it could happen to us. . . . Usually, the focus is that drivers should be careful so they don't get into a crash [and] hurt themselves, or their car. But the Stencil Project was the first and [was] very effective in that it raised awareness of pedestrian safety issues. You think about safety in the streets, you think about violent crimes, not about crossing the street.

What was amazing about this grassroots campaign was that is received a tremendous amount of attention in the press. Pedestrians and drivers couldn't help but notice these crime scene-like images stenciled in the street. It caused an immediate reaction and left an indelible impression. Makarechi explains it this way:

> For a grassroots campaign, it had a huge, huge effect. There were 200 stencils all around the city at one point, and there was an online aspect. The stories of how people perished were told if we knew them and people could go to our site (citystreets.org) to get involved. This project started a while ago, I believe some time in 1997, and it has been adopted by activists and advocates of our ideas in Atlanta, San Francisco, Sydney, Australia, Vancouver and Toronto in Canada, and Amsterdam, and a few other cities around Europe. Sometimes it would be a group, sometimes an individual; they would call us and want to start [the] Stencil Project in their community.

Creating these images was not simple. The creative team came up with a specific way to draw them on the pavement, so they'd have a consistent look wherever they appeared. Makarechi offers the following explanation. "We have a schematic way in which we put stencils down and actual materials that we share. Things to keep the consistency of the idea and so the paint doesn't go everywhere. It takes a little engineering, because it's a full-size outline." In answer to why it received so much media, and even global attention, Makarechi offers this explanation: "As for the reason it got so much press, I think it's because Citystreets, not just the Stencil Project, is so idea- and solution-centric as an organization. A small group of us made it happen. No bureaucracy. We named it; we were the ones to position it. It's proof that a small group of people can have a wide-reaching effect just because of the quality of their ideas and [their] ability to execute on those ideas."

Campaign ideas that target specific audiences yet work equally well for global markets must incorporate a basic truism that is relevant to audiences worldwide. Big ideas can have a universal effect. According to the Saatchi & Saatchi Web site, ideas can even drive change: "We believe ideas have the power to change the world. Not just philosophically, but practically."[13]

More Strategy-Driven Campaigns

Let's look at the Subway "Eat Fresh" campaign. Exactly how did it break into a category driven by burger and pizza titans like McDonald's, Burger King, and Wendy's, as well as Pizza Hut and Little Caesar's? How did a sandwich chain go head-to-head with the recognized giants when its sales were stagnant? Ron Berger explains it this way:

> The interesting phenomenon is [that] you have a target audience of three types of people. First, there are the heavy users, who go to fast-food places around ten to twelve times a month. Second are the medium users, who go six to eight times a month. Third are the light users, who go two to three times a month. . . . The role of advertising in this category is not to get someone who never went to a fast-food restaurant and get them to go. It's to get those who [do] go to go more often. Either they go because they like it or their kids like it or someone they work with likes it. Someone without an opinion is not where marketing dollars are spent. . . . You want the heavy user to go more often. The medium user to become the heavy user. And the light user to become the medium user. This will make the cash register ring.

Berger then explains the way many people toss about the daily question "Where do you want to go for lunch?" Of course, location is always a consideration.

That's why most fast-food restaurants are near each other. People simply don't have time to go all over town (figure 9.17). He shares how Subway becomes a possible choice:

> The next point is in relation to that, you want to nullify the "veto vote" to the question "Where do you want to go? How 'bout Burger King?" Someone answers, "Oh, I don't want a burger." You need something on the menu for the "veto vote." . . . The last point is that the biggest meal for most fast-food places is lunch. People start thinking about where to go for lunch around 11:30 to 12:30. It's not a long conversation. . . . The role of advertising for Subway was to get them in the conversation. They were not in the conversation of burgers or pizza. They were a fringe player. They needed to get into the conversation and into the consideration set.

So, exactly how did the Subway campaign go about doing that? Here is Berger's answer:

> We did it by looking at the category: the strengths and weaknesses of the competition. The weakness was the heavy users were having weight problems. Our offer was a fresh and plentiful option. A sandwich made while you were watching it being made. And it's a hero sandwich, so you'll be

FIGURE 9.17 "Baked and Built" print ad created by Euro RSCG for Subway. Image courtesy of Euro RSCG

satisfied. "Eat Fresh" was a clear articulation of that. The fresh idea is fresh turkey, fresh cheese, fresh lettuce, fresh tomato, and you see it being made fresh. At other fast-food places, your order is made it in the back. It gets wrapped, and you don't see it. "Eat Fresh" is a clear statement of what Subway is and what it isn't.

Campaigns with Clear, Strong Messages

One Girl Scouts of the USA TV commercial, created by The Kaplan Thaler Group, also spoke directly to the audience (figure 9.18). This time the target was parents of young girls. In a warm and endearing spot, a little girl asks her dad a very commonly asked question: "Daddy, why is the sky blue?" When he offers a playful answer, "Well, to match your pretty eyes," the little girl answers, "Nope, not even close," and explains to her father, "See, all colors have wavelengths that are diffused by nitrogen and oxygen. Since the blue is the shortest wavelength, it diffuses up to ten times more." He asks, "Who taught you that?" She replies, "Mommy." This spot demonstrates the child's intelligence and grasp of science. By presenting this little girl as a scientist in training, the commercial

FIGURE 9.18 "Girls Go Tech" TV spot from the math/science campaign created by The Kaplan Thaler Group for Girl Scouts of the USA. Photo courtesy of the Ad Council

makes parents rethink their daughters' futures. The spot closes with this powerful line: "It's her future. Do the math."[14]

For Continental Airlines, The Kaplan Thaler Group created "Bowing," a TV spot in which a group of Japanese businessmen are all bowing as they meet an executive who fell asleep while bowing. No one wants to stand up until the guest does, and no one wants to wake him, so everyone is politely stuck in a bowing position. It's a very funny image that transcends the need for cultural translation.[15]

In a spot for Panasonic, "Car Wash," The Kaplan Thaler Group showed a young couple in a convertible car, driving through the car wash with the top down. They start to get soaked and begin shaving with their Panasonic shavers, using the suds from the car wash as lather. He's shaving his face, and she's working on her legs using the car wash suds. The spot is a lighthearted twist on a normally realistic slice-of-life type of spot.[16]

All campaigns, regardless of the medium, must be on strategy and on target in order to be successful. Add to that ingenious creativity, and you have a recipe for some groundbreaking work that captures both the imagination of the public and the attention of the press.

■ EXERCISE

Visit several agency Web sites and look for case studies that show exciting on-strategy campaigns that have demonstrated impressive results. Which other media could you incorporate into the campaign? What kind of promotion could you introduce online? Is there another audience that you would also target? If so, why? ■

■ PROJECT

How could you continue this campaign? Develop a series of three additional messages that spin off the original concept. What could you do to make your new campaign ideas more memorable? Use any of the techniques discussed in chapters 2 and 3. Consider the meaning of colors as explained in chapter 8. Remember to use the Web-safe color palette for your online promotion. ■

Notes

1. Deutsch, www.deutschinc.com (accessed August 3, 2005).
2. Tom Denari, personal communication, July 20, 2005.

3. Linda Kaplan Thaler, personal communication, January 4, 2006.

4. Norm Grey, personal communication, November 8, 2005.

5. Sharoz Makarechi, personal communication, November 2, 2005.

6. Noel Haan and G. Andrew Meyer, personal communication, November 30, 2005.

7. Linda Kaplan Thaler and Robin Koval with Delia Marshall, *Bang! Getting Your Message Heard in a Noisy World* (New York: Doubleday, 2003), 6.

8. Jeffrey Wolf, personal communication, November 4, 2005.

9. Lisa Fortini-Campbell, *Hitting the Sweet Spot* (Chicago: Copy Workshop, 2001), 15.

10. Jeffrey Wolf, private communication, November 4, 2005.

11. Think Tank 3, http://thinktank3.com (accessed July 17, 2005).

12. Ron Berger, personal communication, October 28, 2005.

13. Saatchi & Saatchi, 2004, www.saatchi.com/worldwide (accessed November 29, 2005).

14. The Kaplan Thaler Group, "Portfolio," 2006, www.kaplanthalergroup.com/portfolio/index.php (accessed November 11, 2005).

15. The Kaplan Thaler Group, "Portfolio."

16. The Kaplan Thaler Group, "Portfolio."

Learn the Latest through Inventive Case Studies with Impressive Results

> No matter how you word them, most processes end up sound-ing alike. Following a specific process is great if you're making homogenized milk or government cheese. But that's about it. We don't even like the word process. Instead we have a simple 3-part procedure. Hence the 3 in our name. We can even tell it to you in 3 words. THINK. PLAN. DO.
>
> —SHAROZ MAKARECHI[1]

Case Studies in Innovative Thinking

Volvo "Revolvolution"

Situation   As we saw in chapter 9, Euro RSCG's "Revolvolution" campaign spoke directly to the target audience by reaching them in their everyday lives while they used their BlackBerrys or other PDAs, and while they surfed the Web. According to Euro RSCG's Web site, Volvo's integrated campaign was designed to (1) increase awareness of the new S60 T5, (2) establish it as a creative force in new media, (3) test that new media against more traditional advertising vehicles, and (4) increase the Volvo database of prospective future buyers.

Solution   The solution was "The Road to the Volvo S60 T5," a fully integrated campaign that ran during the two-week annual NCAA college basketball tournament. The communication vehicles included the Internet, television, interactive TV, PDA, and WAP-enabled mobile phones. These promotional messages were all focused on enticing people to log on to the Web site to register to win a Volvo S60 T5 and a trip to the Final Four. The promotion built up to a strong finale: a live webcast announcing the winner of a Volvo S60 T5 on the day of the NCAA Championship basketball game.

Results   The results were impressive. In just a two-week period, "The Road to the Volvo S60 T5" message was featured across media more than 250 million times. And with 62,000 entries, paired with more than 20,500 "opt-ins," Volvo could build a database of 10,000 consumers who revealed their interest level in purchasing a Volvo in the near or not-too-distant future.[2]

Subway's "Eat Fresh" Campaign

Situation   Before that campaign was launched, sales were flat for Subway and the average consumer was over thirty-five years old. It was sitting in a category with burgers and pizzas with immediate name recognition like McDonald's, Burger King, Pizza Hut, and Papa John's. The company wanted to attract a younger, more voracious fast-food audience. It did not have a single focused message that would resonate with local, as well as regional and national, markets. Although many people saw the Subway "Eat Fresh" campaign, the real question was, what impact did it have on sales?

Solution   How did Euro RSCG, Subway's agency, turn this around? What creative approach did Euro RSCG use to speak directly to its targeted audience? How did Subway go from being overlooked to being a definite option? The solution was to focus on what Euro RSCG called Subway's core equity: freshness. It projected this through the message, the images, and the slogan, "Subway. Eat fresh." The campaign also focused on the trend toward a healthier diet and positioned Subway as the choice for excellent taste and healthier eating. Freshness was the focal point of the communication message. It addressed the consumer's health concerns in every opportunity to reach the audience, as well as in all media, including television, local promotional activities, and on-site merchandising. National ads were developed so they could easily be tailored in local neighborhoods.

What ultimately was the result of this campaign? Did it reach its audience and persuade the younger market to take action and stop by Subway? Did it drive sales and take some of the spending dollars away from its competitors? Here's what Euro RSCG reported.

Results   The results were impressive, showing a 30 percent increase of sales in just two years. In fact, Subway enjoyed the quickest annual growth in the food industry, with public awareness up even higher than McDonald's, whose daily budget was almost $2 million.

With an increase of almost 25 percent in overall awareness (from early 2000) and 4 percent in top-of-mind awareness, Subway experienced heightened traffic. It suddenly became a contender in the lunch-decision process, especially with the younger heavy-user market.[3]

Aflac (American Family Life Assurance Company)

Situation   Most of the time, when people think someone is trying to sell insurance, they have an immediate negative reaction and want to avoid the conversation. In fact, many are unreceptive, even borderline hostile, toward insurance salespeople's pitches. So, to make any insurance company even the slightest bit appealing is a huge challenge.

When The Kaplan Thaler Group began working with Aflac, it was a forty-five-year-old multibillion-dollar insurance company with virtually no name recognition. But that was before the Aflac duck commercials (figure 10.1) appeared on TV, quickly turning Aflac into a household name.

Solution   The Kaplan Thaler Group created quirky, humorous commercials using the Aflac duck in offbeat scenarios. These included the "Synchronized Swimmers" TV spot, in which a group of synchronized swimmers were discussing the need for insurance. It's funny because most people wouldn't consider synchronized swimming a sport, let alone a dangerous one. But during the performance, the Aflac duck joins the routine shortly after one swimmer strikes another in the head with her hand, proving that even in a seemingly safe sport, accidents happen. Another spot showed a Frankenstein-like experiment taking place in which the scientist was about to put the voice of a beautiful young woman into the Aflac duck. When asked why he would do that, the scientist answered, "To tell the world the benefits of Aflac with sex appeal."

Results   Not only did the campaign break through the insurance "avoidance armor" most people had up, but in just three years it caused awareness to soar from a paltry 12 percent to a staggering 90 percent, high enough to rival Coca-Cola's brand recognition. Just six days after the commercials began to air, the Aflac Web site had more hits than it had previously received over a one-year period. In three years, sales grew by 20 percent and continued to climb, reaching $1.2 billion in 2005. The campaign's lovable duck also helped garner millions of dollars in free publicity. In addition to giving the company instant name recognition, the duck also became woven into the country's

FIGURE 10.1   The Aflac duck in the "Broken Leg" TV spot created by The Kaplan Thaler Group for Aflac. Photo courtesy of Aflac Inc.

vernacular and appeared on everyday apparel like t-shirts as well as children's toys.[4]

Clairol Herbal Essences

Another campaign by The Kaplan Thaler Group that caused a buzz was "The Totally Organic Experience."

Situation   Clairol's Herbal Essences, once the third most popular shampoo in the 1970s, fell into obscurity by the 1990s. With a budget that was below 15 percent of its leading brand rival, the campaign had to rejuvenate the brand. Although women enjoyed showering and saw it as a private retreat from everyday hassles, they didn't see it in a serious light. It was just something they personally enjoyed.

Solution   Playing off a hilarious and sexy scene from the film *When Harry Met Sally*, "The Totally Organic Experience" portrayed shampooing as a nice yet naughty pleasure. Though bold, the campaign was lighthearted and playful, with a youthful sensuality. Yet with all its humor, it still focused on the product's benefits of a naturally botanical formula that delivered healthier hair.

One TV spot showed a young woman shopping in a supermarket. An announcer encouraged shoppers to go to aisle five for Clairol's Herbal Essences and promised that the product would "take you to where no shampoo has gone before." After imagining herself shampooing her hair and getting lost in sensual delight, she came to her senses. At that moment the well-known sex therapist Dr. Ruth handed her another product and said, "If you think that's great, try the body wash." It was very funny, especially because of Dr. Ruth's delivery.

Results In just two years, Herbal Essences moved from near oblivion to the second position in U.S. sales. The brand now earns almost $800 million in global sales and is sold in more than one hundred countries.

Like Aflac, "The Totally Organic Experience" became part of everyday speech. In fact, it was even integrated into some jokes made on late-night talk shows and *Saturday Night Live* skits. One American Greetings card referred to the campaign, whimsically urging the recipient "to have as much fun on your birthday as the woman in that shampoo commercial."[5]

South Auckland Health Foundation

Situation Saatchi & Saatchi wanted to vividly demonstrate how the overcrowded conditions in neonatal intensive care units prevent many infants in critical condition from being admitted and receiving appropriate care. The campaign needed to touch potential donors who were already facing "compassion fatigue," and to urge that this particular problem be placed at the head of Auckland's agenda over a two-week period.

Solution The campaign clearly highlighted the crowded facility in several dynamic visuals. One piled baby dolls one on top of the other into an overcrowded phone booth (figure 10.2). Another used dolls lying side

FIGURE 10.2 "Telephone Booth," created by Saatchi & Saatchi New Zealand for the Auckland Health Foundation Neonatal Intensive Care Unit. Image courtesy of Saatchi & Saatchi

by side to create eyelids around an open blue eye. Using dolls metaphorically to depict babies carelessly abandoned created a visual alarm, an undeniably urgent call to action.

Results In just two days, awareness of the campaign skyrocketed to 100 percent, and the campaign received a 90 percent positive response from the community. This was topped off with historic public and governmental contributions, resulting in an additional NZ$2 million earmarked for the expansion and improvement of one neonatal intensive care unit.[6]

Lexus LS430

Situation In 2001, the audience was already aware of the status of Lexus but was unconvinced of its overall supremacy in the luxury car market. The campaign's objective was to sway the target's opinion and convince consumers that Lexus had surpassed its competitors with this stellar model.

Solution To show that it knew the audience recognized the similarity in most luxury vehicle advertising messages, Saatchi & Saatchi created type-heavy direct-mail pieces that gently poked fun at the typical high-end car ad. One promotional piece, "Which Logo," stated it was for a luxury car and asked which logo belonged at the bottom of the page. Another piece, "Finest Luxury Sedan," left a blank space in the headline for the recipient to fill in the name of the luxury car. The ads spoke to the audience in a slightly irreverent tone of voice. Although they explained why it was the supreme luxury car, the ads showed Lexus wasn't above having a little fun.

Results The direct-mail campaign exceeded expectations and delivered a 0.8 percent response rate, 0.3 percent over projections. In addition, the campaign generated a flurry of press coverage, plus almost 300,000 visits in totality to the Web site.[7]

Whiskas

Situation The Berlin office of TBWA\Germany was faced with the problem that lower-priced generic products were quickly becoming increasingly popular. Whiskas needed to be positioned as a brand that offered great value.

Solution To combat its competitors' lower pricing, the TBWA\Berlin team developed "The Best Ever Offer" for Whiskas in 2004. The overall idea was to say, "Your cat's favorite food, now in a giant offer." The approach paired the brand's core identity—a definitive end-user preference—with an unbeatable offer. The campaign used exaggerated visuals. One ad showed a huge fish flying out from a body of water, and another featured an enormous sheep.

Results Whiskas cat food was swept off the shelves by eager consumers, resulting in an increase of 38 percent in sales of Whiskas' multipack.[8]

> Lovemarks form a key pillar in what we believe. Lovemarks are super-developed brands that inspire loyalty beyond reason. The relationship Lovemarks have with the people who buy them is not built on function, but on emotion . . . and function.
>
> —SAATCHI & SAATCHI[9]

Pedigree

Situation TBWA wanted to position Pedigree as the dog food company that loves dogs as much as every dog owner does. If the audience could truly believe in Pedigree's passion for man's best friend, then they would entrust the daily nourishment of their beloved dogs to Pedigree. On its Web site, TBWA discusses the power of ideas that interrupt the target audience's lives. This is what TBWA defines as "disruptive ideas." John McNeel, TBWA's worldwide managing director explains it like this: "This is the story of a brand and a company renewing with the universal truth that is at the very core of its DNA. In our network's largest ever Disruption process—spanning eight cities and five continents—we confirmed that Pedigree has the power to make the 'love of dogs' a global rallying cry for the brand."[10]

Solution Under the leadership of Lee Clow, TBWA's chairman and chief creative officer worldwide, two different offices in Sydney, Australia, developed a global multimedia campaign that included television and both outdoor and interactive advertising, as well as point-of-purchase marketing.

The comical "Yellow Mania" consumer promotion playfully urged people in Australia to become "dognappers" so they could have a chance to win the Yellow Mania contest. By kidnapping a dog, they could pretend to be dog owners and go out and buy large amounts of Pedigree. Winning the contest was suddenly so important that ordinarily honest people were coaxed into becoming dog thieves: "If you don't have a dog, get one." The idea was such an obvious exaggeration that it tickled its targeted audience.

Results   During the quarter while the campaign ran, sales of Pedigree Meaty-Bites rose 11 percent above those of the same quarter in 2002. Sales of Pedigree canned food increased even more—by 12 percent from the same period the prior year. In addition, it catapulted Pedigree into its "highest four-week volume share of total wet dog food in 12 years."[11]

Burger King

Situation   The purpose of the "Subservient Chicken" campaign was to introduce Burger King's new TenderCrisp Chicken Sandwich to its targeted audience of eighteen- to thirty-four-year-old males.

Solution   To emphasize Burger King's long-running slogan "Have It Your Way," Crispin Porter + Bogusky launched a "beta" Web site on April 8, 2004, and e-mailed friends and relatives the URL address, www.subservientchicken.com. Then, a webcam was set up so Burger King lovers could log on and interact with a man dressed in a chicken costume (discussed in chapters 1 and 6). People enjoyed giving him commands that he would execute immediately. They could watch the chicken stand up, sit down, spin in circles, flap his wings, or do whatever else they commanded. Now they had a "Subservient Chicken" whose responses reflected Burger King's promise to "Have It Your Way."

Besides the Internet, the campaign also included television spots, print ads, and even action figures designed by Kid Robot, a company that creates mini-figures, limited edition art toys, action figures, and more (www.kidrobot.com).

Results   By the end of the very first day, 193,831 unique visitors and 8,219,498 hits had logged on the Web site, with visitors interacting for more than seven minutes. In less than two weeks after the beta site was posted, the Subservient Chicken had attracted an amazing number of hits and extensive media coverage, including (1) five featured segments on *Fox & Friends* on Saturday, April 17, (2) recognition from *CNN Headline News,* which called the Web site "a unique and successful online 'viral' marketing campaign," (3) commendation from the *Wall Street Journal* in an article that praised the campaign's unique and creative approach, (4) inclusion on CNN in a report by Jeannie Moos, (5) a Subservient Chicken appearance on *The Dennis Miller Show* in July, (6) a scoop on a channel in Singapore, and (7) a parody of the chicken on www.subservientpresident.com.[12]

Two weeks after launch, these key figures were compiled:

Subservient Chicken Statistics[13]

100,000,000+: number of hits to subservientchicken.com
7,000,000+: number of broadcast impressions
30,000+: number of results from a Google search on "Subservient Chicken"
63: number of national, regional, and local broadcast segments
20: number of national, regional, and local print and online articles
15: Visitors spent roughly fifteen times longer on the site than they spend watching a thirty-second commercial.
7 minutes 35 seconds: average time each visitor spent on the site
Total unique hits since launch: 12,142,314
Total hits since launch: 348,420,426

MINI Robots

Situation   Many car commercials resemble each other, leaving audiences sometimes unable to determine which car company is being advertised. Realizing this, the creative team at Crispin Porter + Bogusky was determined to set the MINI apart from its competitors. This is what the creative team has to say about its approach to the MINI:

> Our goal was to break through the clutter of traditional car advertising and create awareness for MINI. This translates to new people becoming interested in the brand. "Robots" continues to define M's brand personality. And it invites people to interact with the brand in a way that creates desire. We have received several e-mails from people who say they enjoyed it so much they are going to the dealer. That doesn't happen too often with a bus shelter advertisement.[14]

Solution   The team invented "interactive fiction," a novel type of creative format that introduced Dr. Colin Mayhew, a fictitious retired British scientist. He allegedly created robots out of MINI parts (figure 10.3) and then used them to conduct highly secretive car experiments. Dr. Mayhew also posted a daily "vlog" (video blog) of short clips on his Web site, showing his covert car experiments.

Even though the character was not a real person, all the information presented on the Web site and in a subsequent book was factual. It gave MINI a platform to showcase its engineering achievements, product features, and unique design "all wrapped in the spirit of motoring." The team also explains that "at the core the robots are about improving driving culture. But at no time is a MINI logo or any type of actual MINI branding evident."

Eventually, Dr. Mayhew revealed that the robots were designed to help humankind. Then a second site was launched, which showcased the robots' good deeds. They were like metal Robin Hoods. Then a short novel, *Men of Metal,* was released (figure 10.4). It investigated the robots' appearances and focused on the author's pursuit to unearth this secretive scientist. The book was distributed at the New York Auto Show and given to anyone who made a purchase at Hudson newsstands. It was converted into inserts, which appeared in issues of *Rolling Stone*, *Men's Health*, *Men's Journal,* and *Motor Trend.*

Other Dr. Mayhew sites were created, including two home pages: one for the book's nonexistent publishing firm, and another for its fictional author, Rowland Samuel, who wanted to find the elusive Dr. Mayhew. The sightings, investigations, and site postings led visitors through a seemingly plausible plot, which was then spread through other communication vehicles, like outdoor boards, bookstores, airports, and MINI dealerships.

Results The press covered the campaign with dozens of written articles about the robots. There were hundreds

FIGURE 10.3 The r50r robot from the "Robots" campaign created by Crispin Porter + Bogusky for MINI Cooper. Photo courtesy of MINI USA LLC

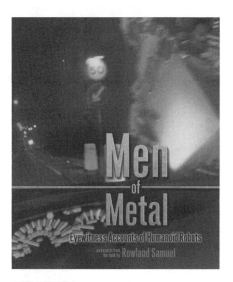

FIGURE 10.4 The r50r *Men of Metal* front cover insert, created by Crispin Porter + Bogusky for MINI Cooper. Photo courtesy of MINI USA LLC

of e-mails to Dr. Mayhew, and thousands of inbound links were traced to the r50r robot. In addition, it generated tremendous activity on the MINI Web site, including almost 10,000 downloads of the giant printable robot and close to 15,000 downloads of *Men of Metal,* and 25,000 robot configurations were saved. In all, the campaign generated almost a million unique visits to the site.[15]

American Legacy Foundation®

Situation   The objective of this campaign was to decrease the number of teenage smokers. The problem was threefold. First, other anti-smoking campaigns that sounded dictatorial had not been effective in impacting teenagers' decisions about smoking. Second, tobacco companies were spending more than $9.6 billion in advertising and promotion of their products. Third, attempting to influence the naturally rebellious teen attitude was a daunting task. After all, teenagers often think they know everything and no one should tell them what to do. That is why smoking can be an overt act of defiance.

Solution   In order to attract teen support and to engage their participation, Crispin Porter + Bogusky, in collaboration with Arnold Worldwide and the American Legacy Foundation, created a brand just as the tobacco industry had. Here is what they reveal about their thinking behind this creative campaign: "We had to make the act of not smoking just as rebellious as smoking. We wanted to direct teens' natural desire for rebellion at the manipulative tobacco industry. So our message became industry manipulation—depicting a real, manipulative adult institution that is worthy of rebelling against."[16]

Together, the two agencies and the foundation developed an anti-smoking message that exposed all the propaganda handed to them from Big Tobacco. The "truth®" commercials revealed the truth about the dangers of smoking as well as the fact that the tobacco industry has been aware of these dangers for many years yet continued to market its products to youth. To illustrate this, the spots showed shocking images. One commercial showed body bags being piled on a city sidewalk outside the offices of a major tobacco company (figure 10.5). Another showed a traffic jam of gurneys being wheeled into a hospital (figure 10.6). Saying smoking is dangerous to your health is not nearly as powerful as seeing body bags piled up in the street or throngs of people on stretchers in front of a hospital entrance practically vying for admission. Crispin Porter + Bogusky's goal was to create "a brand that would provide teens with the knowledge, motivation, and power to deconstruct the myths, lies and deception of the tobacco industry. A brand that teens could watch on TV, interact with on the

FIGURE 10.5 "Body Bags" TV spot from the "truth®" campaign, created by Crispin Porter + Bogusky and Arnold Worldwide for the American Legacy Foundation®. Photo courtesy of American Legacy Foundation®

Web, talk about, wear, have fun with and simply believe in."

Results The campaign caused a remarkable reaction. By 2002, the number of teenage smokers declined by approximately 300,000. This ultimately means that thousands of lives were saved, because almost one-third of people who smoked when they were young die later on from tobacco-related illnesses.[17]

Statistics Don't Show Viral Buzz

Although there are many online campaigns, only a few of those create a real stir in the marketplace. The agencies getting all the attention are

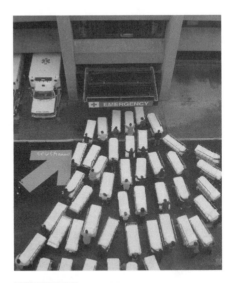

FIGURE 10.6 "Hospital Beds" TV spot from the "truth®" campaign, created by Crispin Porter + Bogusky and Arnold Worldwide for the American Legacy Foundation®. Photo courtesy of American Legacy Foundation®

those that are rethinking interactive media as a whole. Some campaigns that have redefined interactive marketing were ones we've discussed, including "Are You a Mitchum Man" by Deutsch NY, Burger King's "Subservient Chicken" campaign by Crispin Porter + Bogusky, and "Revolvolution" by Euro RSCG. They were successful for many reasons. But the primary reason is that they engaged the audience's participation and paired honesty with a touch of familiarity. The brand, like a good friend, was invited into the consumer's circle of trust.

Ad Spending Trends

Many advertisers have reprioritized their ad budgets to concentrate on online advertising rather than advertising in other media. In 2005, Internet spending increased 1.1 percent, while overall spending including all media increased 4.1 percent. For the first half of 2005, TNS Media Intelligence presented a report that showed national advertising spending had increased to $70.5 billion, up 4.5 percent, with online advertising showing a 9.4-percent increase during the same period, ultimately reaching $3.6 billion. So, who were the big Internet spenders for 2005? TNS listed the following companies as the twenty biggest Internet spenders.[18]

1.	Vonage	$20,632 million
2.	Classmates	$15,510 million
3.	Ameritrade Brokerage	$8,355 million
4.	Superpages.com	$6,761 million
5.	Netflix.com	$6,413 million
6.	Overstock.com	$6,369 million
7.	Amazon.com	$5,462 million
8.	Monster.com	$5,420 million
9.	LowerMyBills.com	$5,251 million
10.	RealArcade Games	$4,698 million
11.	Scottrade Stock Brokerage	$4,644 million
12.	Love@AOL	$4,560 million
13.	Dell VAR Computers Products Direct	$4,347 million
14.	Circuit City	$4,145 million
15.	Capital One	$4,043 million
16.	University of Phoenix	$4,000 million
17.	Harrisdirect.com	$3,770 million
18.	Earthlink	$3,734 million
19.	Careerbuilder	$3,715 million
20.	Freecreditreport.com	$3,704 million

Although many of the firms are primarily e-commerce sites, others are also offline advertisers including General Motors (number twenty-nine), Sheraton Hotels (thirty-three), Verizon (thirty-six), and Wal-Mart (thirty-eight).

Four factors were responsible for this rise of online spending: (1) the increase of overall ad budgets, (2) the shift in marketing spending from more traditional media to the Internet, (3) the incorporation of online spending into campaign budgets, and (4) the rise of media costs for ads and direct response mechanisms like paid searches.[19]

■ EXERCISE

Find two interactive campaigns that captured your imagination and engaged your attention for several minutes. Look for any kind of advertising or promotion that guided you from one medium to another. It could be a promotion, a sweepstakes, a contest, a quiz, a survey, a sponsored blog, vlog, podcast or anything else, even a rebate. Now ask, what caused you to participate? The offer? The information? The creativity? In the future, each time you find an interactive campaign, jot it down and maintain a running reference log for future inspiration. ■

■ PROJECT

Choose a product that you know well. It could be something you use or intend to buy. Now, create an innovative and interactive multimedia promotion that would make you respond. Remember always to ask yourself, "What do I need to hear to take action?" You must think like the consumer, so you can create an irresistible campaign. When you're looking for an ingenious idea, also ask, "Would this get press?" If it's just another "me too" idea, it won't.

Try to think about using both old and new advertising vehicles in imaginative ways, as the agencies we've discussed have done. Rethink taxi-top ads (VIDs), street stencils, floor talkers, projected wallscapes, billboards with live people tethered to them, product mobiles (Oscar Mayer Wienermobile), gas pump stickers, vending machines, and any other communication vehicle you've seen. Now, can you think of a media vehicle that hasn't been used? ■

Notes

1. Think Tank 3, http://thinktank3.com (accessed July 17, 2005).

2. Euro RSCG Worldwide, "Volvo NCAA Integrated Promotion," www.eurorscg.com/h/s/ow_cs_2.asp (accessed October 26, 2005).

3. Euro RSCG Worldwide, "Subway: Eat Fresh," www.eurorscg.com/h/s/ow_cs_9.asp (accessed October 28, 2005).

4. Tricia Kenney and Erin Creagh, personal communication, January 6, 2006.

5. The Kaplan Thaler Group, "Portfolio," 2006, www.kaplanthaler.com/portfolio (accessed November 27, 2005).

6. Saatchi & Saatchi, 2004, www.saatchi.com/worldwide/works (accessed November 29, 2005).

7. Saatchi & Saatchi.

8. TBWA\Thursday by JDM, "Featured Thursday: Cats and Dogs," www.tbwa.com/index.php/jmdthursdays/7;18 (accessed November 27, 2005).

9. Saatchi & Saatchi, 2004, www.saatchi.com/worldwide (accessed November 29, 2005).

10. TBWA\Thursday by JDM, "Life Takes Visa," www.tbwa.com/index.php/disruptiveideas (accessed December 7, 2005).

11. TBWA\Thursday by JDM, "Featured Thursday: Cats and Dogs."

12. Steve Sapka, personal communication, December 8, 2005.

13. Figures courtesy of Crispin Porter + Bogusky.

14. Steve Sapka, personal communication, December 8, 2005.

15. Steve Sapka, personal communication, December 8, 2005.

16. Sarah Howard, personal communication, December 14, 2005.

17. Sarah Howard, personal communication, December 14, 2005.

18. "Who's Advertising Online?" November 14, 2005, www.eMarketer.com (accessed November 14, 2005).

19. "Who's Advertising Online?"

See Which Self-Promotions Really Work

> Direct-mail pieces are risky. A good one gets someone's attention. But a bad one does too. But not in the way you want.
>
> —PIPPA SEICHRIST[1]

The development of a self-promotion is one of the most difficult, yet often most rewarding, challenges you could tackle. But the fact is, every agency and freelancer needs to be able to create materials to solicit new business. Today, many brochures and direct-mail pieces have been replaced by digital formats. Most major agencies have Web sites, as do small design firms, freelance writers, and photographers. Even many recent graduates of advertising programs and portfolio schools have their own sites. Years ago, the portfolio was critical to the interview. Now, it's different. Here's what Norm Grey, executive creative director of The Creative Circus, has to say about large portfolios: "It's been years since self-promotion pieces have been used. And it's been eighteen months since students have created big black portfolios, you know, the old standard. What people want now is an instant examination of a student's or grad's work on a Web site or in a PDF they email. If they like what they see, they'll have the students come in for an interview and look at their mini-book."[2]

But most students send out a digital version to show their work before they interview. So, now the question is, do they need to bring in their mini-book for the initial meeting? According to Grey, "If they have a big portfolio, they should bring it to the interview. I also tell them don't assume that they [the interviewers] don't want to see a book because they saw the electronic version. Or the mini. Sometimes, they need more than a mini-book because of detail and because they want to show your work to other people in the shop. A big book isn't always necessary, but if you have it, bring it."

Today, advertising students are wondering if they should at least create a clever promotion to just get their foot in the door. Are these still effective? Grey answers: "Part of a self-promotion now is how to get across who you are and what you do. It used to be that a gimmick might get you through the door, but that doesn't hold much water any more. It's the gestalt—the whole package— the Web site, mini-book, and cover letter to request an interview."

Pippa Seichrist, president and cofounder of Miami Ad School, has polled agencies all around the world. She explains what she learned about what agencies want to see:

> They said they'll look at work online (on a Web site). Six out of seven said they'd pop in a CD of work. The other one said the CD would just get lost, so don't bother sending one. They all said a mini-book is a must because they can show it to the other creatives and discuss the work. . . . The smartest thing is to have all three: the portfolio, the CD, and an online portfolio of your work. Promotions or a direct-mail piece are not really necessary. They can even be risky. Every contact you make with an agency tells them something about you, so any direct-mail piece has to be as good as the best piece in your portfolio. If you have a really terrific self-promo idea, then go ahead and send it. Though a good book, steady, polite persistence, and follow-up will get you the job. . . . When I discuss mini-books in class, I cross out the letters "ini" and replace them with "any" ["mini" to "many"]. It's not referring to size. Your book shouldn't be small. The book needs to be the size of the work. If the ad you're showing is 8.5 by 11 inches, your book needs to be that big. If your book is too small, the person you're interviewing with won't be able to read the copy, see the logo, [or] even understand the concept. Make it easy for someone to understand your ideas. . . . Some students interview with their mini-book. Others have loose pieces in a portfolio case. In either case, you need to leave a mini-book after the interview. It has to be shown to several people before a hiring decision can be made. Most agencies keep the mini-books on file. They might not

be hiring when you interview there, but the next week or month a position could open up. You want your book there, so you can be considered for the position.

Self-Promotions That Work

Although creative directors and portfolio school faculty might disagree whether or not self-promotions are a viable marketing tool, the consensus is that anything done superbly will always have an impact. Creating predictable, uninspired self-promotions that don't deliver a "wow" is pointless. The purpose of any self-promotion is to generate interest in your creative talent, not convince someone of your lack of originality. So, if you're uncertain of how it will be received, it's better not to send it.

When asked if student self-promotions are still effective tools for landing jobs, Seichrist answers:

> One girl did a creative direct-mail piece. She sent her wallet to creative directors. She went out and bought interesting wallets, so they would stand out. One was lime green with embroidery. Inside, where the photo section was, she put little pieces of her work. The change section held coins, ticket stubs to movies that she saw, business cards from galleries she found interesting, an ID to something—so they saw her picture and what she belonged to—and a barrette, because she always wore them. She even put in a card from a photo exhibit with one of the photos she liked. Everything in there felt like her. . . . She would ship the wallet to a creative director she really wanted to work for. When they opened it, they got an idea of what she was like. Her self-promo got the attention of the creative director at Fallon, and he gave her a job. But an assistant at Wieden called her and said he had her wallet and should he send it back? Obviously, he didn't get it. Some got it and some didn't. . . . Direct-mail pieces are risky. A good one get someone's attention. But a bad one does too. But not in the way you want.

Setting the Example: Playful Yet Powerful Self-Promotions

It is always difficult to create a self-promotion that is playful yet works. Seichrist explains a recent promotion for Miami Ad School. It was a magazine ad with perforated trading cards that readers could punch out to play an advertising game (figures 11.1 and 11.2).

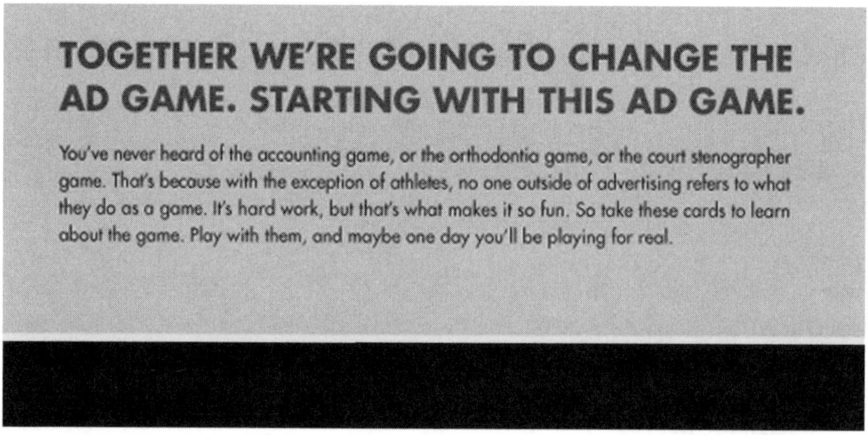

TOGETHER WE'RE GOING TO CHANGE THE AD GAME. STARTING WITH THIS AD GAME.
You've never heard of the accounting game, or the orthodontia game, or the court stenographer game. That's because with the exception of athletes, no one outside of advertising refers to what they do as a game. It's hard work, but that's what makes it so fun. So take these cards to learn about the game. Play with them, and maybe one day you'll be playing for real.

FIGURE 11.1 "Trading Cards" self-promotion magazine ad created by Miami Ad School. Image courtesy of Miami Ad School

We're doing trading cards, like Pokémon cards. The character on each card is a really famous industry person—famous creative directors, photographers, and account planners—that advertising students should know about. All of them are involved with Miami Ad School. Each of the characters has different powers. There are points for charisma, dexterity, skill, spirit, and will. There are a few other characters, like a dentist and accountant. They both have low charisma and spirit points. The cards have the person's photo and a quote from them. It tells why they are famous in the industry and how they got involved with the school. It's a fun way to learn about the business. Someone looking at them says, "Oh, that's who Lee Clow is. I read about him." Leo Burnett is in it. So are Howard Gossage, Alex Bogusky, and Jane Newman. We also did the cards as

CLOW
380
38
"I've never found a client's business problem that could be solved solely through advertising."
Lee has taken Miami Ad School students under his large wings as interns.

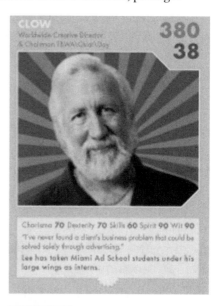

FIGURE 11.2 Lee Clow Card from the "Trading Cards" self-promotion magazine ad created by Miami Ad School. Image courtesy of Miami Ad School

an insert in a magazine. You could tear out the page, punch out the cards, and play the game.

If your piece can engage its recipients' participation, it succeeds in interrupting them and forcing them to take notice. If the piece is creative enough, it will elicit curiosity and stimulate a response. If it's really wonderful, it will be shown around the office. And if it's nothing short of amazing, it might even get media attention and create a buzz.

> We believe passionately in the power of ideas to create sustainable growth for our clients. We're also driven by the simple belief that NOTHING IS IMPOSSIBLE. We can go deeper into what we believe right here.
>
> —SAATCHI & SAATCHI[3]

Innovative, Interactive Self-Promotions

When agencies want to prove their creative capability to prospective clients, their self-promotions must demonstrate this. They must have the power to create a "wow" reaction. Saatchi & Saatchi's self-promotional "Ideas Showcase" (figure 11.3) does exactly that. Placed inside a case that looks and opens like a

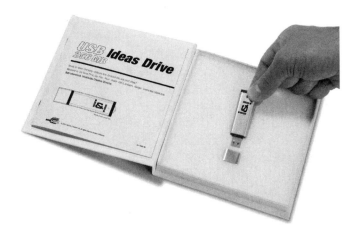

FIGURE 11.3 Saatchi & Saatchi self-promotional "Ideas Showcase." Image courtesy of Saatchi & Saatchi

book, with simulated pages on the side, the jump drive sits vertically over the cap. Together, they actually create an exclamation point.

The cover headline reads "Saatchi & Saatchi—Ideas & Ideas Book." Once opened, the left side says "Ideas Drive" in bold type, accompanied by "USB 256 MB" in outlined type. The right side houses the actual cap and jump drive, which contains visuals of the agency's work in one compact and easy-to-use format. Issued in a limited edition and reserved for new business prospects only, this piece drives home Saatchi & Saatchi's undeniable creativity. Here's what the agency says about this self-promotion piece:

> For Saatchi & Saatchi, the urge to present its work in an original way is irresistible. The Ideas Showcase, shown here, used a USB pen drive (housed in a fake "book") to present the Saatchi & Saatchi Network's best ideas across all disciplines: Film, Radio, Print, DM [direct mail] & Ambient, Design, and Interactive. It's hard to imagine how such disparate content could have been put together successfully in any other way, making the Saatchi & Saatchi "Ideas Showcase" something of an ideal marriage between functionality and originality.[4]

Self-Promotions Are Still Popular with Designers

Just look at some recent awards annuals, and you will see that self-promotions are far from dead. In fact, designers, design firms, and photographers and other freelancers are still using them in innovative ways. A quick glance at "Designer's Guide to Self-Promotion" in *HOW*'s 2005 *Self-Promotion Design Annual* will offer you useful tips. One of the top winners was Knock Knock, the Venice, California, design firm whose product catalogs used humorous comments in circular dials with cutout windows named "Sex Flash Cards" and "Wheels o' Wisdom." The dials in the "Dial-an-Excuse" wheel offered answers to different excuses posed in the little windows (figure 11.4) ("Because a Bad Excuse Is Better Than No Excuse") and "Find It" (figure 11.5) ("A Compass for Chronic Losers"). In addition, it created a flip book with a wood grain cover that sports a different color wood each year.[5]

Knock Knock owner and creative director Jen Bilik explains how the self-promotion was conceived: "The 'Wheels o' Wisdom' were created for sale rather than promotional purposes, as a sort of more-than-a-card, less-than-a-gift morsel. I love old paper products, and I enjoy spreadsheets and lists. And the wheels combine the pleasures of both, as the information contained in the wheel is basically in the form of a spreadsheet. The aesthetic was inspired by old circus

FIGURE 11.4 The Dial-an-Excuse dial from the "Wheels o' Wisdom" product catalog self-promotion created by Knock Knock. Image courtesy of Knock Knock

posters and Victorian ads."[6] The flip book with the wooden cover also reflected design aspects from an earlier period. According to Bilik: "The flip book was also created out of a love for vintage paper products. Sadly, while people delighted in the FB's [Flip Book's] aesthetics, many couldn't figure out which way to flip it, or how."

When asked to explain why Knock Knock created these self-promotion pieces, Bilik answered: "Knock Knock's business is 90 percent wholesale, selling

FIGURE 11.5 The Find It dial from the "Wheels o' Wisdom" product catalog self-promotion created by Knock Knock. Image courtesy of Knock Knock

to retailers and buyers ranging from single-rooftop boutiques to chains, and the catalog is our primary selling tool. We do not create a direct-to-consumer retail catalog; our Web site serves this function. We create a catalog for each of our four selling seasons (spring, spring holiday, fall, and winter holiday) and have done so since the business launched in 2002."

Each season, catalogs showcased the newest offerings, while still including some discontinued items. So, Knock Knock ended up having several different catalogs out at the same time, which became a problem for the sales staff and customers. Bilik explains how the problem was solved: "The solution to this problem was to create an expandable catalog, so that subsequent releases would function as inserts or updates, and the pages of discontinued items could simply be removed. . . . At Knock Knock, we enjoy repurposing standard office supplies. Two-pronged fasteners are a favorite device. We divided the catalog into the three sections of our product—everyday product, cards, and holiday—and separated the sections with tabbed dividers, another homage to office products."

Explaining the overall design, Bilik states that the piece reflected earlier catalogs for design continuity. She adds, "Additionally, the catalog pages follow closely the format of our previous catalogs, with running footers to communicate specs as well as include novelty information such as quotations. This works very well for information organization."

The question now was, exactly how did Knock Knock distribute its catalog to its targeted audience of retailers, buyers, and sales reps? Here's Bilik's answer: "Our catalogs are distributed by mail to sales reps and existing customers and buyers, as well as at trade shows and on rep sales calls. We created a special tuck-top mailer box for the catalog to help it stand out from the postal crush."

Lastly, what kind of response did this piece generate, especially because it was designed for a specific audience to solve an ongoing problem? Bilik reports:

> The jury is still out as to whether the expandability feature is a success. We've heard from others in the gift industry that expandable catalogs don't work, as people lose the catalogs and don't manage to incorporate the updates. Since mailing the original piece, we've sent out two updates, and so far so good. Part of our goal was to create enough of a treasured keepsake, aesthetically speaking, that people wouldn't lose it. In terms of design and organization, the catalog has generated very favorable response. The "Wheels" have been one of our most successful product lines.

Design firms and illustrators have different reasons for sending out self-promotions. Randal Grey, president of Randal Grey Design & Illustration, created a holiday direct-mail piece, which arrived in mid-December. The piece (figures 11.6 and 11.7) included holiday ornaments designed by Grey, which were perforated and pre-punched so they could be separated, strung, and hung on a Christmas tree. This piece allowed recipients to see his illustrative style as well as his design ability through one eye-catching piece. According to Grey, it met its objectives: "I had three goals: to gain more clients, have people remember my illustrations, and create a high-quality print piece I was proud of making."[7] When asked how he selected his audience, he replies that he didn't. He bought a mailing list and didn't narrow it down. "I sent it to advertising agencies, graphic design firms, and corporate people. I mailed it to just about everybody."

He makes this surprising comment when asked what kind of response he received: "When I mail something out, I hear back from the person I least expect." Although he has created other self-promotions, this was the most elaborate one he has developed. He adds: "Last year I sent a diorama. That's where you cut people out and stand them up against a background. It had a holiday party theme." Just like this year's "Cosmic Designer Holiday Ornaments" self-

FIGURE 11.6 Cover of "Cosmic Designer Holiday Ornaments" self-promotion, created by Randal Grey Design & Illustration. Image courtesy of Randal Grey Design & Illustration

FIGURE 11.7 Inside spread of "Cosmic Designer Holiday Ornaments" self-promotion, created by Randal Grey Design & Illustration. Image courtesy of Randal Grey Design & Illustration

promotion, last year's holiday party cutouts also engaged the audience. Even if the recipients didn't take the promotion apart and play with the pieces, they would be stimulated by the designer's enticing invitation to have fun.

Modern Dog Design's "Logo Book" (figure 11.8) was also recognized and featured in *HOW* magazine's 2005 *Self-Promotion Design Annual*. Robynne Raye, the design firm's cofounder and designer, explains the impetus behind the piece: "People really know us from doing other types of work. It's easy to overlook the identity work because it's just not as glamorous as the posters and packaging jobs. We wanted to let others know this is a solid part of our business and has been since the beginning."[8]

When asked what other work her design firm is known for, Raye says: "We are most known for our

FIGURE 11.8 "Logo Book" self-promotion created by Modern Dog Design. Image courtesy of Modern Dog Design

posters because that is the kind of work that gets picked for the design annuals, and it's the kind of work that is easily collected—both by the individual and by museums and galleries. The other type of design work we are known for is packaging."

Asked if Modern Dog Design has a Web site to promote its work, Raye answers, "This [the "Logo Book"] is in addition to our Web site. We don't have a portfolio. When someone needs a physical sample, we send them something specific, depending on what they're looking for. For packaging or brochures, we send actual work. For identity or custom lettering, we have this book. It also makes a nice giveaway at lectures."

For distribution, Raye avoided a blanket or "shotgun" mailing and sent the piece only when current and prospective clients wanted to see examples of the firm's work. She explains why she sized the piece as she did: "We've never done a mass mailing. When people ask for lettering or identity work, I send them our little book of logos. We wanted something small, portable, and easy to ship. It's 7 by 5.25 inches. I think there are around fifty-five logos in there."

How successful was the "Logo Book"? Raye says, "People loved it. The cover is screen printed and the inside guts are digitally printed. With screen printing, it's possible to get ink coverage and color saturation you could never get with an offset press. The end result is a custom-made promo. And although it may not be expensive to produce, it does feel special because the recipient can easily recognize that we didn't make five hundred gazillion of these things. . . . Screen printing used to be called silk screen because it originated in Japan, where the ink was pushed through silk. We have been screen-printing our posters for nearly twenty years."

Graphic design firms, as you can see, are effectively using self-promotions to market their talents to existing clients and other targeted markets. When the pieces are clever, engaging, and reflective of the quality of the firm's work, self-promotions do exactly what they are designed to do: promote sales and high-light innovative designers.

How Student Self-Promotions Can Help

If students have not created a "killer" book, they will not be considered seriously for a creative position. Therefore, courses that encourage them to develop a self-promotion enable students to market themselves as they would a product. Often, this assignment is the most difficult one of all—first, because it takes a great deal of introspective contemplation and second, because it forces them to highlight their own unique selling proposition. If this piece displays originality and skillful execution, it might even land them job interviews.

The interviews might only be for internship positions, but these can turn into full-time positions, as has happened for several Florida International University students. Some students' innovative self-promotions have actually landed them jobs at major New York agencies. One FIU graduate, Natalia Cova, a former franchise owner of Fast Track Kids, flew to New York with several copies of her self-promotion. Without an appointment, Cova went from agency to agency, hoping to land an interview. Not only was she interviewed, but she was offered four positions, all from the strength and creativity of her self-promotion. Cova says: "I landed a job at Bates in New York. But I was also offered positions at J. Walter Thompson, Deutsch, [and] Saatchi & Saatchi."[9]

She interviewed for a position in account services, because without a port-folio, she knew that she wouldn't be considered for a creative position. What was her promotion? It was the final assignment of the advanced print concepts class she took with me. She explains it like this: "It was a stuffed animal. A brown dog with big floppy ears. He had a little newspaper in his mouth. Like he was bringing in the morning paper. I wrapped the paper in plastic and sewed it in his mouth, so it wouldn't fall out. The front of the newspaper was the cover letter. Inside was my resume written in newspaper format."

She says everyone who saw it loved it. Then, after two years in New York, Cova returned to Miami and applied for a position at Zubi Advertising, a leading Hispanic agency. "I also created a second self-promotion when I returned to Miami and applied at Zubi Advertising. That time I had a drum and it said, 'Marching to my own beat.'"

When asked if she found that her self-promotions were helpful in her search for a position in advertising, she answers: "I got every job I applied for. And it's because if you can sell yourself, you can sell whatever product or service you're planning to advertise. How can you convince someone else that you're creative if you don't show it? I learned that from you. At the end of the day, it's about knowing your audience. In this case, it's a creative agency. Therefore, you should show you can give them what they want—that is, that you're a creative person who can think outside the box."

Although the positions were in account services, she and other students without portfolios, CDs, or Web sites ended up working in creatively invigorating environments where they absorbed invaluable lessons in strategic thinking. Today, more than ever, it's almost impossible to land a creative position without showing several examples of heart-stopping creative work.

With that said, there are many creative positions in major corporations with in-house advertising and promotions departments, including radio, TV, and cable stations; retail, discount store, and restaurant chains; tourism-based corporations like cruise lines, car rental firms, and hotel chains; and electronics and computer companies, as well as home improvement chains.

A self-promotion can show any potential employer your ability to conceptualize and execute an idea. For example, one graduate applied to a Miami creative boutique, Global Impact (owned by the author), for three years in a row. He reapplied each year but was so nervous during each interview that he appeared immature and unprepared for his dream copywriting job. Finally, in the third interview, he showed up with a miniature wine crate. The creative director opened the small handmade crate to find a wine bottle with a label that boldly read, "Hire me. I've aged." She was so impressed that she immediately offered him a job. Cova, recalling this self-promotion from class discussions, comments that it is still a viable creative idea today. "I think the wine promotion can still work because of its simplicity and the play on words. It's taking something so obvious like the value of a mature wine and making it 'ownable.' In other words, thinking outside the box doesn't necessarily mean thinking crazy or having to reinvent the wheel; it can also mean taking something that's already known and turning it around to make it your own."

Some Strong Student Self-Promotions

Creative track ad majors at Florida International University who wouldn't have portfolios developed by graduation were required to create a self-promotion as their final project for the same class Cova took with me. Although they all complained it was too hard for a final assignment, they managed to surprise their classmates with their imaginative solutions. Here are some examples of their self-promotions.

1. In the "Idea Creator," Paola Ferrer created a pack of gum that served as her portfolio. Once opened, each stick wrapper showed one miniature example of her work. Its compact size and easy portability made for an original yet simple promotion (figure 11.9).

FIGURE 11.9 "Idea Creator" self-promotion created by Paola Ferrer, graduate of Florida International University. Used with permission of the School of Journalism and Mass Communication, Florida International University

2. A spin-off of the Rubik's Cube created by Roberto Gonzalez served as an innovative way to show various samples. Each time the cube was reconfigured, the various sides combined to highlight another set of creative work (figure 11.10).
3. Jodi O'Brien's "Gotta Wear the Right Gear" was a box within a box. On the left was a little "closet" of clothing and on the right was a cardboard doll waiting to be dressed. The clothing stayed on with Velcro strips. It had some whimsy, but it also included several creative examples. The packaging was clever, and the execution showed a command of layout and design (figures 11.11 and 11.12).

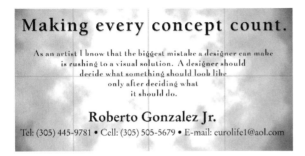

FIGURE 11.10 "Rubik's Cube" self-promotion created by Roberto Gonzalez Jr., creative services/marketing at Estefan Enterprises, graduate of Florida International university. Used with permission of the School of Journalism and Mass Communication, Florida International University

4. A real basketball with a built-in zipper that housed creative work was how Matthew Ubriaco displayed his interest in working in the promotional department of a sports team. Just the communication vehicle alone was an attention grabber. He refined the zipper compartment and is using it for interviews.

FIGURE 11.11 "Gotta Wear the Right Gear" self-promotion, a sample page, created by Jodi O'Brien, graduate of Florida International University. Used with permission of the School of Journalism and Mass Communication, Florida International University

Students with unusual names created self-promotions that drew attention to their forenames or surnames, in the same way that the gecko reminds people of Geico Car Insurance. For instance, Eliza Pastrana created a three-dimensional "Pastrana" (pastrami-like) sandwich that opened like a portfolio of work, in which each example was displayed as a different layer of the sandwich. Another student, Jackie Morjan, created a "Jackie-in-the-Box," a doll that greatly resembled her and that popped up when you turned the handle of an actual jack-in-the-box. Because something actually popped up, it caught the viewer by surprise. The

FIGURE 11.12 "Fix It Time" page from "Gotta Wear the Right Gear" self-promotion created by Jodi O'Brien, graduate of Florida International University. Used with permission of the School of Journalism and Mass Communication, Florida International University

doll inside held a mini-book, which housed her creative work. The outside of the box was colorfully decorated with comments about her creative abilities.

Other students with extensive experience in a specific industry and a desire to land a job in that field showcased their expertise in their self-promotions. For example, Nicole Gallie, who has a strong acting background, created a *Playbill* magazine that included examples of her work as print ads, plus a realistic-looking ticket with all her contact information. Katherine Penner, who had worked for eleven years in the liquor industry, created a self-promotion by designing a label on an actual spirits bottle and attaching a brochure to the neck. The copy wove industry terms throughout the piece. Her slogan was "Raising the Bar in Marketing Spirits."

If there is a company or an industry you are targeting, it is best to create a self-promotion that clearly demonstrates your experience and interest in that field. For example, some students who worked in the cosmetics industry while pursuing their degrees wanted full-time positions with the same firms. They created unique makeup kits filled with the companies' products accompanied by artistic labels that identified product features and then related those traits to their own talents. For example, they would use phrases like "I can highlight product's best features," for a cosmetics industry self-promotion.

Focusing on one agency, corporation, or industry will help you design a self-promotion that is unique yet relevant to your target audience—your future employer. Avoid creating a piece that is too predictable, like using a wolf because your last name is Wolfe. Instead, try to develop an idea that has an element of surprise or a "reveal" that leaves something to be discovered by the recipient.

Changes in the Ad Industry

Anyone following the news can see that there have been many changes in the advertising industry. But what changes are taking place in the hiring process? Norm Grey from The Creative Circus explains the shift he sees as follows:

> It's a whole new thing now. They don't have time to hire and fire anyone. When they do make the time to meet you, they want you to meet nearly everyone on staff. 'Cause they're inviting a stranger into their family. It may be a dysfunctional family, but it's their family. And you're the stranger. . . . So, what a boss wants today is approval from everyone. It's a different dynamic now in the hiring process. Now, it's a two-week or two-month trial internship to see if it works out. They'd rather "date" first. Then get "married." It used to be the other way around. It sometimes ended in a messy "divorce."

Besides the hiring process, what other changes are taking place in the work environment? Grey offers this observation: "Now you can live in one place and work in another. The world is exciting and frightening at the same time. How different it is, because now when they [agencies] come to see our students' portfolios, they entertain the kids and court them to go to work at their agency. Some are treated like top draft choices. Not in every case. But we do see it often enough."

Interns now have opportunities to develop work that will be accepted by clients. Pippa Seichrist offers as an example one stellar experience with a creative team from Miami Ad School's internship program, which finds more than two hundred prospective positions a year. "An art director/copywriter team of students interned at DDB. One of their assignments was to concept a TV spot for McDonald's. The client liked the commercial so much they produced it. The students missed their graduation because they had to go to Sydney for the TV shoot. It was the first ever global TV spot McDonald's ever did. It's on our Web site, www.miamiadschool.com."

■ EXERCISE

Look at as many outstanding self-promotions as you can find. Study graphic annuals and magazines, especially the awards issues, to see how other creative talents are marketing their firms. Examine promotions by design firms, photographers, freelance illustrators, and copywriters. Sources could include:

1. Magazines like *HOW, Print, Communication Arts, Graphis, Dynamic Graphics,* and *Graphic Design USA,* especially awards issues
2. Annuals like *The One Show, American Showcase, Showcase Illustration, The Big Logo Book, Society of Publication Designers' Publication Design Annual, The Best of Brochure Design, Best of Business Card Design, Design Annual, AIGA Year in Design, The New York Festivals, International Advertising Awards, International Design Yearbook, American Graphic Design Awards, Design Innovations Yearbook* (product design), *American Corporate Identity, International Yearbook Communication Design, Art Directors Annual, Publication Design Annual,* and *Typography: The Annual of The Type Directors Club*
3. Portfolio school Web sites, including Brainco (www.adschool.com), Chicago Portfolio School (www.chicagoportfolio.com), The Creative Circus (www.creativecircus.com), and Miami Ad School (www.miamiadschool.com) ■

■ PROJECT

Design or redesign a new self-promotional piece for yourself, a design firm, ad agency, photographer, illustrator, or any other freelancer. Decide which colors to use, which fonts to apply, and which graphic icons or typographic treatment to implement for the main message. How will that element "spin out" in the piece?

Consider your target audience. Who's receiving this? What do you want them to do once they look at it? Be sure it's as interesting on the outside as it is on the inside. Compel the recipient to open it. Tempt them to respond. ■

Notes

1. Pippa Seichrist, personal communication, November 30, 2005.

2. Norm Grey, personal communication, November 8, 2005.

3. Saatchi & Saatchi, 2004, www.saatchi.com/worldwide (accessed November 29, 2005).

4. Monica Hudson for Bob Isherwood, personal communication, January 5, 2006.

5. Michelle Taute, "Self-Promotion Design Awards," *HOW,* October 2005: 64.

6. Jen Bilik, personal communication, December 29, 2005.

7. Randal Grey, personal communication, December 13, 2005.

8. Robynne Raye, personal communication, December 20, 2005.

9. Natalia Cova, personal communication, December 7, 2005.

Be Inspired by Creative Tips from Conceptual Thinkers

It will help you recognize a big idea if you ask yourself five questions:

1. Did it make me gasp when I first saw it?
2. Do I wish I had thought of it myself?
3. Is it unique?
4. Does it fit the strategy to perfection?
5. Could it be used for 30 years?

—DAVID OGILVY[1]

W hen you're attempting to understand how agencies arrive at their creative solutions, hearing explanations directly from them can provide insight and guidance. Here you will read comments by the creative teams responsible for the work from interviews, comments posted on agency Web sites, and statements reported in magazine articles.

How They Work

Before any creative work is begun, agencies can spend a great deal of time preparing to solve the creative problem presented by the client. First, the audience is analyzed, observational research is conducted and evaluated, the creative brief is absorbed, the various media vehicles are analyzed, and the personality of the product or service is reassessed. Agencies generally work from the creative brief as a guide to develop on-strategy and on-target creative solutions.

The Deutsch Web site explains that designers are involved early in the creative process in order to help infuse the entire campaign with visual insight: "The design group is brought in at the beginning stages of the creative process, both to absorb the strategic direction and to provide artistic guidance to all creative disciplines."[2]

Delivering the Message

Andrew Keller, creative director at Crispin Porter + Bogusky, states in *Adweek* that the message alone does not deliver the full impact to the audience. There are other factors that are equally important: "It's not just what you say. It's how you say it, where you say it and when you say it. Each piece has the ability to exponentially affect the power of the idea."[3]

In the same article, Rob Reilly, assistant creative director at Crispin Porter + Bogusky, reveals the driving impetus behind the team's creative thinking for Burger King's "Subservient Chicken" campaign. By defining the tone of voice as a specific character, the creative team could measure its ideas by evaluating if the tone was in keeping with this particular personality: "For Burger King, the voice, we always say, is like a cool uncle, so we'll go through creative ideas that are coming in, and [Andrew Keller] will say, 'Well, that doesn't sound like what a cool uncle would say to you.'"[4]

> I think the first and most important thing in advertising is to be original and fresh.
>
> —BILL BERNBACH[5]

According to Sharoz Makarechi, there is an integral relationship between creative ideas and the media in which they will appear. In expounding on what contributed to the impact of the Citystreets pedestrian safety campaign and why the "Stencil Project" resonated so well in the public's consciousness while attracting media attention, Makarechi says, "I would say that it's because the thinking and the media are relevant to one another. Inherently integrated thinking. It's how I encourage my students to think at School of Visual Arts and my staff at Think Tank 3; it's how our agency creates advertising. It puts you in the crosshairs that much faster. You hear the word 'integrated' a lot in context of marketing and advertising. It's difficult to deliver on, but those who do stand out. Which is why you're talking to me, I suppose."[6]

David Ogilvy, who died in 1999, left some nuggets of copywriting wisdom in his famous book, *Confessions of an Advertising Man*. He considered the headline the single most important element to reach your audience. He also discussed the necessity of creating a brand personality. Fifty years after Ogilvy wrote this, the establishing of a unique brand personality has continued to receive attention. "There isn't any significant difference between the various brands of whiskey, or cigarettes or beer. They are all about the same. And so are the cake mixes and the detergents, and the margarines. . . . The manufacturer who dedicates his advertising to building the most sharply defined personality for his brand will get the largest share of the market at the highest profit."[7]

Stimulating Creative Thinking

G. Andrew Meyer and Noel Haan, exective vice presidents/group creative heads at Leo Burnett USA, offer a few ways to get the creative juices flowing. Meyer says:

> We both drink a whole lot of coffee. A big shot of espresso can get your brain in gear. With creativity, you do it naturally at first, and, then you make a living at it, and then you find you have to ask your brain to do it on demand. But it's like learning how to hit a golf ball 250 yards. You can't do it consistently right away. It's a kind of muscle memory. You train your brain to be creative on demand by doing it a lot. Everyone has flashes of creative thought. You have to learn how to push that button.[8]

Haan says, "Your best ideas come when you're walking or when you're doing something other than being at the office. In order to train your brain, you need to incorporate a regimen, so as a creative thinker you can come up with ideas at any place or time. Embrace your regimen and work on that. You need to build your creative stamina. A lot of people think they have to come up with ideas at the workplace. Not necessarily."

Meyer discusses the importance of focusing on relaxing and letting the mind run free: "Gather information. Concentrate and think hard about the problem you're trying to solve. And then let go. Free your mind to find the ideas. If they don't come right away, be patient. Surprisingly, the ideas will show up, usually unannounced. It's the notion of the creative muse, letting things come to you. You have to find that kind of Zen state. So that's the weird thing—applying an artistic process to solve business problems." However, in an article in *Adweek*, Meyer admits that his mind is always working on some concept. "There's always some idea percolating in your head whether you want it to or not."[9]

Many design firms refer to visual stimulants to get themselves into the creative zone. Jennifer Minnich, creative director at M2Design in Hollywood, Florida, says: "Combing through design annuals is one way to spark exciting visual ideas. Also, going to museums and looking at great artwork is another terrific imagination catalyst. Even strolling through an outdoor art festival can ignite some wonderful creative solutions."[10]

Saatchi & Saatchi's philosophy is that people who love what they're doing create great work because they're passionate about it. "It's our belief that Peak Performance calls for love and passion. Peak Performers love what they do. Love doing what they do better. And better than anyone else. They live in the now. They think in the next. Peak Performers dream it. Then they do it. Then they aim higher."[11]

Getting the Big Idea

Finding the idea that goes "bang" in the marketplace is what The Kaplan Thaler Group strives for and has achieved with the Aflac duck's quack and Herbal Essences' "Totally Organic Experience." Linda Kaplan Thaler and Robin Koval's *BANG! Getting Your Message Heard in a Noisy World* offers insight into the development of what they call "Big Bang" campaigns. "A Big BANG! is an idea that enables a brand to explode into the marketplace virtually overnight. A Big BANG! cuts through the clutter, gets into the culture and gets people to sit up and take notice. A Big BANG! helps you to make the sale, to close the deal."[12] The agency's Web site also discusses their special kind of thinking. "Call us old-fashioned. We believe advertising should rocket sales. And we know it can when it creates a BANG! in the marketplace. We call our unique, powerful approach 'Big Bang Communications!'"[13]

Being open to far-out ideas helps creative talents stimulate a new way of thinking. If you're restricting idea generation in any way, you'll be relegated to already-run concepts. According to copywriter Steve Dildarian at Goodby,

Silverstein & Partners in San Francisco, "Cliff Freeman & Partners kind of instilled a renegade spirit toward the way I look at work. He taught me, you know, nothing is unrealistic, nothing's too far or too much. I don't do things 'cause you're supposed to, 'cause that's the way everyone does it."[14]

When delivered, the message must really touch the audience on an emotional level. All the features are fine, but if the consumer is not excited about owning the product, it won't sell. Ben Walker, an art director at Wieden+Kennedy, says, "The new Civic is as much about the heart as the head. We want people to feel the car—really feel it. And you can't do that by just showing it going 'round a winding road."[15]

> A Big BANG! is highly disruptive, forges strong emotional connections, is embraced by the culture, and gets big results . . . fast.
>
> —LINDA KAPLAN THALER[16]

Breaking a Creative Block

Guy Seese, executive creative director at Cole & Weber, explains how he gets past a creative block this way: "Silence. There's more that happens when nothing is happening than when something is. Creative ideas happen between the spaces. That's the best way to sit back and be open to the universe."[17] Seese goes on to say that having a negative attitude is an annoying block to creative thinking: "Negativity . . . it's such a blocker. People saying 'I can't' is infinitely more disturbing than those who say 'I can' and aren't able to."[18]

A Baker's Dozen of Tips

Bob Isherwood, worldwide creative director at Saatchi & Saatchi, offers what he calls "a few beans" of wisdom that might be an inspirational catalyst when you're developing new client relationships as well as creating powerful messages.

A Few Beans from Bob Isherwood[19]

1. People out there are not waiting to hear from you.
2. Advertising has to be more than information in fancy dress.
3. If your message doesn't make an emotional connection, you won't make a sale.

4. Visit your client's factory. It's where creative insights are made. It's where ideas are hiding.

5. Get out there. Your agency isn't the real world. Be a sponge. Collect facts. Collect stories. Collect experiences.

6. Not keeping it simple is stupid. (See point 1.)

7. Your ideas impact on a brand's character. So unless you want to change the character, be sensitive to it. If you're not, you'll probably end up bitter and frustrated because your ideas won't go through.

8. Please never believe you ever achieve perfection with an idea. (Is the music track absolutely 100 percent right?) Keep nagging at it until outside factors conspire to make you stop. Then take your dissatisfaction (a natural characteristic for a creative) on to your next brief.

9. Accept that the old chestnut "How do you come up with ideas?" is an unanswerable question, similar to "Why is blue?"

10. On the other hand, imaginative minds just can't help creating.

11. Humor is a serious business. It can be painful getting it right, but not as painful as when you don't.

12. Clichés make creative minds cringe.

13. You haven't had your best idea yet.

■ EXERCISE

What quote in this chapter, book, or elsewhere had the greatest impact on you? Write the quote on a card, add graphic elements for greater impact, and hang it in your creative space for inspiration. ■

■ PROJECT

Obtain a small notebook that you can carry with you. Every time you find an inspiring quote, jot it down along with the source. Now, design a visual icon or graphic element to accompany each message. ■

Notes

1. David Ogilvy, *Ogilvy on Advertising* (New York: Vintage Books, 1985), 16.
2. Deutsch, www.deutschinc.com (accessed October 7, 2005).
3. Mae Anderson, "Creative All Stars," *Adweek*, January 24, 2005: 20.
4. Anderson, "Creative," 21.

5. Denis Higgins, *The Art of Writing Advertising: Conversations with Masters of the Craft* (Chicago: NTC Business Books, 1965).

6. Sharoz Makarechi, personal communication, November 2, 2005.

7. David Ogilvy, *Confessions of an Advertising Man* (New York: Ballantine Books, 1963), 89.

8. Noel Haan and G. Andrew Meyer, personal communication, November 30, 2005.

9. Christine Champagne, "Outshining the Past," *Adweek,* August 15, 2005: 17.

10. Jennifer Minnich, personal communication, January 4, 2006.

11. Saatchi & Saatchi, 2004, www.saatchi.com/worldwide (accessed November 29, 2005).

12. Linda Kaplan Thaler and Robin Koval with Delia Marshall, *BANG! Getting Your Message Heard in a Noisy World* (New York: Doubleday, 2005), 6.

13. The Kaplan Thaler Group, 2006, www.kaplanthalergroup.com (accessed August 5, 2005).

14. Eleftheria Parpis, "Creative All Stars," *Adweek,* January 24, 2005: 22.

15. Christine Champagne, "Outshining the Past," *Adweek,* August 15, 2005: 16–18.

16. The Kaplan Thaler Group, 2006, www.kaplanthalergroup.com (accessed August 5, 2005).

17. Mae Anderson, "Guy Seese on the Spot," *Adweek,* May 30, 2005: 32.

18. Anderson, "Guy Seese."

19. Monica Hudson for Bob Isherwood, personal communication, January 4, 2006.

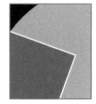

Glossary

ABA the reintroduction of a previously seen component; Verbal ABA is when the last line of the copy refers back to the headline to bring closure to the writing. Visual ABA shows contrast and repetition of graphic elements. Typographic ABA clearly divides type into groups that are alike and different (see box 2.3).

alliteration the repetition of the first letter or sound

all-type ad when there are no visuals at all in the ad, only *typography*

ascenders the lines that rise above the body of the letter, as in the letters *b, d*, and *h*

asymmetrical layout when one half of the design is disproportionate to the other, with one side having more typographic or graphic items than the other, creating an energetic result

bar a solid rectangular box of varying widths that can be used as a graphic icon or as a text box with reverse type

benefit how the product rewards the consumer, also called W-I-I-F-M: what's in it for me?

brainstorming an idea-stimulating technique that can be done alone or in groups. It encourages everyone to participate, promotes wild and crazy ideas, discourages criticism, and fosters equal acceptance of all ideas. The purpose of this collaboration is to dream up as many ideas as possible in a short time period. Working with a tight time constraint helps safeguard against idea censorship.

brief a short outline of the creative strategy, which answers the following questions: (1) What is the brand? (2) Why is it advertising? (3) Who is the audience? (4) What do they (audience members) currently think? (5) What do you want them to think? (6) Why should they buy this product/service? (7) What is the big message you want them to know? (8) What kind of tactics (specific ad/promotional techniques) do you want to use? You should also be able to answer this question: who is the competition?

Looking at the second question—Why is the brand advertising?—you need to understand what an ad strategy statement is. It's a formula that has the following components. Just fill in the blanks with the appropriate words:

The brand is advertising to say something to _____ (VERB—persuade, convince, inform, educate) the audience (MEN, WOMEN, AND CHILDREN CONSUMERS) that this _____ (PRODUCT, SERVICE, OR BRAND) will _____ (STATE THE BENEFIT) because (FEATURES THAT EXPLAIN WHY AUDIENCE SHOULD BELIEVE IT).

Also, think of the brand as having a personality. Then, define what kind of person it would be.

bullets icons used in front of word lists, like asterisks, check marks, dots, circles, and wingdings

buttons the use of a clever line to close the copy

buzz when a lot of attention is generated by many people, who are talking to each other about the same topic, product, or experience

caption a line of text that describes the image (like a photograph or illustration)

chroma the intensity of a color's brightness or dullness, also called *saturation*

color the use of specific colors and color combinations for specific products and emotional responses

comps comprehensive layouts that look precisely like the final version of the ad, brochure, flyer, newsletter, annual report, billboard, and so on

concept the driving idea behind the message of the ad, campaign, or promotional piece

connectors conjunctions and other words that tie sentences and paragraphs together

contractions using a more natural way to write that combines two words into one shorter one. Examples include "It's" instead of "it is," "you'll" in place of "you will," "we've" rather than "we have."

contrast the inclusion of opposing items that differ in weight, size, color, texture, lightness and darkness (value), and so on

copy block the text set in columns within the layout

corporate speak the language of corporate America, for example, "Bring it to the table" means to suggest. "Face time" means a face-to-face conversation. "Feedback" means someone is waiting for a response.

Critter a specific font in which each letter is created in the shape of an animal (for example, a *P* looks like a python, and *T* looks like a tiger)

cross-promotion the teaming up of advertisers by sharing costs and media exposure

crowding compressing the type together, making it look as if it needs more space

descenders the lines that hang lower than the body of the letter, as in the letters *j, p, q,* and *y*

direct mail promotional material that is sent directly to the consumer through the mail

direct response any promotional device that urges a response from the audience, for example, coupons, 800 numbers, and reply panels

double truck a layout (also called a spread) that goes across two pages, like a two-page article or ad

drop shadow the inclusion of a soft line that gives dimension to the type or image (like a picture hanging on the wall with a shadow just below it)

feature a specific product quality or characteristic, like extra-long life in a battery

floor talker an advertising message that appears on a floor, often used in supermarkets

flow writing that moves effortlessly from beginning to end

font a particular typeface

format what kind of promotional material it is, for example, a business card, letterhead (for stationery), print ad, coupon, shopping bag, or billboard

ghosting back the fading of the type or visual (by using a percent of the color), so it appears translucent like tracing paper

grid the underlying division of the layout (like an invisible checkerboard that holds the design's structure) that makes it more comprehensible

gutter the space between two facing pages

headline the main concept or message of an ad or other promotional vehicle, like a billboard, for example

head-vertiser the placement of a company logo on a person's forehead to serve as a walking billboard

hue the actual name of a color

kerning the space between the letters or characters

t h i s   i s   o p e n   k e r n i n g

layering the overlapping of one component over another, like type over type, type over visual, or visual over type

layout the arrangement and relationship of all the components to each other (how the type, color, visuals, and icons work together)

leading the amount of space between lines of type (open leading could be three lines apart, close leading could be less than one line apart)

This is open leading.

Notice how far apart the lines are.

legibility the ease at which readers can decipher each letter

letter-inspired layout where a letter drives the layout in any number of different ways: (1) As a visual—an oversized letter *o* could be a donut and work as the word "oh" in the headline. (2) As a design—the type could be set in the shape of the letter *o*. (3) As a form—here the type could be the letter *c*, wrapping the side of a curved image.

line art a drawing that depicts the outline of the image, without interior shading or background

margins the open space around the page

marriage of a headline and visual the integration of both into one inseparable concept

masthead the newsletter's name (can be set in all type or designed like a graphic logo)

medium the vehicle where the message will appear, such as billboards, radio or TV spots, online banner ads, print or magazine ads, direct mail (promotional materials sent through the mail) and so on

morphing when one image gradually blends to become another (like one face on the left side that changes into a different one on the right); for example, some music videos and television commercials use this technique

negative space the background area in a photograph or the supporting or secondary sections in a layout

novelty type whimsical *fonts* with unusual character design

OpenType A new font with greater capability like including more characters per font set. That allows users to (1) stay in the same font for accent marks in other languages and (2) have letters with swashes, which the font would automatically choose depending on the surrounding letters. So, if the word had an *r* with a swash next to a vowel, like "brown," it would use the swash. But, if the *r* with a swash sat next to a letter with an ascender or descender, like "quirky," it would automatically omit the swash to avoid a typographic collision. Open Type has blended Postscript fonts (used mostly by graphic designers and agencies in the past) with True Type fonts (used mostly by Windows users or those who developed Internet communications), enabling users to (1) work in multiple formats, (2) greater ease of use for *PDF* and Internet files, (3) better font protection, and more. In general, it offers greater overall font applicability and portability in both print and onscreen formats.

outlined type when each letter has an outline around it (imagine a red line that exactly follows the shape of the letter)

overall impact the impression the overall design leaves with the audience

Pantone Matching System (PMS) the universally accepted color reference that assigns every color a Pantone number with a precise formula, specifying color percentages needed to create each color

parallel construction the repetition of a word, phrase, or part of speech, for example, "The Energizer Bunny keeps going and going and going."

PDF Portable Document Format, which enables Mac and PC users to read files with both images and text through a program called Acrobat Reader. Before this program was introduced, users would have a problem reading documents with fonts or programs their systems did not have. So, if someone created a document in a design program (QuarkXPress, Adobe Photoshop or Adobe Illustrator, etc.), the recipient had to have the same program and all the same fonts to open the file and view it with the original fonts.

positive space the primary subject in a photograph or the main visual or headline in a layout

proximity the closeness to other graphics or type in the layout

readability (1) how long readers can read without eye strain, because of well-organized type, and (2) how easily readers can comprehend the message. When you add extra words and long, boring sentences that go on and on and on, or when *the passive voice is used,* the reader struggles to follow the writer's thought, and the copy is less readable. When you write clearly and *use the active voice*, the copy is more readable, and the reader absorbs the message faster.

related word association an idea-generating technique that consists of creating lists of words that are related to the product or company you're advertising. After creating a list, do the following: (1) find words that rhyme, (2) group words that have the same first letter (alliteration), (3) select words that are opposites (like "top" and "bottom") and (4) look for abstract connections between words. Then, try to create headlines or phrases using rhyme ("nonstop mop"), alliteration ("luscious lobster linguine"), opposite ideas ("top-of-the-line products, rock-bottom prices"), and abstract connections ("rock, rattle, and stroll" for a baby store).

reverse type light type over a darker background (for example, white type on a black background or yellow type on a dark blue background)

ringtone the ring of a mobile phone that can be programmed to reflect the owner's individual taste, personality, and style

rough true-to-size layouts, often containing hand-drawn visuals with headlines that used to be hand-lettered, but are digitally set in the computer

screen a percent of a color that creates a shaded or darkened area in a layout

shape the inclusion of a particular geometric shape used to organize or divide the page, for example, using a donut as a large letter *O* in an ad to emphasize a point, as in "Oh, boy! Twice the donuts, half the price!"

shell the basic template for every ad in a campaign, also the placement and use of typography, colors, visuals, and tone of voice are consistent

slogan the main message of the entire campaign, like "Got Milk?" also called *tagline,* theme line, and catchphrase

spin out an idea that works well in a series and in different media, so it could work as several ads or in various billboards. It's based on one big idea that can keep going to create a campaign with related components.

strategy the overall objective of the promotional and/or marketing campaign

symmetrical layout one half of the design matches the other in the weight, number and arrangement of typographic and/or graphic items, creating a tranquil effect

stopping power ability to demand viewers' immediate attention

subhead the supporting line of copy that further explains the headline

tagline same as *slogan*

teaser campaign a series of ads that do not include the company's name or logo until the last ad in the campaign (For example: an *all-type* teaser campaign for the Florida lottery started with only one word in the first ad: "Ha." The second ad read "Ha. Ha." The third ad said, "Ha. Ha. Ha." The ads continued until the final ad had a stacked headline of the word "Ha" repeated over and over. The last ad revealed the advertiser and read something like this: "Ha. Ha. Ha. Ha. Ha. Ha. Ha. Play Florida Lottery and Laugh All the Way to the Bank.")

text wrap having the type go around an image or type block and follow the shape (see box 2.5)

texture the creation of visible patterns that are created by (1) grouping shapes together (like rows of circles); (2) contrasting light with dark areas; and (3) visually depicting textures like sand, fabric, rocks, wood, and so forth, in the design, so readers can almost feel the page

thermography ink that is raised through heat (thermo) in the printing process, so you can touch the letters—usually found on quick-print business cards

thumbnails miniature-size layouts that can be one-fourth or smaller than the final, allowing the artist and client to see the work in one quick look

tone of voice the way you address the audience, for example, friendly, formal, authoritative, or concerned

translucent an effect that makes the image or type appear sheer, like tracing paper

transparent the reader can completely see through, clear like glass

type foundries design companies that develop new fonts

typography the selection, manipulation, treatment, and placement of type to create text portions and graphic components

value (1) In *design*, it is the use of dark and light areas to draw the reader's attention (closer objects, dark and bright areas are noticed first). For example, in an all-dark ad with one white area, viewers see the white space first. (2) In *color*, the value is how light or dark it is, also referred to as its shade, tone, or tint. (3) In *message*, value means what consumers are willing to pay for something. Think of value as what it's worth to them.

vellum translucent paper that you can print on and looks like tracing paper

vernacular casual, everyday speech: "yeah," "betcha," "hey," "okay," "wanna," and so on

vibrating type when type appears to be moving or bouncing, caused by using two colors of the same intensity side by side

viral marketing a word-of-mouth (or word-of-Web) technique to generate product buzz

visual hierarchy the arrangement of all the components by order of their importance to help readers navigate across the page

visual techniques like (1) layering, (2) ghosting back type or images, (3) using repeat graphic elements, (4) applying bullets (icons used in front of lists of words), (5) including illustration (realistic, abstract, cartoon, line art, etc.), and (6) incorporating photography

volume the portrayal of three-dimensionality with the use of shadows behind objects and borders around images

weave the integration of the main concept throughout the copy

white space areas in the layout that are blank and give the reader's eye a rest

wingdings symbols that can be used as graphic elements or bullets in front of words in a list

Selected Bibliography

Applegate, Edd. *Strategic Copywriting: How to Create Effective Advertising*. Lanham, MD: Rowman & Littlefield, 2005.

Bendinger, Bruce. *The Copy Workshop Workbook*. 3rd ed. Chicago: Copy Workshop, 2002.

Berman, Margo. "In Advertising, Don't Write Copy. Compose a Sonata." *Journal of Advertising Education* 3, no. 2 (Fall 1999): 57–59.

———. "Teaching Grammar through Lyrics, Film and Literary Quotes: The Grammar Controversy." *American Society of Business and Behavioral Sciences* 10 (February 1998): 67–73.

———. "Tips for Developing Sticky Taglines." *Journal of Advertising Education* 6, no. 1 (Spring 2002): 54–57.

Birren, Faber, ed. *The Elements of Color: A Treatise on the Color System of Johannes Itten*. Trans. Ernst Van Hagen. New York: Van Nostrand Reinhold, 1970.

Blakeman, Robyn. *The Bare Bones of Advertising Print Design*. Lanham, MD: Rowman & Littlefield, 2005.

Bly, Robert W. *The Copywriter's Handbook*. Updated ed. New York: Henry Holt, 1990.

Bovée, Courtland L., John V. Thill, George P. Dovel, and Marian Burk Wood. *Advertising Excellence*. New York: McGraw-Hill, 1995.

Boyle, Cailin. *Color Harmony on the Web*. Gloucester, MA: Rockport, 2001.

Carter, David E. *American Corporate Identity #10*. New York: Art Direction Books, 1995.

———, ed. *Blue Is Hot Red Is Cool*. New York: HBI, 2001.

Carter, Rob, Ben Day, and Philip Meggs. *Typographic Design: Form and Communication*. 2nd ed. New York: John Wiley & Sons, 1993.

Drate, Spencer, and Jutka Salavetz. *Extreme Fonts: Digital Faces of the Future*. New York: Madison Square Press, 1999.

Eiseman, Leatrice. *Pantone Guide to Communicating with Color.* Cincinnati, OH: Grafix Press, 2000.

Higgins, Denis. *Art of Writing Advertising: Conversations with Masters of the Craft.* Chicago: NTC Business Books, 1965.

Itten, Johannes. *The Elements of Color.* Trans. Ernst Van Hagen. New York: Van Nostrand Reinhold, 1970.

Kaplan Thaler, Linda, and Robin Koval, with Delia Marshall. *BANG! Getting Your Message Heard in a Noisy World.* New York: Doubleday, 2005.

Klein, Erica Levy. *Write Great Ads.* New York: John Wiley & Sons, 1990.

Landa, Robin. *Graphic Design Solutions.* Albany, NY: Delmar, 1996.

Lester, Paul Martin. *Visual Communication: Images with Messages.* 2nd ed. Belmont, CA: Wadsworth/Thomson Learning, 2000.

Lüscher, Max. *The 4-Color Person.* Trans. Joachim Neugroschel. New York: Simon & Schuster, 1977.

———. *The Lüscher Color Test.* Trans. and ed. Ian A. Scott. New York: Simon & Schuster, 1969.

Meggs, Philip B. *A History of Graphic Design.* 3rd ed. New York: John Wiley & Sons, 1998.

Nelson, Roy Paul. *The Design of Advertising.* 7th ed. Madison, WI: WCB Brown & Benchmark, 1994.

Newman, Michael. *Creative Leaps.* Singapore: John Wiley & Sons, 2003.

Ogilvy, David. *Ogilvy on Advertising.* New York: Vintage Books, 1985.

Peterson, L. K., and Cheryl Dangel Cullen. *Global Graphics: Color—Designing with Color for an International Market.* Gloucester, MA: Rockport, 2000.

Poynor, Rick, and Edward Booth-Clibborn, eds. *Typography Now: The Next Wave.* London: Booth-Clibborn, 1994.

Resnick, Elizabeth. *Design for Communication: Conceptual Graphic Design Basics.* Hoboken, NJ: John Wiley & Sons, 2003.

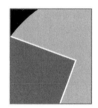

Index

About the Author

As an associate professor at Florida International University, **Margo Berman** teaches creative courses in advertising and public relations. Margo is a creativity and marketing expert with more than twenty years of experience as an award-winning creative director. She founded her own ad agency, Global Impact, which handles American Express, Alamo Rent A Car, and Banana Boat. Margo also produced and hosted an interview talk show in Miami called *Artists about Themselves*.

She is the inventor of *tactikPAK®*, a patented system of learning, and has coauthored three books on spirituality. In addition, she has written articles for national trade journals and reference publications, including the *Encyclopedia of Advertising*. Margo is a corporate trainer of interactive seminars such as *Creative Problem Solving, Great Ads That Sell, Killer Copy*, and *Mental Peanut Butter®*. She has won numerous advertising awards, including Addys, Tellys, Andys, Clarions, Angels, FAME Awards, and International Radio and International Film Awards, plus Outstanding Teaching Awards. She was named the 2001 Woman of the Year in Communications Education. Her Web site, www.unlocktheblock.com, won a 2003 National Clarion Award, and she is a 2005 Kauffman Faculty Scholar.